Security

Security
A Critical Introduction

Lee Jarvis
and
Jack Holland

 palgrave

First published 2015 by
PALGRAVE

Palgrave in the UK is an imprint of Macmillan Publishers Limited, registered in England,
company number 785998, of 4 Crinan Street, London N1 9XW.

Palgrave Macmillan in the US is a division of St Martin's Press LLC, 175 Fifth Avenue, New
York, NY 10010.

Palgrave is a global imprint of the above companies and is represented throughout
the world.

Palgrave® and Macmillan® are registered trademarks in the United States, the United
Kingdom, Europe and other countries

ISBN 978-0-230-39195-6   ISBN 978-0-230-39197-0 (eBook)
DOI 10.1007/978-0-230-39197-0

A catalogue record for this book is available from the British Library.

A catalog record for this book is available from the Library of Congress.

Typeset by Cambrian Typesetters, Camberley, Surrey, England, UK

Contents

List of Illustrative Material

Figures

Tables

Boxes

Preface and Acknowledgements

As will become clear in the following pages we set out to write a different type of introduction to the field of Security Studies (if it is, indeed, a field): one that begins with the big questions, rather than theories or issues of security. Our interest in doing this is, of course, enormously influenced by all of our current and former colleagues at Leeds University, Oxford Brookes University, Surrey University, Swansea University, and the University of East Anglia. We are also indebted to our own supervisors and teachers as undergraduate and postgraduate students at the Universities of Birmingham, Cambridge, Nottingham and Warwick, with whom we have learned and discussed material upon which this book draws. We would also like to acknowledge Oz Hassan, Michael Lister and Matt McDonald for their extremely helpful comments on earlier drafts of this book and material contained within it. Our genuine thanks also go to all of the students we have taught on modules relating to Security Studies in our academic careers thus far. Many of the ideas expressed here draw directly on those experiences, and the insights, knowledge and questions of our students.

To pre-empt themes raised in Chapter 3, the writing of this book has obviously depended on far more people than is implied by the two names on the front cover. We would like to express our deepest gratitude to everyone with whom we have worked at Palgrave Macmillan for their support for this project, including Stephen Wenham, Madeleine Hamey-Thomas and especially Steven Kennedy, who was instrumental in the book's original conception and in seeing it through to completion. The book also benefited enormously from a number of extremely helpful and encouraging anonymous reviewers along the way, and we thank them for their help in getting it to this stage.

Finally, as always, we are grateful to our family and friends for providing us with the encouragement and support that helped us to see this project through to completion.

LEE JARVIS
JACK HOLLAND

Note on the text

To assist readers, and particularly newcomers to the field of Security Studies, each of the following chapters contains a range of pedagogic features including a guide to further reading and key points boxes. The book also contains an extensive glossary, with all terms included in it printed in **bold** type the first time they occur in the text.

List of Abbreviations

AfPak	Afghanistan–Pakistan
AIDS	Acquired Immune Deficiency Syndrome
AK47	Avtomat Kalashnikova
ANZAC	Australian and New Zealand Army Corps
BRIC	Brazil, Russia, India, China
BWC	Biological Weapons Convention
CAQDAS	Computer-Assisted Qualitative Discourse Analysis Software
CCTV	Closed-Circuit Television
CDA	Critical Discourse Analysis
CIA	Central Intelligence Agency
CO_2	Carbon Dioxide
CONTEST	Counter-Terrorism Strategy (UK)
CoW	Correlates of War
CSS	Critical Security Studies
CTS	Critical Terrorism Studies
CWC	Chemical Weapons Convention
DIY	Do It Yourself
DoD	Department of Defense (US)
ELF	Earth Liberation Front
ETA	Euskadie ta Askatasuna
Europol	European Police Office
FAO	Food and Agriculture Organization (of the United Nations)
FARC	Fuerzas Armadas Revolucionarias de Colombia
FGM	Female Genital Mutilation
4GW	Fourth Generation Warfare
FPA	Foreign Policy Analysis
GDP	Gross Domestic Product
HIV	Human Immunodeficiency Virus
HPG	Humanitarian Policy Group
IAEA	International Atomic Energy Agency
ICBM	Intercontinental Ballistic Missile
IED	Improvised Explosive Device
IGO	International Governmental Organization
INGO	International Non-Governmental Organization

IQ	Intelligence Quotient
IR	International Relations
IRA	Irish Republican Army
ISAF	International Security Assistance Force
MAD	Mutually Assured Destruction
MDGs	Millennium Development Goals
MoD	Ministry of Defence (UK)
NATO	North Atlantic Treaty Organization
NGO	Non-Governmental Organization
9/11	11 September 2001 Terrorist Attacks
NMD	National Missile Defense (US)
NPT	Non-Proliferation Treaty
NSC	National Security Council (US)
NSF	National Science Foundation (US)
ODI	Overseas Development Initiative
PhD	Doctor of Philosophy
PLO	Palestine Liberation Organization
PMC	Private Military Company
R2P	Responsibility to Protect
RAF	Red Army Faction
RMA	Revolution in Military Affairs
SALW	Small and Light Weapons
SARS	Severe Acute Respiratory Syndrome
SDI	Strategic Defense Initiative (US)
7/7	7 July 2005 Terrorist Attacks
TCO	Transnational Criminal Organization
UAV	Unmanned Aerial Vehicle
UCDP	Uppsala Conflict Data Programme
UK	United Kingdom
UN	United Nations
UNDP	United Nations Development Programme
UNICEF	United Nations Children's Fund
UNSC	United Nations Security Council
US	United States
USA	United States of America
USD	US Dollar
USSR	Union of Soviet Socialist Republics
WHO	World Health Organization
WMD	Weapons of Mass Destruction
WTO	World Trade Organization

Introduction

Chapter Overview

This chapter introduces readers to some of the challenges involved in the study of security, and outlines the approach to these taken in this textbook. We begin by pointing out some of the paradoxes associated with security, noting that the term is used to describe ways of both protecting and taking life: of making us more and less safe. We then outline a series of fundamental challenges raised by this powerful, yet peculiar concept: including that it can be equally, and as easily, applied in relation to states (in discussions of national security) and individual people (in discussions of human security). The chapter then outlines two major ways in which this textbook differs from alternative introductions. The first is in taking a question-centred approach to security rather than one that focuses on theories or issues. The second is in linking debates around international security to broader controversies across the social sciences. The chapter finishes with a brief introduction to the major theoretical approaches to the study of security, before providing an overview of the remaining chapters.

Chapter Contents

Security: a critical analysis

The concept of **security** is a peculiar one. In daily usage, it invokes safety and the absence of threats, promising some measure of assurance and certainty for those 'secure in the knowledge' of something or other. At the same time, security conjures forth the spectre of weapons,

1

surveillance, martial law and armed conflict. The Security Services and CCTV security cameras gather intelligence on citizens, whilst security fences and walls maintain a boundary between 'us' and 'them'. Countries go to war for reasons of **'national security'**; others introduce draconian, exceptional, legislation in response to terrorist threats, undocumented migration, criminal gangs, and the like. Non-citizens are deported when they are deemed a threat to the security of their host **state**; whistleblowers face espionage charges for the same reasons.

Yet, national security is not the only type of security that comes to mind when we hear this term used. Security makes just as much sense – and is as familiar to us – at the level of the individual person, as well as in relation to families, communities and our other social groups (religious, sexual, racial, and so on). We might, for instance, seek to secure our homes through installing burglar or fire alarms, or through fitting insurer-approved locks on our windows and doors that meet government standards. We might join a voluntary neighbourhood watch scheme in an effort to secure our street from crime and anti-social behaviour. Vigilante groups patrol towns, national borders and Internet sites to identify and deal with threats to themselves and others. Gated communities exist across the world complete with armed guards and barbed wire fences restricting and policing access to the sanctuary 'within'. Short of money, we might secure a loan against the value of our current possessions; or, we might take up a pension to provide for our financial security when we are no longer able to work. And, those in most need could, historically at least, benefit from state-provided social security schemes offering a minimum standard of well-being: income, food, health care, shelter, and so forth.

Security, then, is both paradoxical and complex. Paradoxical, because security seems both desirable and capable of quite terrible things. On the one hand, security implies the absence of danger, the management of future **risks**, and, perhaps some measure of freedom to do what we would choose. If I go to the cinema this evening, for example, my decision to do so is made possible, in part, because of the personal security given to me by my job, my health, low local crime rates, and so forth. In relation to social security, moreover, the term implies some basic measure of well-being for those most in need of support or assistance from the state. On the other hand – and just as importantly – security technologies (such as guns or drones), professionals (such as the employees of **private military corporations**), and **discourses** (such as the 'global war on terror', 'war on drugs' or **'Cold War'**) both perpetuate and help to justify massive inconvenience (think airline restrictions in the post-9/11 period), terrifying incursions on civil liberties (look at the treatment of asylum seekers in many of the world's most powerful democracies), huge opportunity costs (on what else might the War on Terror's estimated $5 trillion have been spent?), and death (think every war that has ever occurred). Security, in short, seems to make us safer and less safe, perhaps even contributing to both at the same time.

Leaving this paradox aside, for the moment, security is riddled with a host of additional complexities that must be addressed in any serious treatment of this concept. First, as implied above, it is not immediately obvious to whom or to what we are referring when we think about, discuss, or seek to achieve security. Should we, for example, focus our efforts on understanding and improving the provision of security for people (as people) or for the states in which those people reside (and are these mutually exclusive)? Moreover, how about the security of other phenomena that fit into neither of these categories: perhaps the environment and the fauna and flora therein, or a collective 'way of life' coming under threat from the erosion of traditional norms and practices? Related to this, is security a zero-sum game – like a pie – so that the more of it I have, the less there is by definition available to you? Or, does increasing the security of one person, community or state – in an era of globalization – mean that the security of others will also grow? For example, does lifting people out of poverty 'over there' improve security from organized crime 'here'? In relation to this, what should we do when the security of one entity comes into conflict with that of another? Is it legitimate, for example, to cause harm in the form of torture to a suspected – individual – terrorist, in order for a potential gain in national security given the information that the suspect might hold?

A second, and no less challenging, set of questions centres on how we decide what counts as a security threat? Do we wish to include any source of potential harm under this category, given that DIY accidents, lightening strikes, neglect of children, and dog attacks all lead to human death on a regular basis? If, instead, we want to limit this category, how exactly are we to do this? And, in so doing, how do we decide which threats to prioritize for our study (as researchers and students of security) and our attention (as policymakers, other practitioners of security, and perhaps as citizens). Third, if we think that security is a good thing of which we want more for ourselves or others, how might we go about trying to achieve it? Does this involve greater military expenditure, spreading democracy, improving access to health care and pharmaceuticals, confronting **sexism** (see **patriarchy**), homophobia and racism, more CCTV cameras, tighter border controls, new or improved International Governmental Organizations (IGOs) or transnational alliances, a more consistent global **human rights** regime, or something else entirely? Alternatively, might we conclude that security will always be temporary – never complete and never forever – and that there is value in learning to live with some measure of insecurity? Indeed, at what point might we conclude that small gains in security are not worth the cost or the inconvenience required to bring them about (see Mueller and Stewart 2011).

This textbook offers an attempt to introduce readers to precisely these kinds of debates, and to the significance of different positions that are taken within them. In writing this book, our aim was to offer a different kind of introduction to the many excellent overviews of **Security Studies** that already exist, and from which we have learned a great deal as students, researchers and teachers (e.g. Sheehan 2005; Fierke 2007; Buzan and Hansen 2009; Peoples and Vaughan-Williams 2010; Collins 2013; Williams 2013; Salter and Mutlu 2013; Shepherd 2013). Two differences, in particular, separate this book from these. In the first instance, we have organized the following chapters around a series of core questions or themes that – in our opinion – run through all discussions of security in the academic subfield of Security Studies and beyond. This contrasts with many other introductions which tend to take their readers on a journey through competing theoretical positions or 'schools' (**political realism** (see **realism**), **post-structuralism**, **feminism**, and so forth), or to focus individual chapters on major contemporary security issues (for instance, war, the international arms trade, climate change, **terrorism**, and the like).

Our emphasis on core themes is, we should underline, not because we believe empirical detail or theoretical sophistication to be unimportant in discussions of security. Rather, it is because we believe there are considerable merits to following a question-driven rather than theory- or issue-driven approach. Such an approach, we argue, offers one way of avoiding and perhaps helping to mitigate the 'schoolism' that has dominated debates around security – and **International Relations** more widely – over the past twenty years or so (Booth 2011: 2). This 'schoolism' – the division of the field into seemingly discrete and clearly defined warring camps (Sylvester 2013) such as 'the **liberals**' or 'the constructivists' – has, in our view, had something of a limiting effect on debate around security for at least four different reasons.

First, it is simplistic. It implies that theoretical positions in relation to the study of security can be clearly delineated and distinguished from one another. This, we suggest, gives newcomers to the field an impression of stasis and order – here is one theory, here is another – which fits very poorly with the vibrancy and fluidity of academic positions and debates. Theories of security are always changing and no textbook – including this one – can hope to do justice to this dynamism. Taking a theory-based approach to security, in other words, risks skipping over the chaos, confusion and changing of minds which are a major aspect of what makes the study of global political life so important and exciting for newcomers to the field as well as for established thinkers. There is no 'liberal position' on international security, just as there is no (single, uncontested) 'feminist position' on the use of rape as a weapon of warfare. Realist thinkers are as likely to disagree amongst themselves about the likelihood of war breaking out in any particular context, as they are with non-realist thinkers. It is, in short, vital to be attentive to internal differences, developments and debates within broad theoretical frameworks and approaches to security rather than overlooking these for the sake of simplification.

Second, school-based cartographies of Security Studies are also potentially misleading. This is because overviews of this sort encourage us to look for – or to 'see' – the differences between competing theoretical approaches to security, at the same time as they hide or help camouflage potential similarities or areas of agreement across different positions within debates. As we try to demonstrate in subsequent chapters, different approaches to security frequently share more than first appearances imply. By the same token, seemingly similar perspectives also – at times – seem to depart from one another in unexpected ways. Straightforward adherence to a typology of theoretical perspectives (or, indeed, issues), in short, encourages us to look at how ideas are packaged and 'badged', rather than to think through the content, similarities, and differences between those ideas, and to question who does the 'badging'.

A third danger is that school-based accounts of any scholarly field can easily become self-referential. Focusing too attentively on developments in one academic discipline can lead to the neglect of developments in other – and potentially equally relevant – fields of study, or in the 'real world' of global politics (such that one exists). As argued throughout, discussions of security have learnt much – and have much still to learn – from discussions taking place within Geography, Psychology, Sociology, Neuroscience, Gender Studies, Development Studies and many other fields besides. Ideas, concepts and **methodologies** and so on from here and elsewhere have had a major impact on how security is studied today. It is important, then, not to forget this porosity of Security Studies' boundaries, and not to foreclose opportunities for further developments.

Fourth, and finally, we also agree with Ken Booth's (2011: 2) recent critique of the 'pigeon-holing, feuding and flag-waving of distinctive ontological, epistemological, and methodological theoretical positions' that tends to dominate discussions of international politics. There is, we suggest, much effort and ink wasted in the repeated setting out, attacking, and defending of competing approaches to security. Beginning with questions – rather than theories or issues – again offers one way to counter this: and to focus on the substance rather than packaging of ideas about security and its relation to insecurity. Let us be clear, there is absolutely no harm in critiquing constructivist understandings of the war on terrorism as a security discourse, to give one example on which we have both worked individually and together. Indeed, sympathetic critique and unsympathetic criticism are both fundamental to the academic enterprise and we have gained much from each from teachers, students, and peer reviewers (of this textbook and other works!). But, it is vital that constructivist understandings of terrorism discourse are attacked because of their limitations or inadequacies, rather than because they are – or because they are seen to be – 'constructivist'.

In order to achieve this first aim of a question-based approach to security each of the following chapters takes one 'big' question as its focus:

- What is security?
- What can we know about security?
- How can we study security?
- Whose security should we prioritize?
- What constitutes a security threat?
- Is security possible?
- Is security desirable?

Our argument throughout is that all perspectives on, and debates relating to, security take a stance on these questions: sometimes explicit, sometimes implicit. And, as suggested above, our hope is that by taking these as our focus we can begin to think differently about the importance of differences or similarities between answers to any of them. In the final section of this introduction we outline in a little more detail how we set about attempting to answer these questions in the chapters that follow.

The second major difference between this book and many other introductions and textbooks is its attempt to connect discussions of security to broader debates taking place across the social sciences. Security Studies is often thought of, and approached, as a subdiscipline of International Relations (IR). This was its 'home' in its earliest incarnations throughout the twentieth century, and it is from IR that studies of security have frequently taken their research questions, theoretical frameworks and methodologies. Most students taking modules in

Security Studies still do so in the context of a degree in International Relations or Political Science (or in International Security more specifically), and most of the now 'classic' or pioneering articles on security were published in journals associated with these disciplines. While it is important to remember this – and, indeed, to think critically about the implications of this historical relationship – our own view is that discussions around security cannot – and should not – be divorced from what is taking place in other fields of study and their own debates. There are two reasons for this.

First, as alluded to above, although it is often overlooked, the boundary between Security Studies and other fields of enquiry has always been a fluid one. As outlined in Chapter 3, for example, many of the most interesting and innovative research **methods** employed by contemporary 'critical' researchers studying security were initially developed within other fields such as anthropology or gender studies. Failing to engage with ongoing debates elsewhere, therefore, risks, first, failing to recognize the significance of unfamiliar or overlooked ways of thinking and researching security issues. And, second, it risks taking a snapshot of Security Studies as it is presently set up, and presuming this tells the truth about what this field looks like, how it is organized, and how it is related to others. A snapshot of Security Studies today, for instance, would look very different to one that was taken only twenty-five years ago at the end of the Cold War era. The challenge – in both senses of the word (what needs to be done, and the difficult nature of attempting to do this) – is therefore to remain open to the range of possible future directions in which analyses of security might go. In the book's concluding chapter, we point to a number of ways in which this might be possible.

Beyond this disciplinary fluidity, a second reason for engaging with debates in other fields is that so doing helps us to unpack the underpinning assumptions, rationales, logics, questions and values of competing positions within, and debates on, the study of security. This is particularly the case in relation to social and political analysis, and to the philosophy of social science. Engaging with these, we argue, helps us to think through the stakes involved in, and implicit claims of, competing perspectives on each of the above 'big' questions. This is, not least, because disputes around security are rarely, if ever, purely empirical: a matter of making better or worse calculations and the like. Instead, such disputes involve theoretical disagreement – how do we define 'war' or democracy; methodological disputes – how useful are mathematical models of intra-state wars; analytical disagreements – how many case studies provide us with reliable knowledge of the causes of famine; and much else besides. As outlined in Chapter 7, for example, debates around the 'new terrorism' of al Qaeda and its difference to the 'old terrorism' of the Provisional IRA are as much debates about the dynamics of historical change as they are about the minutiae of these two organizations.

In short, this book offers an accessible yet intellectually rigorous overview of contemporary debates within Security Studies, surveying this landscape by reference to key questions or themes rather than around dominant 'schools' or empirical case studies. In doing this, we attempt to tie these big questions to broader debates and developments taking place across the Social Sciences, and to illuminate conceptual discussions on security by reference to relevant, and contemporary, examples. These include, amongst many others, terrorist violence and insurgency; climate change and environmental disasters; undocumented migration; global poverty; disease pandemics such as HIV/AIDS; gendered violence; the proliferation of weapons and the international arms trade; and transformations in warfare including with reference to recent conflicts in Afghanistan, Iraq and Libya. Our hope is that by the end of the book readers will be better positioned, first, to engage critically within disciplinary debates around Security Studies. And, second, to engage with developments and debates beyond the discipline including, but not limited to, those discussed in the following chapters.

Security: approaches and issues

Our organization of this book around key questions or 'problems' associated with security means that readers will be introduced to various theoretical approaches at appropriate points in the following chapters. No prior understanding of these approaches is expected, or required, and there are a number of very good textbooks for those wanting a more detailed account of the origins, development and contours of these (e.g. Doyle 1998; Weber 2005; Steans *et al.* 2010; Burchill and Linklater 2013; Daddow 2013; Baylis *et al.* 2014). At the same time, we recognize that some readers may want something of a springboard before plunging headfirst into the waters of international security. As such, this section offers a very succinct sketch of some of the major conceptual approaches that have dominated studies of international security. These approaches, importantly, are far from exhaustive and others such as **post-colonialism**, Queer Theory, the **English School** and Green Theory might also have been included and are referred to in places throughout the following chapters. The approaches in Table I.1, moreover, are also, importantly, not necessarily mutually incompatible. It is quite possible, and not uncommon, for instance, to be both a feminist as well as a post-structuralist, realist, constructivist or liberal (see Sjoberg 2009). Our hope, however, is that the following discussion offers a helpful sketch of some of the ideas to which we subsequently return. But, to be clear, the book has been written in such a way that those preferring to throw themselves straight into the deep end will be able to swim rather than sink without it.

Table I.1 offers a very brief summary of some of the major approaches on which this book draws. The key concepts and texts identified are far from comprehensive, but are intended to give some flavour of the emphases and orientations of these approaches, as well as a guide to further reading for each. To work our way down from the top of the table, we encounter first political realism and liberalism (sometimes referred to within International Relations literature as idealism). These approaches represent the mainstream of Security Studies, as they do of most sub-areas within global politics. Together they share a heritage that extends to the turn of the twentieth century within the academic discipline of International Relations, although both draw on political philosophers far further back than this. Political realism and liberalism should be thought of as broad 'families' of shared ideas – rather than single perspectives – and there is much disagreement within each of these families.

To simplify greatly, political realism offers a pessimistic under-standing of global politics as an arena that is dominated by self-inter-ested states encountering one another in an anarchical environment. In this environment, the behaviour of states, and the outcomes of their encounters with one another, are decided ultimately by differences of **power** (usually understood in terms of material capabilities). Understood in this way, it is either survival or power that states desire above all other goals. Realism, then, tends toward an understanding of world politics that embraces statism – the **normative** prioritization of the state as the actor that *should* be privileged and secured – and, at the same time, state-centrism – a focus on states as the primary actors that drive international dynamics (see Bilgin 2002: 102). As a conse-quence, political realists tend to focus on the conditions and likelihood of military conflicts between states, and have been repeatedly criticized by other approaches for the narrowness of this emphasis. These criti-cisms have included, *inter alia*, the importance of intrastate or 'civil' wars in comparison to inter-state war; the importance of non-material sources of power; and, the importance of factors other than power for determining behaviour, including the role that international organiza-tions might play in shaping national interests. In spite of these and other criticisms, however, political realism continues to dominate

Table I.1 Approaches to security

	Key ideas and concepts	Key texts
Political Realism	International anarchy *Realpolitik* National security National Interest Survival Balancing Bandwagoning	Thomas Hobbes, *Leviathan*, 1651 Hans Morgenthau, *Politics Among Nations*, 1948 Kenneth Waltz, *Theory of International Politics*, 1979
Liberalism	Democracy Democratic Peace Thesis Free markets International Governmental Organizations Liberty	Immanuel Kant, *Perpetual Peace*, 1795. Bruce Russett, *Grasping the Democratic Peace: Principles for a Post-Cold War World*, 1993 Robert O. Keohane, *After Hegemony: Cooperation and Discord in the World Political Economy*, 1984.
Constructivism	(Social) construction Norms Identity Rules Roles Language	Alexander Wendt, *Social Theory of International Politics*, 1999. Nicholas Onuf, *World of Our Making: Rules and Rule in Social Theory and International Relations*, 1989. Peter Katzenstein, *The Culture of National Security: Norms and Identity in World Politics*, 1996.
The Copenhagen School	Securitization Desecuritization Securitizing actors Security sectors Regions	Barry Buzan, Ole Wæver and Jaap de Wilde, *Security: A New Framework for Analysis*, 1998. Thierry Balzacq, *Securitization Theory: How Security Problems Emerge and Dissolve*, 2010. Ole Wæver, Barry Buzan, Morten Kelstrup and Pierre Lemaitre, *Identity, Migration and the New Security Agenda in Europe*, 1993.

	Key ideas and concepts	Key texts
Feminism	Gender Femininity Masculinity Patriarchy Performativity Sex	Cynthia Enloe, *Bananas, Beaches and Bases: Making Feminist Sense of International Politics*, 1989. J. Ann Tickner, *Gender in International Relations: Feminist Perspectives on Achieving Global Security*, 1992. Christine Sylvester, *Feminist International Relations: An Unfinished Journey*, 2002.
Critical Security Studies (CSS)/ The Welsh School	Emancipation Community Critical theory Imminent critique	Ken Booth, *Critical Security Studies and World Politics*, 2005. Ken Booth, *Theory of World Security*, 2007. Richard Wyn Jones, *Security, Strategy and Critical Theory*, 1999.
Human Security	Development Freedom from want Freedom from fear Indivisibility	United Nations Development Programme, *Human Development Report 1994: New Dimensions of Human Security*, 1994. Mary Kaldor, *Human Security: Reflections on Globalization and Intervention*, 2007. S. Neil MacFarlane and Yuen Khong, *Human Security and the UN: A Critical History*, 2006.
Post-structuralism/ Post-modernism	Discourse Deconstruction Genealogy Subjectivities	David Campbell, *Writing Security: United States Foreign Policy and the Politics of Identity*, 1998. David Campbell, *National Deconstruction: Violence, Identity and Justice in Bosnia*, 1998. R.B.J. Walker, *Inside/Outside: International Relations as Political Theory*, 1992.
Paris School/ International Political Sociology	(In)security (In)securitization Practice Security professionals Security fields Security technologies	Jef Huysmans, *The Politics of Insecurity: Fear, Migration and Asylum in the EU*, 2006. Michael Williams, *Culture and Security: Symbolic Power and the Politics of International Security*, 2007. Didier Bigo et al., *Europe's 21st Century Challenge: Delivering Liberty and Security*, 2010.

studies of international security, not least because of its ability to evolve and adapt in relation to a changing world and to challenges from other approaches.

Part of realism's success as the dominant **paradigm** within Security Studies can be explained by the efforts of realists to grapple with developments in the 'real world' of international politics (Schmidt 2004: 429). This is in contrast to more contemporary approaches which often focus on how this world might be radically transformed. Recent attempts to incorporate terrorist groups within this state-centric framework offer but one example of this adaptability (Brenner 2006). The plurality of theoretical positions political realism supports is another important reason for its successes (see Bell 2009; Booth 2011: 10–11; Buzan 1996; Glaser 2003; Legro and Moravcsik 1999; Walt 1997: 932), with 'neo-classical realism' and its attention to the ideas and foreign policy preferences of political leaders representing the most significant recent development here (see Rose 1998). As Ken Booth (2011: 9) argues, realism may therefore be better understood as a 'a body of ideas with some family resemblances rather than a coherent research project' (see also Ashley 1981: 206–7; Walker 1987).

Many of the most prominent criticisms of realist approaches to security have tended to come from liberal thinkers. Although traditionally seen as its major competitor, liberalism tends to share realism's view of self-interested states inhabiting a world of **anarchy** without anything equivalent to a world government. As Jervis (1999: 43) put it, contemporary variants of realism and liberalism alike, 'start from the assumption that the absence of a sovereign authority that can make and enforce binding agreements creates opportunities for states to advance their interests unilaterally, and makes it important and difficult for states to cooperate with one another'. Where these approaches tend to differ from one another, however, is that liberals typically offer a more optimistic account of the prospects of cooperation between states, or of the necessity of conflict between them. For liberals, free markets, democracy, and IGOs such as the United Nations or European Union all affect the behaviour of states seeking national security: not least because they increase the costs of conflict and the benefits of cooperative behaviour. Furthermore, liberal approaches also tend to differ from those associated with political realism because of the significance they attribute to **non-state actors** – such as charities and non-governmental organizations – and the role that such actors play in shaping the dynamics of international politics.

Constructivism offers a similarly broad family of approaches, and one that has exerted a major influence on the evolution of contemporary Security Studies as well as many other areas within the social sciences (Jarvis and Lister 2013c). Indeed, as one critical engagement puts it, the phenomenon of constructivism 'has become inescapable' (Zehfuss 2002: 2). Constructivist analyses emphasize the importance of norms, ideas and identities in the shaping of global political outcomes, arguing that brute material forces do not explain everything. Viewed through a constructivist lens, actors in international relations – usually, but not always or necessarily, states – act in accordance with their understandings, or constructions, of the world and the things within it: rather than reacting directly to the basic 'stuff' from which it is made. So, from a constructivist perspective, the United States might choose to intervene in a conflict because it views itself as a beacon of freedom or defender of the powerless, as much as for purely material gains (see also Weldes 1999b). Similarly, whether conflict breaks out because of the actions of one state – to increase military spending, to develop nuclear weapons, and so on – will depend on how other states view themselves, their potential foe, and the actions undertaken (for example, Howard 2004). Constructivist insights have been applied to a huge diversity of security issues and contexts and are far less restricted to military affairs than is typical within the mainstream approaches.

Constructivist approaches share with liberalism an emphasis on the importance of international institutions in the quest for international security. In the case of the latter, International Governmental Organizations (IGOs) such as the European Union, World Trade Organization or NATO are seen to have genuine possibility for encouraging cooperation between states within an anarchical environment. This can happen in a number of ways including helping to resolve disputes when they arise, reducing uncertainty about the behaviour of other states, and making it more difficult for states to 'cheat' others. In constructivist approaches, institutions which might be formalized in the case of IGOs or less so in the case of international regimes, also have capacity to improve security by stimulating a sense of shared identity. At its most consolidated, this can lead to the emergence of **'security communities'** whereby 'states become integrated to the point that they have a sense of community, which, in turn, creates the assurance that they will settle their differences short of war' (Adler and Barnett 1998: 3).

The **Copenhagen School** framework is a more specific example of constructivism which focuses in particular on how political issues are **securitized** or created as security matters (Buzan *et al.* 1998). Lots of things have the potential to cause harm to humans, states or other **referents** – nuclear weapons, unemployment, sharks, men, and so on – but these potential threats only become matters of security when a privileged actor talks about them in this way, and relevant audiences accept this. For example, domestic violence causes far more fear, insecurity, physical harm, and death than terrorism does in the United Kingdom, yet terrorism – and not domestic violence – is widely seen as a security threat to which vast amounts of resources are dedicated. For advocates of securitization studies, this suggests that security should not be thought of as a condition or experience. Instead, it is a 'speech act': it is the act of labelling something 'security' that produces the 'thing' as a security issue. Importantly, in this tradition security is also generally seen as undesirable for two reasons. First, because it stifles political debate about how and whether to deal with the issue at hand. And, second, because speaking about political issues as matters of security – and therefore both urgent and important – helps to legitimize exceptional responses to those issues in order that they might be dealt with.

Feminist approaches again vary dramatically, although they share an interest in the ways in which international politics and security are inherently gendered. For some feminists this means demonstrating the importance of women's (typically hidden) experiences within political contexts: such as the prevalence of domestic violence in the home or the workplace, or the ways in which women are treated within armed forces. In this sense, feminist security studies has sought to recognize, highlight, and begin addressing sources of insecurity that are themselves intrinsically gendered. For instance, forms of violence targeted specifically at women – such as the use of rape in wartime – are widespread (Card 1996; Hansen 2001; Sjoberg 2009: 198). As are non-militaristic violences such as **female genital mutilation** (FGM), which a recent UN (2010: 135) study found that 38% of women in Yemen aged between 15 and 49 had undergone in 2006. For Burkina Faso the figure was 77%, in Mali 86%, and in Guinea, Egypt and Eritrea the number approached 100%. Less dramatic, but no less significant, is the extent to which women suffer disproportionately from other forms of harm, violence and want, including poverty, insufficient access to food and clean water, and illiteracy (UN 2010).

Other feminist researchers focus their work on how gender is constructed and employed in the framing of security politics. This includes, for example, the ways in which military interventions in other states are frequently justified by arguments about the treatment of women therein. Following the 9/11 attacks, for example, 'the Bush administration began talking about the abuses that Afghan women faced under the Taliban regime and argued that the war on terror would also be fought to protect the rights and dignity of women' (Hunt 2006: 51). Importantly, feminist approaches look at performances and practices of masculinity as well as femininity, and have been responsible for critiquing aspirations for 'gender blindness' within mainstream approaches to security. They have also, as argued in Chapter 3, been particularly important for bringing new methodologies and concepts to this field of study.

Critical Security Studies (CSS) or the **Welsh School** approach to Security Studies sees security as an inherently desirable condition. From this perspective security exists in a positive, mutually reinforcing relationship with emancipation: 'the freeing of people (as individuals and groups) from those physical and human constraints which stop them carrying out what they would freely choose to do' (Booth 1991: 319). As this suggests, the focus in this approach is on the security of individuals rather than states, although with a recognition that individuals are located within communities. Security, seen thus, is both a 'real' and desirable condition because it gives people the opportunity to do more than simply focus on their own survival: the opportunity to choose to visit the cinema this evening as in the example above. In the words of Ken Booth (2007), one of its main advocates, security is '**survival-plus**': it is about being able to choose how one would wish to live one's own life. As a consequence, our role as scholars and citizens – for CSS – is to advocate and fight for progressive political projects (for example, global human rights regimes) because these hold the greatest potential at present for enhancing the emancipation and security of the world's most dispossessed. CSS takes much inspiration from developments within **Peace Research** as well as a particular body of Marxist political thought, known as the Frankfurt School.

The **Human Security** approach also focuses on the individual human, and again sees security as a desirable condition. The approach famously came to prominence in a United Nations Development Programme (UNDP) report of 1994 which argued for a very broad understanding of security as freedom from want and freedom from fear (UNDP 1994). Although there are several interpretations of this term (Newman 2001), human security advocates tend to be interested in addressing the full range of threats to human well-being – environmental destruction, crime, economic precariousness, and so forth – and in so doing often argue that security should be thought of as an indivisible 'good' such that it cannot be achieved by one at the expense of the security of others. In one powerful framing of the term, for example, 'human security describes a condition of existence in which basic material needs are met, and in which human dignity, including meaningful participation in the life of the community, can be realised. Such human security is indivisible; it cannot be pursued by or for one group at the expense of another' (Thomas 2001: 161). Although seemingly far removed from traditional concerns that many of us would associate with discussions of national security in particular, several important states including Canada and Japan have used this language in their foreign policy approaches. This uptake, however, has been criticized by some as evidence that the progressive potential of arguments about human security can be too easily be co-opted by states as a smoke-screen for more traditional national interests.

Post-structural approaches – closely related to, but distinct from, **post-modernism** – set out to deconstruct or otherwise destabilize dominant forms of security knowledge and practice. In some variants, this involves exposing the assumptions, hierarchies, and omissions of security discourses: for example, in demonstrating how arguments about national security and order rely upon implicit claims about international insecurity and anarchy (for example, Ashley 1988). As R.B.J. Walker (1987: 69) puts it: 'Civil society, the conventional argument goes, *may* be the site of progress and the pursuit of justice, but international politics simply *is* the realm of contingency and conflict' (original emphasis). Other versions seek instead to uncover or construct historical genealogies of security issues and practices: to root contemporary phenomena in the often hidden contexts of the past (for example, Dillon 2002). What these different post-structural approaches share, however, is a suspicion toward claims to 'truth' and 'authority' that so frequently surround security and insecurity. Or, put otherwise, they share a desire to problematize the privileging of particular ways of speaking and doing 'security'.

The **Paris School** is amongst the most recent of additions to Security Studies, and draws its inspiration from fields of research including migration studies, sociology and policing studies. This approach builds on the discussions of securitization that we encountered above, but sees security and insecurity as inseparable, rather than opposites, and using the term (in)security to capture this relationship. CCTV cameras, for example, might reduce the risk of crime. At the same time, they might make citizens feel anxious about being watched by the state. Similarly, while armed police officers at transport hubs might reduce anxieties about terrorism, they might also encourage us to believe that we should feel insecure. This is especially likely to be the case, of course, if we have had unsatisfying encounters with the police or the state more generally. The Paris School approach draws on the work of sociologists, especially Pierre Bourdieu, and pulls our attention to the role of security technologies (such as full body scanners) and professionals (such as border control guards) in the production of (in)security within particular 'fields'. In this sense, it offers an important alternative to constructivist and some post-structuralist work which has tended to focus on the importance of language.

This brief sketch, of course, does very little justice to any of these ways of thinking about international security. It cannot, and nor is it intended to, convey the complexities within any of these 'schools'. Our hope, however, is that readers use it only as an initial springboard, or as a point of reference when thinking through some of the issues thrown up by discourses, practices and issues of security in subsequent chapters. In this sense, we also hope that this sketch produces as many questions as answers; and perhaps even as much confusion as clarification at this stage.

Chapter overview

The remainder of this book is organized around eight chapters focusing on the 'big' questions identified above. Chapter 1 – What is Security? – introduces readers to major **ontological** controversies within efforts to define this most contested of terms. Is security about survival or emancipation, for example? Is security a material and 'real' phenomenon, or is it something that is constructed through social practices such as language? The chapter locates these and other definitional debates within their historical contexts, and points in particular to the changing nature of Security Studies throughout and after the Cold War period.

Chapter 2 – What can we Know about Security? – introduces readers to **epistemological** questions about our knowledge of security. The chapter begins by contrasting the views of those who see Security Studies as a scientific enterprise, on the one hand, with, on the other, their critics who are sceptical of any such comparisons between the social and natural sciences. The chapter then turns to two really important questions that have been raised by contemporary approaches to security including feminism and post-colonialism. First, can we gain objective or 'truthful' knowledge of security and insecurity, and if so how? And, second, does security mean the same thing in different times and places: or is it a variable phenomenon? This question, we argue, raises further issues about how legitimate it might be to speak on behalf of the security of others.

The book's third chapter – How can we Study Security? – provides an overview of some of the most important research methods that are available to those seeking to study international security. These include statistical techniques such as **regression analysis** as well as non-mathematical methods such as **discourse analysis**, **focus groups**, research **interviews** and **ethnographic observation**. The chapter argues that we should welcome the recent interest in research methods within 'critical' approaches to security in particular for a number of reasons. Not least, because thinking about how knowledge of security is produced helps us to assess the claims that academics, policymakers and others regularly make about security threats and issues.

Chapter 4 – Security For Whom or For What? – provides an overview of different referents that can be invoked in discussions of security. We begin by exploring why the state – and national security – are traditionally privileged when we think about the concept of security, before outlining some major problems with this approach. These include the sheer diversity of states that exists, and the increasingly tenuous link between states and their peoples. We then turn to major alternatives that are posed within contemporary efforts to rethink security, exploring debates around 'human security', 'societal security' and 'ecological security'. The chapter argues that the whom or what of security does not exist before or beyond security threats. Rather, identifying or creating security threats is vital for the creation of security's referents.

Chapters 5 and 6 investigate the range of security threats that exist in contemporary global politics. Chapter 5 focuses on military issues, including the changing nature of warfare, the role of weapons in the **international system**, and international terrorism. Chapter 6 then explores the importance of so-called '**new security challenges**' and '**structural violences**' with case studies on climate change, famine, poverty, organized crime and gendered violence. The chapter concludes by exploring how security threats are identified and measured, and the political dynamics that are central to the prioritizing of some issues over others.

Chapter 7 – Is Security Possible? – asks whether, and how, security can be achieved in light of the range of potential threats discussed in Chapters 5 and 6. The approaches explored include military balancing or bandwagoning in which states align themselves with or against others for protection; the spread of free markets and international governmental organizations; development programmes such as the United Nations' Millennium Campaign; and international human rights regimes. We argue in this chapter that different approaches to security's possibility reflect different understandings of the possibility of change within the international system.

The book's final chapter – Is Security Desirable? – explores the normative issues that are raised by the study of security. It concentrates, in particular, on two questions. First, is security a 'good' thing: to be pursued wherever and whenever possible? And, second, what should we do when researching, speaking and practising security as students, scholars and citizens? As we shall see – and perhaps as we might hope – there are a huge range of answers to questions such as these, but the chapter makes two arguments in particular. First, that every serious discussion of security and insecurity must engage with these issues. Indeed, ethical commitments and claims are contained, we suggest, within every approach to security, even if they remain only hidden or implicit. And, second, that scholars of security should be as explicit as possible about their own commitments, and as open as possible to alternative ways of thinking and doing security.

In the conclusion we offer a brief recap of the book's arguments and rationale before outlining some of the future paths open to Security Studies. In so doing, we argue that Security Studies benefits from its diversity and heterogeneity, so long as dialogue is maintained with others working across and outside of the subdiscipline. We also note that Security Studies scholars and students must be reflexively aware of the contexts in which security and insecurity are spoken, studied, practised and experienced.

Conclusion

As the above suggests, this textbook has been written to introduce readers to debates around, issues within, and ways of thinking through the politics of security. Our argument throughout the discussion is that controversies around security do not exist in a vacuum. Rather, they are connected to developments in the 'real world' of global politics (as argued in Chapter 1) as well as to broader and competing assumptions about how the world works and how we should study it. Table I.2 summarizes some of these and how they play out in the domain of Security Studies (for a more substantive overview see Hay 2002).

One final thought with which we would like to finish this introduction: what, exactly, makes this book a *critical* approach to security? This is a more complicated question than it needs to be because – as you may already have noticed – some approaches to security explicitly label themselves (and are labelled by others) 'critical', although usually with a capital 'C', thus: Critical Security Studies. These approaches are those that draw on the Frankfurt School strand of Marxism which emphasize the importance of emancipation. As will become clearer, this book is not 'Critical' in that sense, although those ideas are discussed in the pages that follow. Rather, it is critical in seeking to highlight – and encourage reflection on – the underpinning assumptions, partialities and limitations of all ways of thinking about and doing security. This does not involve attempting to stand 'outside' of the world and asking how it is that the world came to be as it is (Cox 1996: 88): such a level of detachment is, from our point of view, neither possible nor desirable.

Table I.2   *Important controversies within Security Studies*

Issue/Debate	Overview	Example
Ontology	What is the nature of reality?	Is international politics anarchical?
Epistemology	What can we know about reality?	Can we accurately predict the likelihood of war?
Methodology	How can we gain knowledge or understanding of reality?	Does interviewing child soldiers tell us anything important about security?
Structure/ Agency	Is behaviour a product of actors and their interests, or of the contexts in which they find themselves?	Does the lack of a world government compel states to act aggressively?
Ideational/ Material	Are social and political dynamics driven by material 'things' or by the ideas that actors have about them?	If malaria is widely under stood to be a security threat, does it then become one?
Continuity/ Change	Is the social and political world characterized by stability or transformation?	Is 'new terrorism' com pletely different to 'old ter rorism'?
Parsimony/ Complexity	To understand the world, should we aim for detailed explanations with as much information as possible (complexity)? Or, should we simplify and focus only on the most important aspects thereof (parsimony)?	If states are the most pow erful actors in global poli tics, is it legitimate to focus our studies only on these (parsimony)?

Instead, this involves 'de-essentializing and deconstructing prevailing claims about security' (Krause and Williams 1997a: xiv) and constantly asking: where do these claims come from, what are their overt or covert assumptions, and what do such claims 'do' in relation to academic debate and security politics. In this sense, although it draws heavily on 'critical' approaches throughout, the book provides a critical introduction to security as much as it does an introduction to critical security studies – capitalized and otherwise.

Chapter 1

What is Security?

Chapter Overview

This chapter introduces readers to the most debated question within research on security: what is security? The chapter begins by exploring narrow and broad understandings of this concept, and what these mean for the study of international politics. Here we contrast theorizations of security as survival with more expansive understandings, such as those based around emancipation. This helps us to think through what conditions – or needs – must be met in order to achieve security. A second section then asks whether security is a material 'thing', or something that is socially created in part through our language, ideas and identities. The chapter's third section locates these debates around the definition of security both historically and politically. Our argument is that what security 'is' – or what it means to scholars and students, as well as to people and states – cannot be separated from the historical and political contexts in which security is being discussed. Particular attention is paid here to changes within Security Studies in the periods immediately following the end of the Cold War era and 9/11.

Chapter Contents

Introduction

This chapter asks a fundamental question, the answer(s) to which shape the field of Security Studies and this book: what, exactly, is security? What does it mean? It is not possible to answer this question, we will argue, outside of theory and outside of the contexts in which it is asked. First, whether desiring it or not, students and researchers of security require theory to inspire and guide the questions they ask, and the answers they build. Second, understandings of security – like understandings of *anything* and *everything* – are a product of the (political, cultural, and socio-economic) contexts in which they originate rather than the creation of autonomous, isolated scholars and practitioners. Academic disciplines such as International Relations and Security Studies do not exist in a bubble. They are shaped by, and help shape, the history of ideas – or intellectual paradigms – and the history of events and political urgencies. To understand what is meant by the question 'what is security?', and to see why this question is asked at particular times and not others, we need to move between the linked stories of twentieth century world politics and the **historiography** of the subdiscipline of Security Studies. Two types of narrative, above all others, dominate both of these histories: **realist** and liberal.

As Rothschild (1995) has shown, people have been the principal focus of discussions about security through the long sweep of documented human history. And, yet, in the minds of many International Relations scholars and practitioners, the term 'security' often conjures images of the state and its military. This bias is due to the **hegemonic** position political Realism occupied during the foundational and formative years of Security Studies. As shown in Chapter 4, this academic subdiscipline took shape following the **1947 US National Security Act**, with the onset and crystallization of the Cold War. At this moment in world politics, the emergence of **bipolarity** and questions of nuclear **deterrence** were the central preoccupations of governing elites. As such, the codification of **containment** and theorization of **mutually assured destruction** (MAD) were two of the foremost tasks facing practitioners and researchers of security. The proximity of the new subdiscipline of Security Studies to the political imperatives of the American government in a new era of Cold War ensured that the development of the former was conditioned by the demands of the latter. This context was fertile for the development and acceptance of realist ideas in the vacuum left by liberalism's apparent discrediting following two World Wars and an unprecedented global economic crisis beginning in 1929 (Carr 2001).

In the formative years of its study, at the start of the Cold War, security *was* national (i.e. state) security (see Chapter 4). Through a realist lens, security was understood, simply, as the continued survival of the state. And, realists suggested, the principal means to ensure survival was through the acquisition of power, understood as **relative material capability**. There is a compelling **parsimony** to this logic of realism (e.g. Buzan 1996). If a state has a greater military arsenal than potential foes, its chances of survival (if war were to break out) are higher. National security therefore is increased through the militarization of the state. Unfortunately, of course, if all states buy into such logic, **arms races** (see Chapter 4) can occur. What is interesting for our purposes, however, is to note that the principal critics of realism at the time bought into the same vision of international relations and its accompanying logic(s) of security.

Although liberalism – realism's traditional alternative – had substantial grounds for optimism at the start of the twentieth century, its fortunes looked considerably bleaker by the time of the birth of Security Studies in the post-World War II era. Liberals had undeniably been set back by the brutishness and **self-interest** underpinning both World Wars, the crippling of Germany in a punitive post-World War I economic reparations regime, and the rise of protectionist forms of economic nationalism. Thomas Hobbes's 'state of nature', in which life, infamously, is 'nasty, brutish, and short', appeared to have trumped Immanuel Kant's liberal aspirations for 'perpetual peace' (see Box 1.1). As the realist E.H. Carr (2001: 58) had argued on the eve of World War I, 'What confronts us in international politics today is, therefore, nothing more than the complete bankruptcy of the conception of morality which has dominated political and economic thought for a century and a half'. In addition, Realism's apparent ability to explain and predict **superpower** behaviour in the Cold War gave further cause for concern to proponents of International Relation's second principal theory.

By the late 1960s and 1970s, these fortunes were shifting, and liberalism experienced an important resurgence. This, however, came at a cost: a general acceptance of the central tenets of realism, if not their implications. Liberalism's cause, in other words, became the mitigation of realism's central claims; namely, that a logic of international anarchy necessitates a relentless pursuit of power by states seeking survival. Liberalism, during the Cold War, sought to prevent the inevitable descent into arms races and spirals of insecurity that realism's more offensive variants predicted. For Liberals, this inexorable logic could be interrupted through dynamics of economic integration, **democratization**, and international institutions, which would

Box 1.1 Thomas Hobbes and the state of nature

The political theorist, Thomas Hobbes, is a figure of major importance in the development of Realist approaches to security. His book, *Leviathan*, set out to explain and justify the emergence of 'the state' as a form of political institution. To do this, he conducted a thought experiment to imagine what life would have been like before its emergence. This hypothetical condition – the 'state of nature' – is one of continual fear and danger in which all 'men' are enemies and, 'the life of man [is] solitary, poor, nasty, brutish, and short' (Hobbes 1985: 186). Many realist approaches to International Relations begin with the assumption that the international system is a similar state of nature. States, just as 'men', are self-interested and a potential danger to the survival of one another.

These assumptions about the state of nature were developed by the Genevan philosopher Jean-Jacques Rousseau in his 'stag hunt' analogy. In this analogy, we are to imagine four hunters in the forest pursuing a large stag. If caught, the stag would provide enough meat for the village through several tough winter days, and all four hunters would certainly get enough to eat. To catch the stag, however, all four hunters must work together in order to successfully trap and kill it. If any one hunter does not cooperate the stag will go free and the hunters go hungry.

The dilemma arises because each hunter has two options: (i) to cooperate and catch the stag; or (ii) to look after their own interest by leaving the stag hunt and 'go it alone' for the easier (and smaller) prize of a hare which would provide sufficient food for the individual hunter. Consider now what you might do in this situation. If you opted to cooperate, and seek to catch the stag together, you had better hope your fellow three hunters did likewise, or it will be a long, cold, and hungry evening. It is this inability to rely on others that realism suggests makes it logical for individuals – whether hunters or states – to act selfishly in order to ensure their own survival.

Realists have gone on to use Game Theory to demonstrate the mathematical logic of defecting (not cooperating) in scenarios such as these. It was the mathematician John Nash (made famous by the film *A Beautiful Mind*) after whom this logical outcome was named: the Nash equilibrium. When we see states renege on treaties or violate international law norms it is often possible to develop a realist explanation of this behaviour as self-interested because of a lack of trust in others. This is particularly true of the international system for political realists because there is nobody 'in charge' to force states to work together. It is this condition – the lack of a world government – that is termed anarchy.

Box 1.2 Realism and its variants

'Realism' is an inadequate label to capture and do justice to the variety of 'realisms' within International Relations and their competing explanations of state interaction. While they do share important common characteristics, such as a focus on self-interest and scepticism about the reliability of others, they are also divided by significantly divergent emphases. The most important of these differences is that between (classical) realism and, its later incarnation, neo-realism (sometimes called structural realism). Where (classical) realism, associated with Thomas Hobbes, emphasizes the role of human nature within political outcomes, neo-realism shifts the level of explanation to structural causes of state behaviour. While both agree that men and states are rational, self-interested, utility-maximizers, for neo-realists states behave as they do due to the anarchic nature of the International System, not the inherent selfishness of man. This anarchy – the lack of a world government – inspires states to look after themselves, potentially at the expense of others. This, neo-realists suggest, is a more scientific theory of International Relations, than that offered by their classical forebears.

To complicate matters, neo-realism itself is not a unified theory, but in fact splits into two predominant strands: offensive and defensive realism. Offensive realists, such as Mearsheimer, suggest that the accumulation of power (in the pursuit of hegemony) is the foremost concern of states, who act accordingly. Defensive realists suggest alternatively that states prioritize survival over power, and act accordingly. The reasons for both are structural. For offensive realists, the international system enables the pursuit of power and aspirations to hegemony (although this is rarely achieved) because there is no world government to prevent a state seeking to do this. For defensive realists, the international system tends to punish such behaviour, for example through heavy military defeat, and thus states tend to pursue the more modest goal of acquiring sufficient power to survive.

During the 1990s, a new variant of realism, named neo-classical realism, gained in popularity. This strand of realism began with neo-realism's structural assumptions, but added insights from classical realism to mediate this structural determinism. Neo-classical realists suggest, for instance, that the agency of state leaders and context of a state's history and foreign policy relations matter. It would, for example, make a big difference if your President were Al Gore or George W. Bush, or your Chancellor Angela Merkel or Adolf Hitler.

bind (accountable) governments together into collective, mutually beneficial arrangements. Today, despite its current woes, the European Union stands as the greatest ever example of an 'international community' founded upon the three legs of the **Kantian Tripod**. The three legs of this tripod – democracy, institutions, and economic interdependence – are the liberal's powerful remedy to the realist's focus on self-interest and survival through military pre-eminence (see Chapter 8). For liberals the stability derived from the coexistence of these legs has the potential to foster the conditions necessary for peaceful cooperation between states.

As this suggests, the 1970s was a time in which realism and liberalism moved steadily towards each other, converging on common ground in their later, newer, variants: **neo-realism** and **neo-liberalism**. This **neo-neo synthesis** looked remarkably more harmonious than the debates between liberals and realists in the interwar years (see Chapter 3). It was marked and made possible, in part, by agreement on the central tenets of Security Studies. For both, the state was the principal actor on the world stage and national security was the primary goal. The risks to security came in the form of external military threats, which could either be mitigated through the **rationality** of deterrence or the mutual binds and benefits of institutions. Within the neo-neo synthesis, the central task of Security Studies was to help prevent the outbreak of (nuclear) war (between superpowers). At the time of this theoretical narrowing, the answer to the question, 'what is security?', appeared readily apparent: security was the continued survival of the United States, through the avoidance of nuclear apocalypse.

Key Points

- Although originally focused on the individual human, the term security has become increasingly associated with the survival of states.
- Central to this change of meaning was realism's dominance of IR and Security Studies in the Cold War era.
- The increasing proximity between realism and liberalism from the 1970s onwards both followed and made possible general agreement on the fundamental tenets of Security Studies.

Security: a narrow or broad phenomenon?

We contend that to pursue security is to do more than avoid nuclear annihilation, prevent war, and/or protect the state through military strength. In making this argument, we align ourselves with critical approaches to the study of security, which tend to adopt a more expansive understanding of the concept and its possibilities. In this section, we explore narrow and broad accounts of security, tracing justifications for each, and what they mean for the study of international politics more broadly. Here, we contrast conceptions of security as a synonym, simply, for survival, on the one hand, and, on the other, more expansive theorizations associated with **Peace Studies** literature and debates around human security and Critical Security Studies (CSS). In so doing, we ask whether the continuation of life is sufficient for security, and, if not, what conditions – or basic needs – must be met for security to be achieved. These are fundamental ontological questions, which must be considered alongside the epistemological concerns of Chapter 2 which focus not on what security *is*, but rather on what we can know about security.

Perhaps the simplest way to define security is as a condition where the survival of someone or something is not at risk. Colonel Gaddafi's Libyan regime, for example, was far more secure before the emergence of the popular uprising that led to his overthrow (and death) in 2011. My personal security, similarly, is far greater if I am stood on top of a grassy hill than on the side of an erupting volcano. At the same time, however, while I might be secure from the threat of lava stood on top of my hill, there might be other – more pressing – dangers that threaten my life in this context: a poisonous snake near my feet, perhaps, or I might be allergic to the stings of those honey bees swarming above my head. Then again, perhaps beginning with my security is to mix up our priorities in this little scenario. Maybe we should be focusing not on the likelihood of my own survival in this instance, but instead, on the security of those bees from the threat I pose to them, and the danger they face whether they sting me or otherwise.

What this contrived story is intended to illustrate is that to study security involves making a series of choices about what this term means. Although we will have much more to say about each of these choices in subsequent chapters, some of the most important include the following. First, does security – as in the above example – mean the same thing as survival? Or, does it mean more than simply staying alive, or continuing to exist? If I had been bitten by the snake and needed my leg amputated but avoided the honey bees, would my security have been greater? Second, does everything with the capacity to cause harm to someone or something constitute a security threat? And, if not, how might we differentiate between, for example, the threat posed by popular uprisings and natural disasters? And, third, accounts of security also involve identifying a 'who' or 'what' that is either secure or insecure: this might be the individual human, the state, or (in our example) the honey bee. What matters, however, is that whichever 'who' or 'what' we prioritize – whichever referent, in the language of Security Studies – will greatly influence our view of the possibility or desirability of security.

The traditional response to many of these questions within Security Studies has been to keep the meaning of security as narrow – and therefore as simple – as possible. So, this has tended to involve focusing on the security of the state (discussed in Chapter 4), from the military threat posed by other states (discussed in Chapter 5). This 'traditionalist agenda' (Buzan 1997) associated with political realism in particular, is one that approaches (national) security effectively as synonymous with the survival of the state from these external threats. Because of this, the role of non-military threats (see Chapter 6), and the insecurities experienced by groups or actors other than the state have had a very limited influence on the development of this subfield of study. Instead, the military value and use of particular weapons dominated much work that was done on security, especially in the Cold War period (Baldwin 1995: 123). The ultimate question underpinning this work, was how might the state guarantee its survival – its security – under conditions of anarchy (see Chapter 8). And, for advocates of this 'minimalist' approach to security, doing so would involve a state prioritizing its own territorial integrity and sovereignty, at the expense of more expansive concerns beyond its borders (compare Suhrke 1993; and Meernik 2004).

Although this traditional – narrow – approach to security as the survival of the state has long dominated research in this area, it has not gone entirely uncontested. Even during the Cold War it was possible to identify dissenting voices for whom this framework was unnecessarily restrictive. One major challenge came from students of 'Third World security' (see Bilgin 2003: 205–7). These authors argued that the emphasis on military conflict and interstate crises within the traditional agenda meant that the security needs of developing states, and people within them, had been largely neglected. For these thinkers – and arguably for foreign policy elites in many 'Third World' states at the time, too – security meant something quite different to simply surviving within the unfavourable status quo of the international system. Instead, it meant pursuing radical changes to this system and the economic, political and social inequalities which it perpetuated (ibid). For these authors security was linked to the need for development, and (often) to grassroots movements and practices.

The importance of 'Third World' Security Studies notwithstanding, it was a related Peace Research literature that really helped to generate momentum for the broadening of the meaning of security beyond mere national survival (see Rogers 2013). The notion of 'structural violence' developed by Galtung (1971, see also Chapter 6) was particularly important here, as a way of bringing attention to, and helping to theorize, the diversity of harms that can threaten security. Structural violence refers to those largely unintentional, but avoidable harms that human beings suffer beyond the direct physical violences caused by other people. For example, although more than enough food is produced to sustain the earth's population, there are 870 million undernourished people living today: one in eight of the world's total (FAO *et al.* 2012). Clearly, there is an enormous difference between the current state of affairs, and what could be the case if social, political and economic life were organized differently. There is a difference, in Galtung's words, between 'the actual' and 'the potential'. And, it is structural violence that is the cause of this gap between the actual and the potential: those enduring and entrenched inequalities that cause insecurity for millions of people across the world every day.

This Peace Research notion of structural violence is important because it makes it possible to begin thinking about security in a much broader way than the traditionalist agenda allows. In the first instance, structural violence points to the range of different harms that can affect humans and individuals: hunger, disease, poverty, natural disasters and so forth are as likely to impact an individual's life chances as are direct forms of violence such as war, terrorism, or physical assault (see Chapters 5 and 6). Second, it also suggests that people can suffer violence, or be harmed, in a number of ways that may not lead directly to their death. Individuals or groups, in other words, might suffer insecurity in ways that do not necessarily threaten their survival. While hunger, a lack of access to medication, illiteracy, or the constant risk of unemployment may not lead directly to my death (although several of these ultimately might): my experience of any of them is likely to undermine the extent to which I am secure. Security, in Ken Booth's words, may therefore be understood here as 'survival-plus'. However, the difficulty (perhaps impossibility) of agreeing to the requirements of a 'secure' life helps us to understand why security is so often described as an **essentially contested concept**. What amount or level of food and education, life expectancy, quality of air, employment opportunities, access to the internet, and so forth are necessary for security if security means more than simply staying alive? There are clear parallels here with debates over whether universal human rights exist, and, if so, what they might be.

Two trends emerge from the above examples of narrow and broad understandings of security, both of which speak to a fundamental

Table 1.1   *Narrow and broad approaches to security*

	Narrow	Broad
Water Scarcity	**Referent:** The state. **Threat:** Resource wars/ 'hydroconflicts'; Damage to national agriculture and infrastructure. **Example:** The 1980 Iran–Iraq War was in part motivated by concerns over access to the Shatt-al- Arab Waterway.	**Referent:** Individuals/Communities. **Threat:** Includes harm through drought and famine, and diseases associated with (clean) water shortages. **Example:** 1 child dies from a water-related disease every 21 seconds.
HIV/AIDS	**Referent:** The state. **Threat:** Infections to military personnel; Impact upon national economic performance due to adult illnesses or death rates. **Example:** In Botswana, President Mogae declared HIV a national security threat in 2000.	**Referent:** Individuals/Communities. **Threat:** Ill health and potential death of HIV infected individuals, overrepresented in particular groups. **Example:** Homosexuals, the gay communities and many others in the United States faced an HIV/ AIDS epidemic during the 1980s.
Irregular Immigration	**Referent:** The state. **Threat:** Border control, therefore territorial integrity and sovereignty. **Example:** Recent attempts to limit legal and irregular migration to the United Kingdom and Australia have been premised on cultural and economic arguments about national security	**Referent:** Irregular migrants. **Threat:** Death or physical harm in transit; Economic exploitation; Risk of imprisonment in pro cessing centres; Risk of deportation. **Example:** The Lampedusa boat disaster, in October 2013, claimed the lives of 365 migrants, largely from Eritrea, attempting to travel between Libya and Italy.

divide running through the heart of Security Studies. First, 'traditionalists' and 'broadeners' tend to be divided by their understandings of security's principal referent (see Chapter 4). On the one hand, traditionalists are inclined to study threats – potential sources of insecurity, such as climate change – in terms of their relation to the physical integrity and sovereignty of the nation-state. While these threats, in many instances, manifest as a *security* threat via another source of insecurity, such as migration, the state remains the focus. For these approaches, issues such as nutrition, disease and the environment only enter the (security) debate through their ability to cause violent conflict or otherwise destabilize the state. 'Broadeners', on the other hand, are willing to consider a range of alternative referents beyond the state, such as the security of an individual, or a group of refugees, for example. They are also, moreover, willing to look at causes of harm – poverty, famine, disease, and so forth – as security threats in their own right, irrespective of whether they cause conflict or otherwise. And, in so doing, they are willing to think about security in terms that go beyond the simple continuation of existence. Table 1.1 illustrates how similar issues can spark quite different security concerns across approaches.

As suggested above, it is the narrower approaches to security that have traditionally dominated its study. As Ken Booth (2007: 96) argues, 'over the years, students have been led where the "conventional convictions" of their teachers took them, and this has meant that security became identified as an essentially military terrain'. Security, he suggests, was seen for a long time as a 'common-sense, pre-defined' term; one that was 'unproblematic until examined with a critical eye' (ibid.). For writers such as Booth, the emergence of recent efforts to view security with a 'critical eye' is undoubtedly a positive development. There are, however, potential tradeoffs of which to be aware, and it is important to be keep in the mind the issues involved in broadening one's understanding of security beyond state survival.

A first potential cost is that the wider the term security becomes, the less meaningful it is. If war, terrorism, crime, disease, drought, education, environmental damage, unemployment, famine, energy shortages, and so on all become security concerns, what is left outside of security?

Box 1.3 Case study: Chilean miners' crisis

On 5 August 2010, in the Atacama Desert in northern Chile, thirty-three miners were trapped seven hundred metres underground and approximately five kilometres from the mine's entrance, following a cave-in. 'Los 33' would remain underground until 13 October 2010, emerging jubilant over a 24-hour period, covered live on rolling news footage.

Once the miners were discovered alive, seventeen days after the collapse of the mine's main tunnel, the chances of their survival were considerably higher – although far from guaranteed – than they had been when they were earlier feared dead. If security is the absence of existential threat – the absence of threats to the existence of someone or something – this would imply a massive increase in the security of Los 33 at this time. Yet, the question remains, to what extent could the experience of these men isolated underground without access to natural light, support networks, or any guarantee of rescue – and so on – be thought of as one of security?

In other words, if security is everything, is it also nothing (compare Buzan 1997 and Suhrke 1993)? A second potential cost is one of scholarly expertise. How can any academic subdiscipline be involved in the analysis of all of those aspects of existence – of the state, the individual, the community, and so on – that are necessary for survival and perhaps even more than this? At least the traditionalist agenda had the advantage of concentrating knowledge in the relatively coherent area of military strategy. Third, we might also argue that issues such as education, maternal healthcare, or unemployment – however important – are simply of a different order of things to security issues. Whatever similarity they bear to security issues, perhaps their proper place is under alternative fields of study such as Development Studies, Gender Studies, Political Economy, Human Geography, and so forth.

Key Points

- Narrow understandings of security privilege the state and its military, focusing on the causes of conflict.
- Broader understandings of security offer a wider framework for analysis, potentially including a greater variety of referents, threats, subjects and methods.

Security: material, ideational or discursive?

An important additional factor in conceptual debates over security's meaning is whether security (and therefore insecurity) is reducible to brute material realities. In this section we sketch a range of recent challenges to ontological materialism within the IR and Security Studies literature, pointing to the contemporary prominence of constructivist thought. After a brief account of the breadth of constructivism, we argue that these approaches offer potential for a more complex understanding of security, in which identities, interests and threats exist and interact as social productions, rather than as pre-given entities. Problematizing the realist and liberal approaches outlined in the introduction, we conclude this section by presenting the contribution of Foucauldian approaches to thinking through security's reality.

Approaches within Security Studies and IR occupy a series of distinct, if occasionally overlapping, positions on the importance of material factors – a nuclear warhead, an aircraft, a mountain, and so forth – in determining social and political outcomes. First, realism dominates, replete with a materialist ontology. Second, constructivism claims to have seized the middle ground (Adler 1997), arguing that social reality is comprised of both material 'things' and the ideas we hold about them. Third, post-structuralism has gained relatively recent attention, arguing for an ontology which recognizes that the world is discursively constructed: there is no distance between the world of things and the world of discourse. Of course, labelling and bracketing any of these approaches is a(n) (inter)subjective and violent enterprise: 'realism', 'post-structuralism' and 'constructivism' are all diverse entities with numerous influences and internal debates (although see Debrix 2002).

Despite these difficulties of labelling, realists share an ontological commitment to materialism. The possibility of a war breaking out or being avoided, or the chances of an alliance being formed to balance a threat, is at root an outcome of material capabilities. While epistemological commitment to **rationalism** and a preference for parsimony are also vital, it is a material ontology, focused on the capabilities of states, which undergirds realism's explanatory framework. Material capabilities – or resources – determine the power of particular states in the international system (Berenskoetter 2007: 6). And, it is the relative power of different states at particular moments – which will always act rationally and in their objective, pre-given self-interest – that drives dynamics of conflict and cooperation. War, conflict and the absence of either – fundamental questions of national security for realists – are, therefore, ultimately material phenomena. While evident in the writings of classical realists from Thucydides, through Hobbes and Machiavelli, to Morgenthau, this materialist approach to security becomes very explicit in neo-realist writings. For Kenneth Waltz, for instance, the global system is ultimately anarchical (lacking any *Leviathan*). Its units (states) are **functionally equivalent** in that they do broadly the same things as one another. Questions of survival, rule and domination, therefore, boil down ultimately to physical might. Survival and the pursuit of power, in the face of potential conflict, inspire state action. It is the cold, hard (material) reality of guns, tanks and missiles that ensure any one state's survival (and therefore security), regardless of whether one is studying Israel, Iran or India. For Morgenthau, Waltz, and Mearsheimer, it is material reality that shapes political outcomes across the globe and throughout history. For realism, interests are materially determined and political struggles are decided on material grounds.

Peter Katzenstein's (2003a, b) work is a useful point of departure from realism and into constructivism, as it addresses some of the questions that realism struggles to provide answers for within its deliberately narrow theoretical framework. Realism, and particularly its more offensive variants, has long struggled to account for the dogs that do not bark in world politics (Snyder 1984/5: 93). For instance, German non-participation in the 2003 **Coalition of the Willing** can be challenging for offensive realists, given that the intervention in Saddam Hussein's Iraq was widely viewed to be in the national interest of Western states seeking the spoils of war at the time (e.g. Halperin 2007; see also Kettell 2009). Katzenstein's 'conventional' or 'thin' constructivism remedies this flaw by adding an additional variable to be analysed: the domestic cultural context of a state. For Katzenstein (2003a: 756), decisions to participate in the 'War on Terror' were the 'consequence of institutionalised norms', not only raw material interest. Thus, specific national security cultures and norms made it 'normal' for Germany to interpret 9/11 differently to the United States: with the different histories of these two states a major factor here. As Katzenstein summarizes, Germany 'betrayed a distinctive narrowness in outlook and inwardness in orientation that can be explained only with reference to their historical experiences in the first half of the twentieth century' (Katzenstein 2003b: 53).

Building on the insights of Onuf (1989) and Wendt (1992), Katzenstein's (2003a: 756) work makes important references to the 'bitter lessons from history' that Germany has 'learnt', highlighting the importance of cultural norms and expectations around how Germany should behave on the world stage. For Katzenstein and conventional constructivists, ideas are a crucial missing variable within realist analysis. Germany declined to participate in the Coalition of the Willing because of the existence of a particular set of ideas that were prominent in the country at the time, rather than because of a cost/benefit calculation around the likelihood of victory and potential spoils of war. The broader point here is that states will respond to other actors within the international anarchical system based on their interpretation of those actors. Self-interest and the absence of any global hegemonic power, in other words, do not compel states to behave with aggression or opportunism. Rather, as Alexander Wendt (1992) famously argued, anarchy is 'what states make of it'. Whether this anarchy inspires a zero-sum struggle for survival, a drive to compete economically, or a sense of community and shared interests at any one time, depends upon how the self and others are understood by the actors involved. Consider, for example, Germany's shift from a Hobbesian, fear-driven foreign policy in the 1930s, to more Kantian (and perhaps Grotian) desires to prop-up the European Union in the twenty-first century. For conventional constructivists, therefore, ideas are a crucial component within security dynamics, but the material world is still seen to exist outside of the ideas that are held about it.

Our own view is that conventional constructivism – sometimes also described as 'thinner' constructivism – overemphasizes the 'collective permanence' of intersubjective understandings about the world (Widmaier 2007: 750), as well as the direct, causative impact they have on state interaction. It is problematic to speak of a German culture (in the singular) as well as to argue that such a culture might cause (in an unproblematic, linear fashion) German foreign policy. By adding ideas into the mix, conventional constructivism supplements realism with an important additional variable. This retains realism's parsimony and widens its explanatory scope, but fails to adequately conceptualize what 'ideas' might mean for international relations and our explanations thereof. Fortunately, here, with its mantra that 'ideas matter', constructivism excels. *Critical* **constructivism** emphasizes 'the contingent nature of outcomes by examining how agents frame' events, in order 'to make persuasive claims concerning the need for change' (ibid.). Language, framing and resonance are crucial, and decisions must be communicated persuasively to prevail over alternative accounts of what has been or should be done. In recognizing the importance of persuasion, critical constructivists pursue an approach that emphasizes both ideas *and* language. It really does matter whether Bush or Obama is crafting a narrative for the US population. Their strategies and framings will be different, they will employ different language and, at times, even divergent security policies, despite plugging into the same collection of cultural norms, myths and ideas.

Things get more tricky for critical constructivists when questions are raised as to just how far a researcher has to dig before they hit 'material' (i.e. extra-discursive) reality. Is the world made up of 'ideas all the way down' (Wendt 1999), for example? Or, is there a point at which material properties exist – and have impact upon global processes and events – away from their discursively constructed meanings? This is an important question. On one hand, critics might point to tanks or oil as material 'things'. The rebuttal here is that a tank is a physical manifestation of both liberation and occupation, depending on your particular vantage point. This is more than simply suggesting that a tank means different things to different people. Rather, it is to argue that what the tank actually *is* depends upon the ideas and language that enable its comprehension (see Chapter 2). Oil, for example, was a pointless, sticky mess, prior to knowledge of how to use it for heat, light, movement, and money. Today, it might be seen as a security threat because of its devastating impact on ecosystems in the Gulf of Mexico, as well as its broader role in producing greenhouse gases and contributing to global climate change. Alternatively, oil might be viewed as the guarantor of security through the wealth it brings to oil-rich and some developing states, or the liberating effect it has had on isolated rural communities. Whatever its material qualities, then, oil can be an entirely different phenomenon for different groups, at different times, depending on the discourses in which it is located. Or, at least, that is what critical constructivists argue.

Looking to post-structuralism, we find a similar but slightly different view, whereby notions of 'buying into' a particular discourse are seen to place too high a degree of emphasis on the volition of individuals to choose the meaning of things and, even, themselves. For post-structuralists, discourse is more than 'just' language or political rhetoric; rather, it is a framework – a series of significations – that enables, shapes and constrains the way people think. For a post-structuralist, 'things' only mean anything, as a result of the discourse – the framework – in which they are located. A gun for example can be a weapon, or an ornament; a tool of attack, or defence, or even pest control; and a symbol of freedom (in parts of the United States where membership of the National Rifle Association is particularly high), or a symbol of peace (its barrel knotted, outside the United Nations' Headquarters in New York). The meaning of the gun is generated by its placing within a particular discursive framework.

Post-structural IR was inspired by a dissatisfaction with realism combined with the opportunities that accompanied the breakdown of bipolarity at the end of the Cold War (e.g. Der Derian and Shapiro 1989). Inspired, principally, by the work of Michel Foucault, Jacques Derrida and Judith Butler, its basis was (and remains) a belief that international relations and security is discursively constituted. There is nothing outside of our discourses on global politics: the world and its components can only be understood within these unstable systems of meaning. Post-structural IR takes its normative agenda from a desire to destabilize particular dominant discourses – such as neo-liberalism, **patriarchy**, and political realism, for example – which are seen to be dangerous and silencing of marginalized voices. This (ethical) project therefore seeks to create space for ways of thinking, speaking, and acting otherwise. In stark contrast to realism's material ontology, a post-structural approach discards the notion that 'things' might possess intrinsic or essential qualities as ultimately unknowable and irrelevant. As Wittgenstein suggested, for the post-structuralist, the limits of language are indeed the limits of the world.

Of course, as we have argued elsewhere (Holland 2013b: 13), there are frequent (and unfair) criticisms of an ontology emphasizing the productivity of discourse. One, for example, is that 'material facts' are downplayed or entirely absent and ignored. Adopting a discursive ontology does not mean that a researcher denies the world's materiality, but instead, a different argument is made: that the world becomes meaningful through discourse. The material is not wholly eviscerated. Rather, material and ideational factors are fully interwoven, such that we cannot see either in isolation (see Chapter 2). 'What is denied is not that objects exist externally to thought.' Rather, the different assertion is made that 'they could not constitute themselves as objects outside any discursive condition of emergence' (Laclau and Mouffe 1985: 108). As Richard Jackson (2005a), a constructivist, has argued, 'while everything is text (even a bomb is a text – especially when soldiers write personal messages on them, but also when they are dropped in the name of "freedom" or as a message to other dictators), text is not necessarily everything (bombs are also instruments of death that at the moment of detonation are impervious to any form of deconstruction)'. This is one of the foremost ontological divergences between post-structuralism and critical constructivism. For the former, it is neither necessary nor possible to suggest that material reality exists 'below' the realm of discourse.

For our purposes, it is useful to consider this claim with respect to the interests, identities and ideas that help to shape world politics and security. While realism assumes that interests exist independently of ideas about them – they are fixed and given – post-structuralism argues that they are established through language and other discursive practices which, when relatively stable, produce meaning in a fairly systematic (if always partial) way. For post-structuralists, interests only become apparent against the backdrop of a discursively constructed identity. Consider, for example, debates in the United Kingdom in 1997, when New Labour was torn between two competing notions of what an 'ethical foreign policy' might look like. On the one hand, represented by Foreign Secretary Robin Cook, an ethical foreign policy put human rights front and centre, premised upon an understanding of British identity as atoning for the excesses of the British Empire. On the other hand, represented by Prime Minister Tony Blair, an ethical foreign policy was about reconciling **Realpolitik** and altruism in coalition-backed **humanitarian interventions** for the greater good. This latter variant relied upon a British **national identity** that was not ashamed – perhaps even proud – of the British Empire (Parmar 2006). In both cases, the British national interest was formed on the basis of a constructed national identity, premised variously upon notions of colonial guilt or aspirations for global leadership.

Clearly, in each of these examples, we see that the answer to the question, 'what is security?', depends upon the theoretical approach adopted for its study. For realism, a materialist ontology privileges the material world, and thus the material interests it inspires and with which states act in accordance and pursuit. Constructivists, on the

Box 1.4 Interpreting 11 September 2001

The events of 11 September 2001 were deeply shocking for many Americans (Holland 2009) and others who watched them unfold live on television screens around the world. Over the following days, in response to those events, President George W. Bush asserted that on 11 September 2001, 'night fell on a different world' (Holland and Jarvis 2014). Within this understanding, American national security had been fundamentally changed by the '9/11' attacks. The 'Homeland', for instance, was now a 'battlefield', and an era of relative peace was seen to have ended. How might we make sense of this? Did, as was asserted, the events 'speak for themselves'?

For realism, the events clearly demonstrated a challenge to, and attack on, the United States. The material reality of aircraft destroying centre-pieces of the US economic and military establishment, and killing 3,000 people in the process, was inescapable. Yet, the relative material capability of the Al Qaeda network was such that the challenge it posed to the world's mightiest ever hegemon was insignificant. US survival was never really threatened by this non-state actor. Nor was the hierarchy of states in the global system. How then did a response of War on Terror, premised upon feelings of intense vulnerability and omnipresent threat, take hold of and shape the US policy response?

For constructivists, the material reality of the tragic events is important, but so too are the ideas and language that were chosen to make sense of '9/11'. For thinner constructivists, the security/**strategic culture** of the United States is crucial. Were the attacks to have taken place in a state more accustomed to witnessing terrorism on domestic soil it is possible that a different type of response would have been formulated. For

$\rightarrow$

other hand, in both conventional and critical variants, proffer an ontology recognizing the importance of the interaction of the material with the ideational. The 'truths' of realism, constructivists recognize, only become 'facts' in a particular matrix of ideas. Anarchy, for example, is what states make of it, and the world looks decidedly less Hobbesian for Germany in the twenty-first century than it did in the twentieth. Finally, post-structuralism challenges all approaches in their continued appeals to notions of extra-discursive reality. A post-structural discursive ontology emphasizes the role of language (as well as images) in the production of meaning. Interests, ideas and identities interact as social productions; they are not fixed, pre-determined features of world politics. The implications of this ontology, for studies of security, are particularly stark.

→

critical constructivists, the framing of the events as 'an act of war' was all-important. Narratives of American exceptionalism and a historical calling to defend freedom were crucial in articulating a resonant foreign policy response that garnered the broad support of the American nation (Holland 2013b). George W. Bush was never more popular than in the days after 9/11, reaching public approval ratings of over 90% within the US.

Post-structuralists take this argument further still, arguing that the events were meaningless outside of the discourses that enabled their comprehension. For post-structuralists, events never 'speak for themselves'; rather, they are always located within a discursive framework of meaning. To witness the diversity of understandings of 9/11, it is possible to point to distinct discourses, which constructed the events alternatively as: sponsored by the US Government; sponsored by the Iraqi Government; the punishment of God for American toleration of homosexuality; a (natural) tragedy; the inevitable **blowback** of American empire; the first or latest strike in a **Clash of Civilizations**; or the realization of biblical prophecy. While all of these framings lost traction in the days and weeks after 9/11, Post-structuralists would argue that the 'official', dominant discourse(s) of the 'War on Terror' were no more or less connected to the material reality of the attacks than alternatives. Thus, the official narrative is one, of many, ways of discursively constructing the meaning of those events. As a number of critics have noted, a preferable discursive framing might have emphasized that the events were an intolerable criminal act, rather than an act of war. Such a framing might have inspired a more effective and less damaging form of response (e.g. Bulley forthcoming; Campbell 2001; Jarvis 2009a)

(handwritten margin note: even though people died?)

Key Points

- Realists adopt a materialist ontology, in which interests are pre-given and fixed. Security and insecurity are, therefore, a product of the different capabilities of dominant actors: usually states.
- Constructivists emphasize the interplay of the material and the ideational. Security and insecurity depend upon how actors understand the interests, intentions and actions of others, as well as their role in the world and self-interest.
- Post-structuralists adopt a discursive ontology which recognizes that ideas, interests and identities are discursively constructed. Security and insecurity only exist within discourse, yet this does not mean they are not 'real'.

Putting security into context(s)

This section locates the above debates both historically and politically. Our argument here is that what security 'is' – or what it means – cannot be separated from the historical and political contexts in which security is being discussed. Particular attention is paid to the opening up of Security Studies in two periods: first, the post-Cold War era, and, second, the post-9/11 period.

The post-Cold War era, we argue, was important because it strengthened the position of those arguing that a new, expanded, understanding was required to broaden the concept of security beyond questions of state survival in a context of international anarchy. As the 1994 **United Nations Human Development Report** famously illustrated, this geopolitical shift opened space for: addressing a range of sources of human misery as security issues (including domestic and international sources of harm, and military and other forms of threat); highlighting the impact of these harms at the level of individuals and communities; and rethinking the appropriate mechanisms with which security might be augmented or achieved. Importantly, these developments also encouraged advocates of more traditional understandings of security to reassert and refine the longstanding, realist approaches to this concept for reasons including disciplinary coherence and established expertises.

The impact of 9/11, we argue, was more ambiguous. At one level, these events were interpreted as adding further impetus to the need for a non state-centric, militaristic approach to security (studies). For some, they also reinforced the importance of the linkage between domestic and international security contexts, with the threat posed by 'failed states' becoming increasingly prominent after the attacks. Moreover, their aftermath also opened space for rethinking the obligations owed to the security of others elsewhere around the world – for advocates and opponents of the war on terrorism alike. At another level, however, the attacks and their aftermath were also interpreted as confirming longstanding assumptions about the international system and the nature of security therein. These included the continuing pertinence of military power, national interests and the externality of the most urgent security threats (at least for those in the West). In short, the events of 11 September 2001 raised a number of questions with which this volume grapples, including the nature of security today.

International Relations, dominated by realism, infamously failed to predict the end of the Cold War. The fall of the Berlin Wall and the end of bipolarity came as a surprise, both in the 'real world' of international politics and in the halls of academe. The space that this event afforded Security Studies was considerable. Debates about deterrence,

MAD, and containment were suddenly relegated in significance; instead, concerns about nuclear proliferation and the arms trade were elevated in importance. The greatest beneficiary of these events, however, was the issue of humanitarian intervention. With the overbearing concerns of national security (potential nuclear holocaust) suddenly slightly alleviated, space was created to consider alternative types and drivers of international intervention. The 1990s were, perhaps above all else, the era of humanitarian intervention. As Buzan and Hansen (2009) have argued, it was the shift in Great Power politics, and the accompanying de-institutionalization of the Cold War's strategic priorities, which rapidly filtered through into the reorganization of academic debates.

Just as realism and the neo-neo synthesis had developed and dominated in response to the strategic imperatives of the Cold War, so alternatives, such as the English School, rose to prominence in the early 1990s, as practitioners of world politics wrestled with decisions about 'saving strangers' (Wheeler 2002). The experiences of Bosnia, East Timor, Kosovo, Sierra Leone, and Rwanda, to name only a few, are testament to the importance of humanitarian intervention (or its lack) during the era of **new world order**. Images of genocide, for example, were now broadcast live, and occasionally throughout the day, increasing the sense that 'their' problem was now an issue for 'us', in the Western world. The failure of the international community to act in Rwanda stands out in the list of human rights atrocities from the 1990s. With over 800,000 slaughtered in that conflict, calls to prevent re-occurrences were widespread. Rwanda, however, followed shortly after the bitter US experience in Somalia, where American helicopters were shot down in Mogadishu (see Chapter 5). With the images of murdered American military personnel fresh in the public memory, appetite for a new humanitarian intervention in Africa was extremely limited. The pendulum of public opinion on humanitarian war would swing back and forth throughout the decade. It would be matched in Security Studies and International Relations by English School debates between pro-intervention **solidarists** and anti-intervention **pluralists** (see Chapter 5), accompanied by the emerging doctrine of the Responsibility to Protect (**R2P**).

These debates mirrored the broader expansion of Security Studies, as the subdiscipline realigned itself with the new post-Cold War security environment. The plight of individuals and non-state communities were, at last, considered security issues. And, the significance of the military to the provision of security was de-centred by some security researchers. Debates over the declining utility of military force were initially commonplace (Fierke 2007), and while this may ultimately not have been the case, they do indicate the significance of the paradigm shift that occurred in the wake of the Cold War. Issues such as climate change, nutrition, and health became legitimate topics of enquiry for a redefined and reoriented Security Studies during the 1990s. In 2001, however, many of those shifts were brought into question. Some saw the impact of 9/11 to bring to an end the blissful 'interregnum' that was the era of humanitarian intervention, characterized by concerns about issues of 'structural violence', human rights, and development. The direct challenge to the national security and military pre-eminence of the United States was a difficult fact to ignore, as was the robust reassertion of hegemony from the world's only superpower that followed. Once again, after 9/11, the world appeared a Hobbesian place, where the national interest was paramount in a dangerous dog-eat-dog world. In this new and dangerous world, it was possible to argue that the amount of power the state wielded would be the principal determinant of survival in the face of, what was frequently presented as, an **existential threat.**

The apparent re-elevation of state-centric, military-preoccupied approaches is not without contestation, however. The complexities of international and domestic security, for example, are readily apparent in debates about 'failed' and 'harbouring' states abroad, as well as counter-terrorism legislation and measures at home. Recent events such as the 2013 Boston Marathon Bombings, the 2013 murder of Drummer Lee Rigby in Woolwich, London, and the 2013 attack on the Westgate Shopping Mall in Nairobi, Kenya, have highlighted the intertwined nature of domestic and international grievances, leading, at times, to violent extremism. In these instances, it appears that international political issues and sources of influence interacted with the specific circumstances of national politics and local upbringing. In Woolwich, for example, the juxtaposition of a South London resident, speaking with a thick local accent about 'our (Muslim) lands', raises questions about identity formation that realist approaches struggle (or decline) to take seriously. This book considers the continued importance of military force, as well as the role of ideas and language within contexts such as the War on Terror and Arab Spring; we argue that it is normatively and theoretically important for Security Studies to consider, for example, both IEDs (improvised explosive devices) *and* identity. Both drones *and* discourse are significant in the new post 9/11 security environment. And, as during the Cold and post-Cold War eras, the subdiscipline of Security Studies must respond to – and emerges out of – the complexities of the contemporary period, replete as they are with myriad material, ideational, and discursive elements.

Key Points

- The end of the Cold War created space for rethinking Security Studies away from the state and the military (see Chapters 4 and 6).
- The post-Cold War era brought the issue of human rights and humanitarian intervention to the fore, alongside others.
- The post-9/11 security environment has been argued both to return traditional security concerns to centre-stage, as well as to reinforce the importance of a more expansive, critical agenda.

Conclusion

This chapter has considered what it means to speak of security, sketching some of the potential answers to (and issues in answering) this fundamental, ontological question. We began by considering the realist dominance of International Relations and Security Studies during the Cold War. In so doing, we argued that this dominance was suffocating of theoretical alternatives, whereby even realism's greatest challengers came to accept and adopt the central tenets of IR's pre-eminent theory. The minimalist understanding of security within realism came to shape the contours of the subdiscipline of Security Studies, marking out its relatively narrow boundaries of legitimate enquiry. Within this tightly bounded field, the state and its military were the principal components of a materialist ontology. The fall of the Berlin Wall and the end of the Cold War raised the possibility of **widening** Security Studies. One logical expansion of this increasingly broad understanding of security was the consideration of humanitarian intervention, which extended Security Studies' expertise in issues of war and conflict to the most pressing issues of the day. The intellectual space created by bipolarity's demise also, however, created scope for more diverse inclusions, such as climate change and health (see Chapter 6), which were now studied beyond their potential to cause or impact upon armed conflict.

The impact of 9/11 has been claimed by proponents of political realism, supporting traditional security agendas, as well as those influenced by a range of critical perspectives who have tended to welcome the broadening and **deepening** of Security Studies (see Chapter 4). On the one hand, the importance of military power and national security have undeniably resurfaced to dominate the security landscape of the War on Terror. On the other hand, the ideas, identities, and discourses of our political leaders have rarely been so important in shaping our understandings of security and demarcating the parameters of possible policy responses. In this era of War on Terror and Arab Uprisings, support can be found for a diversity of minimalist and maximalist agendas, as well as materialist, ideational, and discursive ontologies. A useful way of positioning ourselves in these debates is therefore to think more carefully around what we might be able to know about security: the focus of Chapter 2.

Further Reading

Buzan and Hansen (2009) is an excellent genealogical account of how international security studies has developed over time. For a more thematic overview of the field, Dannreuther (2013) is also insightful and worth reading. Fierke (2007) provides an explicitly critical introduction which focuses on issues including representations of danger, and the importance of identity within security politics, while Nayak and Selbin (2010) offer an important rejoinder to the Western-centricity of most overviews of global politics. Not introductory, but important because of its impact on the field, is Wendt's (1999) *Social Theory of International Politics*, which provides a book length exposition of his constructivist approach to international politics.

Internet Resources

It is interesting to compare the vision of security contained within the UN's understanding of R2P which was developed during the 1990s – UN Office of the Special Advisor on Genocide (2014) – with that outlined in the stated aims of the United States Department of Homeland Security (2014), which was established in 2001 following the 11 September attacks. The United Nations Food and Agriculture Agency (2012) summarizes and provides access to their recent report on world hunger, including the headline finding that nearly one in eight of the world's population were suffering from chronic undernourishment in 2010–2012. The World Health Organization (2014) fact sheet on malaria provides a succinct overview of the disease, and its transmission, symptoms, treatment and prevention, while the *Guardian* (2013) – a UK-based newspaper – provides data and resources on the 'world's deadliest migration routes'.

Chapter 2

What can we Know about Security?

Chapter Overview

This chapter focuses on the question: what can be known about security and insecurity? It begins by introducing a range of different approaches to epistemology – different theories of knowledge – and their importance within discussion on security and global politics more widely. In particular we distinguish between positivist views of Security Studies as a scientific enterprise, on the one hand, and, on the other, post-positivist approaches which argue that knowledge of security can never be impartial, detached or unbiased. The chapter then focuses on two questions. First, whether 'our' knowledge of security is objective or subjective. Second, whether we can make universal claims about the experience of security and the conditions of insecurity that are suffered by others around the world. The chapter concludes by arguing that what we think can be known about security is vitally important for two reasons. First, because this shapes the type of knowledge we are able to produce and how we present it. Second, because our epistemological position will impact on the type of methods we are likely to use in security research: the focus of Chapter 3.

Chapter Contents

Introduction

This chapter builds on the discussion of ontological questions in Chapter 1, by focusing on epistemological issues surrounding what can be *known* about security. It argues that different theoretical positions within the field of Security Studies not only reflect contrasting views about the 'stuff' of which international politics is made: who the major actors are, how their interests are formed, whether change is possible, and so forth. But, at the same time, that different positions also reflect competing views on the knowledge that can be acquired about that 'stuff'. So, for example, some scholars believe that a neutral, value-free and objective understanding of security threats is possible, albeit perhaps difficult to achieve. Within such a view, the researcher's task is to discover the (capitalized) Truth of (in)security: what causes famine; how can war be avoided; what will happen when US hegemony ends, and so on. Other scholars, in contrast, view their role very differently, seeing themselves as interpreters or narrators of stories relating to (in)security. Here, doing Security Studies might involve creating detailed – or 'thick' – descriptions of how particular events are understood or constructed by their participants and witnesses, rather than a concise and 'scientific' explanation focused on causes and effects. In this tradition, one might, for example, be more interested in trying to understand how illegal migrants are portrayed as a security risk by some actors, than in trying to explain and predict the transnational movements of people.

The chapter begins by exploring the importance of epistemological issues within studies of social, political and cultural life. In so doing, we identify four very different ways of thinking about knowledge – of anything – and how it might be acquired. These are: rationalism, **empiricism,** (critical) realism, and interpretivism. We then turn to the growing interest in epistemological matters across Security Studies and International Relations (IR): something that has been driven by internal developments within this field, as well as contact with other fields of study. In tracing these developments, we argue that although some scholars (and some students!) bemoan the attention that is afforded to epistemological questions, any attempt to understand or explain security dynamics requires at least some attention to these matters.

The chapter then turns to two major epistemological issues, on which any approach to security will take a stance, if only implicitly. The first is whether the study of security is a subjective or objective enterprise. So, for example, is it possible to accurately identify, measure and compare the security of different referents – whether individuals, communities or states? If so, how might one go about attempting this? Or, do such attempts reflect implicit assumptions, values, preferences and interests that cannot be escaped? To illustrate the importance of different responses to this question we turn to debates around how human security might or should be measured.

The second issue we explore is whether it is possible to make universal arguments about security. We begin here by demonstrating that many of the most prominent approaches within Security Studies believe that it is indeed possible to create transnational and trans-cultural understandings of security that hold true across time, space, gender, class, ethnicity and so forth. As Ken Booth (2005a: 181), for example, powerfully argued: 'what matters is whether ideas are true or false, with the grain of humanity or against it, emancipatory or oppressive: what matters is not where ideas come [from] but how well they travel'. We then contrast this type of claim with critiques from strands of feminist, post-colonial and post-structuralist literature. These approaches tend to be far more sceptical toward universalizing accounts of security, arguing that the experience thereof is intimately tied to one's position, status, interpretations, and so on. The value of approaches such as these, we argue, is they take all understandings of security seriously, including those that are held by marginal or subjugated individuals and groups (see Foucault 1980: 82). This is important because showing that security is a particular rather than universal experience might help to bring into question otherwise taken-for-granted or hegemonic understandings of security, insecurity, threats and referents.

The chapter concludes by arguing that how we situate ourselves in relation to epistemological debates around security is vitally important because this impacts on two further dynamics. The first is the type of knowledge claim we are able to make about security. For example, do we want to think about our research on security as objective truth, narrative, interpretation, political critique, or something else? While this might seem relatively unimportant, how we present our research might have major implications for how seriously it is taken, whether by other academics, policymakers, or others. As Weber (2014: 8) argues, in a discussion of Queer IR Theory, for example, 'Disciplinary IR rarely recognizes boundary-breaking theoretical, epistemological, and methodological approaches to international theorizing as being productive of valuable knowledge about international politics.' Second, our epistemological approach is also likely to have a very real impact on the types of method one is likely to use in order to try to understand (in)security. These methodological questions are the focus of Chapter 3, and tie in to subsequent chapters (especially Chapters 7 and 8) which explore what researchers hope to achieve with the knowledge of security that they produce.

Key Points

- Ontological arguments concentrate on the 'stuff' out of which the world is made.
- Epistemological arguments concentrate on our knowledge of the world and its 'stuff' e.g. where does our knowledge come from, how reliable is it, and what impact does it have?
- Any effort to understand or explain security has an epistemological stance, even if this is not explicitly acknowledged or discussed.
- Epistemological commitments influence how researchers think about themselves and the process of research. This includes influencing methodological decisions about how to study security and insecurity.

Knowledge and security

Research on security – particularly within the International Relations (IR) literature – has traditionally been dominated by approaches with **positivist** epistemological commitments. **Positivism**, used in this way, refers to the view that the social sciences and humanities should aspire toward the type of explanatory sophistication associated with the natural or physical sciences. This means that researchers should attempt to study the social world and its contents as objectively and as accurately as possible, with the ambition of getting ever closer to the truth about it. Positivists therefore attempt to set aside such things as personal experiences, political commitments and normative judgements in order to step back from the world and research it dispassionately. As one critic of positivism puts it:

> The traditional image of positivist international relations is that we take issues – European integration, the Cuban Missile Crisis, foreign policy behaviour, security or whatever – and place them under our social science microscopes. We then try to describe and explain the phenomena on view. (Booth 1994: 1)

In this section we consider two different strands of positivist thinking and their influence on Security Studies: rationalism and empiricism. We then turn to important critiques of these that can be found within the recent growth of 'critical' approaches to security (see Figure 2.1).

Figure 2.1 illustrates the main epistemological approaches explored in this section, and their competing views of where knowledge of the social world comes from. Aspirations toward a science of security diminish as we move from left to right in the diagram.

Figure 2.1 *Epistemological positions and sources of knowledge*

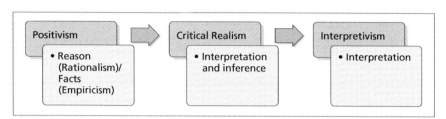

Rationalist approaches to the study of security view knowledge of the world as a product of reason. Because our experiences and perceptions (as researchers *and* social actors) are both limited and fallible, we cannot rely upon these as foundations for understanding events or processes around us. Instead, the researcher must go about their search for knowledge by producing theories of the world from which logical explanations can then be deduced. As a form of positivism, advocates of rationalism most closely resemble the pure mathematician generating and working through abstract formulae in order to better unpack the mysteries of existence. Within Security Studies, this approach underpins neo-realist thinking in particular, and its aspirations for abstract and 'elegant' models of international politics. As its most famous advocate put it, theories serve as an attempt to 'indicate what is connected with what and how the connection is made. They convey a sense of how things work, of how they hang together, of what the structure of a realm of inquiry may be' (Waltz: 1986: 40). Once formulated, the job of the researcher is one of assessing their accuracy via the establishment and testing of hypotheses.

As Smith (1996: 22–3) points out, there are two major problems with rationalist approaches. The first is that reason itself is a particular rather than a universal phenomenon. If knowledge is generated through reasoned **deduction** from grand theoretical principles, different forms of reason – or different types of logic – are likely to lead to different understandings of the world and its workings. How, in other words, do we know that your use of reason is more reasonable than mine (or vice-versa) if we come to radically different conclusions from a similar starting point? A second problem is that the social scientist is quite different to the mathematician in that they already embedded within – and therefore part of – the (social) world they are analysing. There is no neutral vantage point from which to reason about international political dynamics, because there is no way of stepping outside of these. As we will see below, rationalist approaches have attracted quite serious criticism within Security Studies because of these concerns. These have been most striking from those – such as many post-colonial, feminist, and post-structuralist theorists – who argue that knowledge and understanding are always, and inescapably, local and situated rather than general and abstract.

An alternative epistemological position that also shares a positivist commitment to scientific research is empiricism which had a major influence across the social sciences from the 1960s onwards. Empiricism is, effectively, the mirror image of rationalism in that it argues for a 'bottom-up' approach to the construction of knowledge. This begins with the collection or observation of 'facts' by the researcher who is then tasked with building generalizations, theories or laws out of this 'data'. The truth of the world, in this view, is seen as directly accessible to the researcher because empiricists 'privilege experience, assuming (conveniently) that there is no appearance–reality dichotomy and the world presents itself to us in a direct, "real" and unmediated way through our senses' (Hay 2002: 78). The empiricist, then, is less like the mathematician and closer to the biologist collecting samples in the field for later analysis.

As with rationalist approaches, empiricist thinking within Security Studies also has serious challenges which it must confront (Smith 1996: 19–20). The first is that restricting what can be known to those things which can be directly observed or experienced offers a quite limited remit for researchers to work with. If we believe that the world 'out there' contains phenomena that cannot be seen or experienced, then a strictly empiricist position means sacrificing any engagement with these things. These unobservables potentially include important dynamics and elements of the social and political worlds such as class, patriarchy, emotions, or even insecurities, none of which can be 'seen' directly. Second, the empiricist position also reproduces the **subject/object** dichotomy we encountered in our discussion of rationalism above. This is the idea that a researcher (the subject) and the thing they are studying (the object) are independent of, or separable from, one another irrespective of whether they are working on missile defence or people trafficking. The problem with this is that one's ability to experience the world directly – away from one's ideas and thoughts about it – is questionable at best. Although the biologist may be distinguishable from the grasses or flowers they are studying, the social researcher is (again) always a part of the social context they are researching. Third, any effort to study 'the facts' directly needs also to draw on some other criterion (that cannot be directly observed or experienced) that will tell us what events, or phenomena, upon which to focus (Hyde-Price 2007: 5–6). As Michael Moore's film *Bowling for Columbine* implies, far more is needed than a simple list of facts if we are to know – or decide – whether a complex event such as a mass shooting is a product of gun culture, popular music, social alienation, or ten pin bowling.

Despite their limitations, rationalist and empiricist approaches dominated the study of security for a considerable time. Indeed, the search for objective knowledge in this field remains as appealing for many today as it was back in 1991 when one prominent realist argued that Security Studies 'must follow the standard canons of scientific research: careful and consistent use of terms, unbiased measurement of critical concepts, and public documentation of theoretical and empirical claims' (Walt 1991: 222). The challenges of attempting to do this – as Walt (ibid) acknowledges – are not sufficient reasons for abandoning the scientific quest: 'Although no research enterprise ever lives up to these standards completely, they are the principles that make cumulative research possible' (Walt 1991: 222). However, while statistical analyses, complex mathematical models and hypothesis testing continue to dominate the pages of many of the major academic journals on security (see Chapter 3), significant challenges to their scientific aspirations do now exist, two of which we now introduce: critical realism and interpretivism.

Critical realism – as distinct from political realism within IR – is a philosophical tradition which approaches the world as consisting of different layers of reality (see Patomäki and Wight 2000: 223–5). Some of these layers can be directly experienced or observed; others – such as underlying power structures – cannot. This ontological view – that the world exists independently from our knowledge of it (Sayer 2000: 10) – is one which critical realism shares with positivist approaches. In contrast to those, however, critical realism employs a relativist epistemology (see Herring and Stokes 2011: 10–11), in which the (real) world can only be truly known indirectly, through our interpretations of it. This does not, however, mean that all interpretations of the world are equal. To assess their value, we have to partake in a judgemental rationalism, and to test our (fallible, indirect) knowledge against social reality. Thus, while a near-infinite range of different understandings of the conditions that are necessary for human survival is possible, we can meaningfully compare your argument in favour of shelter, food and water against mine which prioritizes ready access to lightbulbs and hairspray. The role of the analyst, in other words, is to seek to get ever-closer to knowledge of social reality, while bearing three things in mind. First, that aspects of this reality will always remain out of reach. Second, that the interpretations we produce also form part of this reality. And, third, that the critical realist's role is one of *critique*: to challenge – and help to change – false beliefs and understandings of socio-political life whether local or global (Sayer 2000: 18–19).

Alexander Wendt (1999: 62–3) – a conventional constructivist who places a strong emphasis on the role of ideas and beliefs within International Relations (see Chapter 1) – explains this critical realist approach to knowledge as a question of reasonableness. In his example, 'Is it *reasonable* to infer the existence of electrons as the cause of certain observable effects, given that electron theory is our best satisfactory explanation for those effects yet might turn out later to be wrong?' (Wendt 1999: 62). In our example, is it *reasonable* to infer shelter, food and water – or lightbulbs and hairspray – as the cause of human security, given that either explanation might turn out later to be wrong? This form of reasoning, he suggests, is a matter of 'inference to the best explanation'.

Moving further from the positivist mainstream on our epistemological spectrum we encounter interpretivist approaches which argue that all knowledge – of security and otherwise – is a product of interpretation. Interpretivism has grown in popularity since the 1970s, impacting disciplines as diverse as anthropology, sociology, history and Security Studies. Although difficult to summarize because of their diversity, interpretivist approaches tend to share some broad epistemological commitments. First is the view that there is a fundamental difference between the social and physical worlds. Where the latter may be reducible to basic material phenomena, the former is made up – at least in part – by the ideas, symbols, languages, discourses, and so forth that give it meaning (Rabinow and Sullivan 1987: 6). For instance, the physical act of placing a ring on another's finger has a very different meaning in the context of a wedding ceremony to that of a playground game: the material reality of the physical act is only a (small) part of the event. To make sense of the human world, then, involves attempting to engage with the meanings it has for those caught up within it, including the researcher.

Second, interpretivists tend to view knowledge as a localized, particular phenomenon, rather than something that is general or universal. In contrast to positivism's search for proofs, laws or other scientific types of knowledge, interpretivists argue that the world takes on meaning – or is known – in very different ways. This implies that there is no single 'Truth' about security or anything else, for security itself takes on different meanings in different times and places, be it a debate in the United Nations Security Council (UNSC), an academic workshop on chemical weapons, or a commercial website advertising home insurance. Importantly, none of these likely different conceptions of security can lay claim to its absolute truth, for, as Peter Winch (1990: 102) famously put it, 'connected with the realization that intelligibility takes many and varied forms is the realization that reality has no key'.

Third, interpretivism tends to shift the purposes of research from an effort at social *explanation* evident within positivist and many critical approaches to its *understanding*. Because knowledge – of the human world, of security, and so on – will always be local, partial and perspectival, interpretivists are sceptical of the truth claims made by formal, 'scientific', explanatory models (Rabinow and Sullivan 1987: 10–15). As Rabinow and Sullivan (1987: 15) argue in a discussion of interpretivist anthropological work: 'This is the art of interpretation. The aim is not to uncover universals or laws but rather to explicate context and world' (see also Hollis and Smith 1991).

The interpretivist interest in exploring how the world becomes meaningful via representational and cultural practices has considerable potential for Security Studies. In one important early discussion, Bradley Klein (1990) explored how NATO's Cold War existence depended on a particular discursive construction of the Soviet threat as implacable, and on a specific representation of 'the West' as a space of order and stability. This is obviously a long way from rationalist explanations of strategic alliances grounded in (relatively fixed) identities and (material, objective) national interests. Price (1995) applies a similar framework – drawing on Michel Foucault's approach to **genealogy** – to the taboo that now exists toward the use of chemical weapons. In his view, this taboo has persisted, in part, because these are understood as weapons of the (uncivilized) weak that cannot be defended against. Other topics explored through interpretivist frameworks include military and humanitarian interventions (Fierke 1996; McCourt 2013), and the importance of conceptions of British identity to its foreign policy (Daddow and Gaskarth 2014; also Atkins 2013; Holland 2013a; Kettell 2013).

Interpretivist studies of security have not passed without criticism. One recurring critique is that they focus on intangibles such as culture and discourse, while neglecting more substantive concerns such as power and interests. A good example can be found in some of the critical realist responses to discursive studies of counter-terrorism. These have argued that the focus on meaning-making practices within the War on Terror (e.g. Jackson 2005b) has meant that the vitally important, *non*-discursive, motivations behind counter-terrorism campaigns – such as the political economy of oil that arguably underpinned the military intervention in Iraq, for instance (see, for example, Stokes 2009) – have been overlooked. In other words, focusing on constructed ideas and identities might mean that 'real' material interests are forgotten.

A second criticism is that interpretivist research can only produce subjective, rather than objective, analysis. If all knowledge of security is merely interpretation, what hope does this leave for answering some of the truly important questions within Security Studies, such as: What makes people insecure? Why do wars occur? And why is the global gap between rich and poor growing? On a normative level, this concern leads to accusations of moral **relativism**. In other words, if security has no universal meaning, we are confronted by two things. First, a potentially infinite range of interpretations of this concept. And, second, the lack of any mechanism or framework to helps us to choose between these.

Third, many researchers associated with critical security studies were attracted to this enterprise because of a powerful normative desire to help 'create an alternative world' in which the injustices and insecurities of the global status quo could be challenged (Hynek and Chandler 2013: 47). This was particularly the case in the earliest debates around the status of 'critique' in the literature and whether some form of emancipatory project was needed (see Introduction). For scholars with these sorts of commitments, a very real danger of depoliticization emerges if Security Studies is reduced simply to the identification, analysis and even deconstruction of competing interpretations of the world. In other words, if there is no truth about (in)security – and no way of objectively adjudicating between competing narratives or interpretations – then what, precisely, is the point to any of this? Why bother studying security at all? As Booth (2007: 178) argues in his critique of post-modernism: 'posturing against metanarratives threaten[s] to marginalise the global downtrodden. Listen to the victims and note how often they have seen their futures as depending vitally on emancipatory grand narratives in favour of female and racial equality, for example.' As he continues: 'While relativism leads to the politics of the bystander, universal values and transnational solidarity provide hope to victims' (Booth 2007: 178).

Key Points

- Rationalist approaches view knowledge of the world – and therefore of security – as a product of reason.
- Empiricist approaches view knowledge of security as a product of observation and experience.
- Critical realist approaches argue that while the world can only be known through interpretation, it is possible to assess the value of different understandings.
- Interpretivist approaches see all knowledge of security as situated and partial.

Why does epistemology matter for Security Studies?

Before turning to more specific discussions on the particular character of claims about security, it is important to reflect briefly on the increasing interest in such questions. This interest might be indicative of a 'growing recognition of the contingency and indeterminacy of what is known and how it is known' (Mustapha 2013: 66) across Security Studies and International Relations (IR) more broadly. This interest is sometimes referred to as the 'third (great) debate' within International Relations (see Box 2.1). Some high profile writers, such as Wendt (1998), have argued that this attention to epistemology is, in many ways, an unfortunate distraction from more pressing concerns. This is because, in his words, 'The central point of IR scholarship is to increase our knowledge of how the world works, not to worry about how (or whether) we can know how the world works' (Wendt 1998: 115). Wendt (1998: 115) continues, having argued that such issues are better left to philosophers and sociologists of knowledge, by suggesting:

> It is simply not the case that we have to undertake an epistemological analysis of how we can know something before we can know it, a fact amply attested to by the success of the natural sciences, whose practitioners are only rarely forced by the results of their inquiries to consider epistemological questions. In important respects we *do* know how international politics works, and it doesn't much matter how we came to that knowledge. In that light, going into the epistemology business will distractus from the real business of IR, which

---

Box 2.1 The third debate

The story of International Relations as an academic discipline is often told as a story of three 'great' debates. The first debate was one between realism and idealism (or liberalism) and focused on ontological disagreements over the nature of 'man' and, by extension, international politics. The second debate took place in the 1960s between those seeking scientific, universal laws of state behaviour, and historicist approaches preferring inductive, particular knowledge claims. The third debate saw positivist and post-positivist approaches pitted against one another. Vital within this was the rise of post-modern and constructivist approaches and their critiques of traditional ways of thinking about the foundations of knowledge in International Relations.

Sources: Navon (2001); Blair (2011).

is international politics. Our great debates should be about first-order issues of substance, like the 'first debate' between Realists and Idealists, not second-order issues of method.

Our argument, in contrast, is that epistemological issues are absolutely fundamental to the study of Security Studies and IR, and anything but a distraction from the 'real business' of these fields of study. In the first instance, this is because one's epistemological stance shapes one's view of what *type* of security knowledge it is possible to aim for (Hollis and Smith 1996). Different epistemological commitments bring with them competing methodological criteria, assumptions and ways of doing research; all of which help to shape how any 'data' is collected and analysed. Although we return to competing understandings of validity, reliability, and so forth within Security Studies in Chapter 3, it is the meta-theoretical – so, ontological and epistemological – commitments discussed in this and the previous chapter that shape what will be seen as suitable research material, as well as how those sources are subsequently treated. These commitments help us decide what – if anything – video games tell us about international conflicts, for instance (see Box 2.2). Likewise, if a politician makes a speech about global poverty should this be seen as a reflection of what they believe? And, do their beliefs – or the speech – even matter (and if so to whom)? These are epistemological questions, and they matter a great deal; primarily, as Wendt suggests, because they are prerequisite to understanding the world and potentially changing it.

Second, epistemological commitments also shape our view of what we think a security researcher is and what they should be doing with their work (Floyd 2007: 335; Jarvis 2013). Positivism – in both its rationalist and empiricist guises – inclines toward a view of the researcher as a

---

Box 2.2 Videogames, meta-theory and war

In a recent analysis, Nick Robinson (2012) calls for greater attention to the role of videogames within social and political contexts such as the War on Terror. This argument depends upon the ontological claim that the videogames sector is an important part of a military-entertainment complex and the militarization of society. Robinson then develops an epistemological argument that such games have the potential to open up new ways of understanding and even critiquing society by allowing gamers to take on particular character identities, for example. Robinson's methodology, finally, is one that views videogames as legitimate – indeed vital – material for engaged social and political analysis.

neutral, dispassionate and objective observer. The task of research here is the impartial discovery of truths about the world: whether in the form of causal laws, empirical correlations, or explanatory models. Critical realists, in contrast, tend to prioritize explanatory analysis, but see this as an outcome of interpretation and inference rather than objective and accurate truth-telling. This is because, as outlined in the preceding section, critical realism conceives of the social and political world as comprising elements that are not directly or objectively observable (Hollis and Smith 1991: 207). Those more sympathetic toward interpretivism, finally, prioritize understanding above explanation and view the researcher as a narrator exploring and interpreting the meaning of socio-political dynamics rather than their truth. However, as noted above, these meanings are always viewed as partial in both senses of the term: being both incomplete, but also situated in a particular time and place.

A third reason to take epistemological issues seriously is that the type of knowledge claim made about security can have important impacts. One of these is upon the discipline of Security Studies itself. The ability of neo-realist IR scholarship to frame itself as a scientific approach (with the connotations of objectivity and truth associated with 'science'), for example, was a major part of its successes in securing dominance within the discipline from the 1970s onwards. This, as Krause and Williams (1996: 236) argued, made it more difficult for those appealing to alternative ways of thinking about and practising security: 'Obviously, if neorealist scholarship can claim the mantle of science, it has a powerful preemptive response to calls for reformulating the research agenda of security studies' (1996: 236). Perhaps more importantly, the impression that neo-realism could offer objective, value-free knowledge about global politics rooted in analyses of national interests was a major part of its successes within foreign policy communities both during and after the Cold War period. Neo-realism's self-image as a science of global politics, in other words, helps to explain its successes in academia and policymaking as much as its substantive claims about how the world works.

Key Points

- Epistemological assumptions matter because they influence what type of security knowledge is seen as possible and legitimate.
- Approaches to epistemology also help shape views of what the security researcher should be doing.
- Epistemological stances have implications for the discipline of Security Studies as well as for the world 'beyond' it.

Security: objective or subjective?

One of the most fundamental epistemological questions to ask about security or insecurity is whether our knowledge of these is objective or subjective. At an individual level, for example, is it possible for me to know whether or not I am currently secure or at risk? Or, is my being secure or insecure rooted in, and inseparable from, whether I *feel* or *experience* security or insecurity? Although this question has generated a lot of interest with the opening up of Security Studies to new perspectives in recent years, it has been around in one form or another since the birth of this subfield. In an essay originally published in 1962, for example, Arnold Wolfers made a memorable distinction between the subjective and objective components of national security, whereby:

> security, in an objective sense, measures the absence of threats to acquired values, in a subjective sense, the absence of fear that such values will be attacked. In both respects a nation's security can run a wide gamut from almost complete insecurity or sense of insecurity at one end, to almost complete security or absence of fear at the other. (Wolfers 2011: 6)

Stuart Macdonald (2009: 99) – a Law scholar – makes a similar distinction in relation to more recent debates around counter-terrorism powers and the balance between liberty and security. In his words: 'It is important to distinguish between objective and subjective security. This is because the two do not always go hand-in-hand; often there can be a discrepancy between how safe people feel and how safe they actually are.'

A common argument in favour of an objectivist approach to security builds on the (ontological) view that security is a condition or experience with tangible, identifiable roots. At the national level, these might include military capabilities, alliances with neighbouring countries, the protection of a regional hegemon, or significant natural resources. At the level of the individual human, these might include the presence of a social safety net of some sort, or access to a basic level of daily nutrition. If security is understood in this way – as the outcome of particular attributes or capabilities – then it becomes at least possible to calculate how secure an actor is (whether a state, a human, or something else), and to make comparisons between actors, and over time. It might be difficult to find appropriate indicators for any of security's component parts, and we might be mistaken in our attempts to identify what those parts are, but the possibility remains that we can accurately and objectively understand how the world works in this context

(Wendt 1995: 74–5). In Chapter 3, we turn to a number of ways in which this might be done.

Objectivist approaches of this sort rely upon what we can call a referential approach to knowledge. This means that knowledge of the world is formed with reference to the world itself. This is important, because it suggests that even if we believe that the world contains phenomena that cannot be directly observed – such as ideas or beliefs – we do not necessarily have to give up our pursuit for objective knowledge of these. One reason for this is the subject/object distinction considered above. For instance, a researcher might be able to study whether homophobia generates anxiety or insecurity amongst particular communities, even though homophobia cannot be directly seen, because it has a social existence outside of the researcher's experience. Patriarchy, nationalism, racism and so forth might similarly be approached – and therefore studied – as social facts, even if they cannot be directly accessed by a researcher.

A second route toward the objective study of unobservables involves rethinking the kind of question we ask in our research. So, rather than asking 'why' questions in studying security – why is the earth's atmosphere warming, why is biodiversity being reduced, why did the US invade Iraq in 2003, and so forth – it might be more useful to ask 'how possible' questions instead: for instance, how was the US able to invade Iraq in 2003 (see Doty 1993)? These kinds of question do not call for a direct causal explanation of events (X caused Y), but rather a detailed explication of the conditions in place that allowed Y to occur. So, in this example, we might point to US imperialism, a pervasive terrorism discourse, or the Responsibility to Protect (R2P) norm within global politics: all of which might be important for understanding the context in which those events occurred.

Opponents of the view that security can be studied objectively point to a number of important criticisms of this belief. A first problem is the importance of *interpretation* within any attempt to understand, measure and classify the world (see Krause and Williams 1996: 236–7). If I encounter a group of young people on the street while walking home alone one night, a number of responses are possible. I might decide to continue as I was, to cross the street and try to avoid eye contact, to step into a shop and seek refuge, or to grab hold of something with which to defend myself if necessary. Which option I chose will depend on: (i) whether I view this group of young people as harmless children or a dangerous mob; (ii) how I see myself and my chances of avoiding, reasoning with, or successfully fighting the group; and, (iii) how I assess the consequences of different outcomes of any encounter. Similarly, using Wendt's (1992: 405) example, humanity would not necessarily believe itself to be in imminent danger following the arrival of life from another planet:

> Would we assume, a priori, that we were about to be attacked if we are ever contacted by members of an alien civilization? I think not. We would be highly alert, of course, but whether we placed our military forces on alert or launched an attack would depend on how we interpreted the import of their first gesture for our security – if only to avoid making an immediate enemy out of what may be a dangerous adversary.

The point here is that threat, danger, security, conflict, insecurity and so forth are a product of interpretation and understanding: they are not necessarily given by the situation itself (Campbell 1998b: 1–3). The meaning and significance of any issue or event are imposed or constructed by those within it: however much any event may seem to 'speak for itself' (Devetak 2009). This is the case for actors and their encounters, but it is also true for researchers and analysts trying to study them. And, importantly, these understandings and interpretations are never themselves neutral or entirely devoid of political considerations and contexts (Jackson *et al.* 2011: 163–4). Thus, although World War II is typically seen in the West as a global confrontation between good and evil, it may also be interpreted as an inter-imperial war or as a collection of conflicts with radically different histories and geographies than the standard narrative structured around the Axis and Allied powers between 1939 and 1945 implies (Barkawi and Laffey 2006: 338–40). This importance of interpretation is also part of the reason that some security issues are given far more attention and resources than others; even if, in crude empirical numbers, at least, other 'risks' might be responsible for far greater levels of harm (see Chapters 5 and 6).

An alternative to referential theories of security knowledge – and one favoured within much post-structuralist and critical constructivist work – is a *relational* one. Here, the meaning of security is seen as something that is produced via its relation to other concepts. So, just as 'civilization' can only mean anything in relation to its opposites – savagery, barbarianism, and so on – and 'Europe' derives its meaning via perceived (or constructed) differences to non-European others – Asia, Africa, etc. – so, too, security only makes sense in relation to its own others: insecurity, risk, danger, threat, and so forth. Approached in this way, security has no inherent meaning at all, and, as such, cannot be identified or studied objectively. What security means is given by what security does not mean, and this will always be socially and culturally determined within broader structures of meaning or discourses, such as the Cold War, War on Terror or War on Drugs. The construction of (in)security within these discourses is not, however, a purely subjective dynamic (Buzan and Hansen 2009: 33–5). The Cold War or War on Drugs had an existence outside the mind of any observer thereof. At the same time, because the threat of communism, terrorists and drugs have been produced or 'made' within these discourses, these processes cannot be said to be objective either. The designation of these things as security threats is not simply a straightforward reflection of reality.

A good example of the importance of these issues can be found in debates on the concept of 'human security' (see Chapters 4 and 6). One approach to human security is to see this as a policy-relevant framework for addressing global inequalities in life chances and conditions. In order to operationalize such an approach, the next step might be to develop a 'simple, rigorous, and measurable definition' (King and Murray 2001: 485) allowing the concept to be put into practice for the purposes of assessing and changing actual insecurities in the everyday lives of people. King and Murray (2001), for example, propose an individual's number of future years of life spent outside of a state of generalized poverty as one measure for doing this. Related attempts put forward the value of a 'threshold' approach which would prioritize causes of harm to human life based on the extent to which they 'surpass a threshold of severity and become not simply human rights violations, environmental problems, or isolated violent acts, but also threats to human security' (Owen 2004: 384).

Another – quite different – way of thinking about this concept is as a political tool that can be used to critique established ways of thinking about, and seeking to achieve, security (Bellamy and McDonald 2002: 376). So, scholars and activists dissatisfied with national security discourses and their militaristic associations might invoke the notion of human security as a way of challenging the dominance of these. This might involve, for example, highlighting the ways in which border control policies designed to foster national security have a major negative impact upon the security of those individuals and their families adversely affected by immigration laws and their surrounding discourses. This use of the term 'human security' as a political signifier is obviously a long way from more policy-related efforts to measure and prioritize different aspects of human security as an existential condition (see also McDonald 2002). As such, measuring the concept accurately is here far less important.

Appreciating the differences underpinning conceptions of human security as either policy tool or political critique does not in itself end the discussion. The question remains: is there any way of adjudicating between these accounts of what human security is, and what the concept should do? To return to the above discussion of epistemological positions, we can distinguish between critical realist and interpretivist answers to this question. The former would be willing to assess – or to make inferences about – the value of these different uses of human security, as well as the extent to which different understandings of this concept adequately capture reality. Interpretivists, on the other hand, would be more likely to conclude their analysis at the point of exploring how competing interpretations of 'human security' are constructed and function in particular social and political contexts. So, they would ask how 'the human' and their 'basic needs' are created in different discourses of human security; what is excluded or left out of these discourses; and, what happens when these different interpretations are put into use.

Key Points

- A fundamental epistemological issue within Security Studies is whether knowledge of security and insecurity can be objective.
- Objectivist approaches often rely on a referential view of knowledge.
- Critics of objectivism point to the importance of interpretation in the production of meaning, as well as the relational nature of meaning.
- Debates over 'human security' as a concept demonstrate the importance of different types of knowledge claim around security.

Security: universal or particular?

A second important question that links to the above issue of objectivity is the extent to which it is possible to make universal generalizations about security that apply across time and space. Is it possible to make claims about the security threats faced by others who we have not met? Or, does the perspectival and partial nature of all security knowledge mean that we have to be much more circumspect in so doing: do we, in other words, have to accept that security and insecurity are heterogeneous and particular? In this section we point to the desire for universal security truths within mainstream and 'capital C' 'Critical' approaches alike. We then turn to post-colonial and feminist writers who are sceptical of these ambitions despite sharing some normative and political commitments with the non-mainstream universalists.

Many realists studying security pursue the possibility of general, overarching claims about the dynamics of world politics and their impacts on the (in)security of states and their citizens. Although they reject the term 'universal', a recent appeal for more theoretical work within the discipline of IR by Mearsheimer and Walt (2013: 432) – two of today's most prominent realist thinkers – is illustrative of this, in which they argue:

> Theories provide general explanations, which means they apply across space and time. Social science theories are not universal, however; they apply only to particular realms of activity or to specific time periods. The scope of a theory can also vary significantly. Grand theories such as realism or liberalism purport to explain broad patterns of state behavior, while so-called middle-range theories focus on more narrowly defined phenomena like economic sanctions, coercion, and deterrence.

As they subsequently point out, no theoretical approach will ever perfectly explain all potentially relevant events, whether we are looking at state behaviour in general, or more specific strategies of coercion, deterrence, or anything else. Outliers will always exist, mistakes may be made in theory formulation, and potentially significant aspects of the dynamic under study may be neglected. Nevertheless, they make a powerful argument for returning to the abstract work, generalized claims, and predictive capabilities that is the stuff of theory (at least as they understand it), given the prominence of empirical, quantitative, hypothesis testing within contemporary studies of global politics.

This search for general truths about security is also found within the Welsh School of Critical Security Studies, and much of the human security literature. As we will see in Chapter 4, these approaches share an attempt to refocus the study of security around the individual person, rather than the state. What is important, for us here, is that these approaches share a belief that humans possess certain basic needs that must be met for their survival (Newman 2001; Jarvis and Lister 2013c). Because these basic needs are seen as more or less universal – the ontological claim – it becomes possible to identify whether, why and how *particular* individuals are secure or otherwise – the epistemological claim. In other words, if we know that a human needs X water, Y food, and a minimum temperature of Z to survive; we can assess the survival chances of any human against this set of criteria. For many advocates of these approaches – as discussed above – there is a further political rationale for making universal claims such as these which involves representing the world's dispossessed. This is part of a **cosmopolitan** ethics that is committed to reducing insecurity for all human beings (Burke 2013: 20; see also Chapter 8).

Some of the most important challenges to these approaches have come from post-colonial and feminist writers on security, and the emphasis many within these 'traditions' place upon local and particularized stories (for example, Wibben 2010). Post-colonialism, in this context, takes as its starting point the **Eurocentric** nature of much of the 'mainstream' scholarship on security (see also Chapter 8). Although such scholarship is often framed in universal (and thereby impartial) terms, post-colonial critics argue that it actually builds upon a very particular, yet unacknowledged and unspoken, historical context. As Barkawi and Laffey (2006: 334) put it: 'conventional security studies, the core of IR, is...shaped by the politics of a particular time and place – the post-1945 Anglo-American world – even as it presents itself in the seemingly neutral and timeless language of social science'. What are seen as universal truths about security, in other words, are simply a reflection of Western views on this topic rooted in the experience of the late twentieth century.

Pinar Bilgin (2010) – another post-colonial writer – also takes Security Studies to task for being Western-centric. In her view, Security Studies remains both *parochial* because it mistakes Western experiences for universal ones, and *peripheral* because it neglects the importance of non-traditional security issues. This blindness to alternative ways of understanding and experiencing (in)security is deeply problematic for two reasons. First, because it leads to an unnecessarily limited understanding of (in)security: one that is grounded in the history and language of a privileged minority. And, second, because this apparently universal approach to security (and its connection to the state and military capabilities) has been taken on by political elites across the world, which has led to individuals and communities becoming even less secure in the process (Bilgin 2010).

This scepticism toward universal truths about security is also evident in some feminist approaches. Laura Sjoberg (2009: 192), for example, argues that feminism takes very seriously the importance of the standpoint or subject position of any speaker of security truths, because feminism recognizes that, 'objective knowledge is only the subjective knowledge of privileged voices disguised as neutral by culturally assumed objectivity, "where the privileged are licensed to think for everyone, so long as they do so "objectively"'. Once this is recognized, then the political character and importance of all attempts to discuss, explain, calculate and provide security become more visible. This is why many feminists are often committed to 'understanding the world from the points of view of marginalized peoples and actors' (Sjoberg 2009: 193). This commitment can be seen as a political and a normative one that involves seeking to re-centre the excluded and disempowered in our attempts to make sense of the world (Sylvester 2013: 613). Hence, the level of contemporary interest in trying to create academic and other forms of space in which 'ordinary' individuals might be able to speak – in their own language – about their own conceptions and experiences of security and insecurity. This is in stark contrast to the traditional experience of such peoples who have been usually, 'studied using someone else's script' (Sylvester 2013: 614; also, Jarvis and Lister 2013c). As Sylvester (2013: 619) continues, this emphasis on localized and particular —rather than abstract and universal – understandings of security renders this type of Security Studies a very different project to that found within traditional International Relations:

> The idea behind studying people's experiences is to learn how the world looks and works according to those who actually, rather than theoretically, face forces of international relations. The point is not to test hypotheses that could help predict how others would react to similar or simulated conditions of international relations, or to gather true and accurate information on the ground. The point rather is to fill in the abstract contours of our knowledge by acknowledging that people are involved in daily and extraordinary activities of international relations – their lives are affected by the forces a field studies, and what they do can affect the world and should affect what IR studies.

Key Points

- Discussions of security from the perspective of political realism, Critical Security Studies and human security are frequently grounded in universal claims.
- Such claims can be justified by cosmopolitan ethics as well as by the epistemological search for scientific truths.
- Criticisms of universalism have come from a number of traditions, including feminism and post-colonialism.
- There is an increasing interest in 'everyday', 'vernacular' or 'lay' understandings of security, partly in response to these criticisms.

Conclusion

Knowledge about security does not emerge in isolation from other social, political, cultural and economic contexts. Buzan and Hansen (2009: 47–65), for example, identify a number of important factors that have helped to mould the development of Security Studies as an academic programme following World War II. These factors – or 'driving forces' in their terminology – included: shifting relationships and distributions of power amongst the major players in the global system; the development of new military and civilian technologies and their impact upon different populations and issues; events and processes that change security knowledge and practice, such as the Cuba Missile Crisis or 9/11; 'internal' academic debate over what the field of Security Studies should look like and do; and, the importance of institutional dynamics and structures such as the role of governments, think-tanks and NGOs in producing, funding and disseminating particular security knowledges.

Our argument in this chapter, and throughout this book, is that we – as students of security and insecurity – cannot but take the production, distribution and consequences of efforts to speak about security and insecurity seriously. Moreover, it is particularly vital that we are cautious of those claiming to be scientific, neutral, dispassionate or objective observers of (in)security. Such claims are particularly powerful, and have a lengthy history – in various guises – within Security Studies, IR and other social scientific disciplines. Challenging them, however, is of fundamental importance for two reasons in particular. First, because their claims about science or the truth of security work to delegitimize alternative, dissenting or oppositional arguments about what security means, where security comes from, and what constitutes a security threat. If I manage to convince the world that the security of all is produced via the manufacture of more guns and bombs based on the sophisticated use of mathematical models, then your arguments about access to antiretrovirals or improvements in maternal health care are unlikely to be heeded irrespective of whichever of us has a more plausible story to tell.

Second, this type of identity claim also helps to camouflage the situated nature of security knowledge – which always comes from somewhere – as well as the broader relations of power and politics in which that knowledge is produced and circulated. While these contexts cannot ever be fully escaped, it is important to reflect upon them and to be conscious of their role in shaping the questions we ask and the answers we offer. Doing so, offers one way of challenging the history of conventional security studies, which, as Barkawi and Laffey (2006: 349) argue: 'takes the perspective of the powerful, of those who have colonised, dominated and competed over the world'. Thus, while they might be right that, historically, 'There is a politics to security studies and it is the politics of the strong' (Barkawi and Laffey 2006: 349), unravelling how this perspective of the strong and the powerful has been framed and shared offers one way of challenging it and of potentially rethinking security.

Further Reading

Bevir, Daddow and Hall (2014) is an edited collection exploring the value of interpretive approaches to issues around global security. Chapters include case studies on the United Kingdom, Russia and the United States. Barkawi and Laffey (2006) provides a post-colonial critique of traditional ways of studying security and is an excellent introduction to this way of approaching global politics. Booth (1994) details his own intellectual journey as a scholar of security, including his increasing dissatisfaction with political realism. Sylvester (2013) offers an account of the current state of IR theory, drawing on her background as a feminist critic, while Lyotard (1984) explores the construction of knowledge in post-modernity.

Internet Resources

For a video of a lecture delivered in 2008 in which feminist questions are asked about security, International Relations, and the post-2003 Iraq war in particular, see Enloe (2008): http://www.youtube.com/watch?v=XXUCL ahznqs. A recent interview with Chris Brown (2013) describes his growing dissatisfaction with relativist approaches to International Relations. And, a discussion of the objectivity of security in relation to the concept of securitization is available via this video interview with Barry Buzan (2014).

Chapter 3

How can we Study Security?

Chapter Overview

This chapter focuses on methodology and methods within Security Studies. Building on the discussion of ontology and epistemology in Chapters 1 and 2 we explore a range of ways in which knowledge on security and insecurity can be created. These include mathematical methods such as regression analysis and formal modelling, as well as 'qualitative' techniques such as ethnography, discourse analysis and focus group research. The practice, value and limitations of these research methods are explored using concrete examples of recent work on security. The chapter argues that the contemporary growth of interest in methodology across Critical Security Studies is to be welcomed for a number of reasons. Uppermost amongst these is that thinking carefully about how knowledge of security is generated improves the quality of security research, at the same time as it strengthens a researcher's ability to engage critically with designations of threat, risk and insecurity of the sort explored in Chapters 5 and 6.

Chapter Contents

Introduction

In Chapter 1, we explored ontological debates that centre around one deceptively simple question: what is security? In Chapter 2, we followed this by exploring epistemological debates around the related question: what can one know about security? Having engaged with a range of responses to each of these, the next question to ask is a more applied one, and may be framed thus: *how* can – and how should – a researcher study and generate knowledge about security? This question – a methodological one – is the focus of this chapter, which seeks to achieve two aims. The first is to introduce readers to a range of the research methods used by those working within Security Studies. In doing this, we provide an outline of the mechanics of different approaches to the collection and analysis of data, as well as some of the limitations and advantages of commonly used methods. Throughout, we identify and reflect upon case studies for each discussed method, exploring how they have been used in prominent, ground-breaking work. The chapter's second aim is to ground this discussion of methods within broader academic conversations about the process, challenges, context, and responsibilities of research, especially in relation to discourses and practices of security. Here, we will introduce different views of what research is – and what it is for – as well as reflecting on contemporary changes within the subfield of Security Studies.

We begin our discussion by defining 'methodology' and 'method', and exploring the importance of methodological issues for those seeking to understand security dynamics. Following this, two arguments are made. The first is that research is a challenging process that is situated in – and constrained by – a whole spread of issues and contexts that are rarely mentioned within a project's published outputs. Doing research, in other words, is not simply about applying (or adapting) a method to a new data set however much academic articles may make it appear thus. It is a pragmatic as well as an intellectual enterprise that involves emotional commitment, personal resilience, material resources and imperfect choices. The second argument we make here is that the type of security knowledge a researcher believes to be possible is likely to shape – although will not determine – the types of technique employed to generate that knowledge. Put otherwise, one's epistemological position is likely to impact upon one's methodological practices.

The chapter's second section then introduces some of the major mathematical research methods that are employed primarily – although not exclusively – by positivist researchers in this field. These include statistical techniques – such as regression analysis – associated with empiricist research, on the one hand. And, on the other, attempts to model security dynamics and relations associated with rationalist work. In the chapter's third section, we then argue that longstanding concerns around the methodological deficit within post-positivist work have become increasingly outdated as critical security studies approached broadly (see Introduction) has gained momentum and prominence. To demonstrate, we identify the diversity of innovative techniques now being used by researchers with these meta-theoretical commitments, many of which originated from beyond the borders of International Relations. These include discourse analysis, **critical discourse analysis (CDA)**, ethnography, interviews, and focus groups.

The chapter concludes by arguing that although these issues are often viewed as less significant or interesting than theoretical or empirical matters, students and scholars of International Security need to reflect on the methods they use, as much as their ontological, epistemological and normative commitments. As such, the recent interest in research methods – especially amongst 'critical' approaches to security – is to be welcomed for a number of reasons. First, because it encourages greater reflection on, and justification of, the origins and status of security knowledge. And, second, because it has also allowed the emergence of novel and interesting techniques for generating or constructing knowledge about (in)security. This, we argue, in turn has potential to open up new ways of understanding or experiencing security. Just as importantly, it also opens up new ways of critiquing, challenging, deconstructing and destabilizing established security claims and practices.

Key Points

- Ontological questions ask, 'what is security?' Epistemological questions ask, 'what can one know about security?' Methodological questions – the focus of this chapter – ask 'how can one get or construct knowledge of security?'
- Security research is always challenging, imperfect and situated in academic and other contexts.
- For contemporary security researchers there are a vast range of available research methods. Many of these come from beyond the traditional 'home' of Security Studies: International Relations.

Methodology and methods of Security Studies

The term 'methodology' should not be taken as a synonym for 'method': the former is much larger in scope and more contested than the latter. Methodology, as approached here, designates an orientation toward the generation of knowledge. One's methodology, therefore, includes the tools applied within a research project, the justification for selecting those tools rather than others, and the decisions that are taken about how to apply them. Put otherwise, methodology is the conceptualization and conduct of the research process: the 'analysis of how research should or does proceed' (Blaikie 1993: 7), or, to adapt Colin Hay's (2002: 63) definition: 'the means by which we reflect upon the methods appropriate to realise fully our potential to acquire [or construct] knowledge of that which exists'.

The term 'method', in contrast, typically has a narrower meaning, and refers specifically to the particular technique used to acquire or generate information (or 'data'). Although widespread, the term is not universally embraced for at least two reasons. The first is the implication of neutrality that it carries with it: the sense that a 'method' is an instrument that can be picked up and applied on a new research project before being put aside until needed again. Thinking about methods in this way neglects the extent to which methods are adapted to, evolve within, help recreate, and are fundamentally part of the context, dynamic or event under study. As Jacques Derrida (1997: 9) famously said of 'deconstruction': 'Deconstruction is not a method or some tool that you apply to something from the outside... Deconstruction is something which happens.' Second, and related, the term 'method' also has clear positivist connotations. It forms part of a scientific vocabulary of experimentation and discovery that does not fit well with some of the critical methodological approaches explored below.

In textbooks and university courses on how to research security or other issues it is common to think of research as a linear process that unfolds across time. Portrayed in this stylized way, this process begins, typically, with research design. This is where a researcher sets out the problem they wish to investigate; establishes their underlying questions or hypotheses; identifies the case study, examples, or data to be explored; and decides upon the methods to be used to access and analyse the information. Next comes data collection in which the researcher gathers their data employing the method(s) chosen in the design stage. Attention will be given here to research ethics, amongst other things. For instance, if the research involves human participants (as interviewees, focus group members, and so on), do they have sufficient information to consent to their role in the study? Third, once the data has been collected comes the analysis stage. How this is done will depend upon the literature in which a research project is grounded – concepts might be taken from this and applied to the case study – as well as the specific research questions, and the type of research material that has been gathered. So, a project exploring constructions of identity in written language might apply predicate analysis to political speeches at this stage to explore how specific nouns – or 'things' – are characterized in certain ways or given particular properties (Åhäll and Borg 2013: 199; Doty 1993; Milliken 1999). Doing this might reveal, for example, that debate around a proposed humanitarian intervention constructed women in the targeted country as 'vulnerable' or 'helpless' as a means of justifying the intervention. Finally, once the analysis is completed comes the dissemination of results and conclusions. This may involve written outputs – dissertations, journal articles, monographs, PhD theses and so forth – or others such as conference papers, poster presentations, blogs or podcasts. Here, much attention in our stylized research process will be focused upon the original contribution that a particular piece of work has made to existing academic knowledge of the phenomenon under study.

This timeline might be a useful heuristic because it helps to differentiate the various stages of doing and sharing research. Engaging in analysis *is* different to disseminating research, although the two might often take place at the same time (for example, in answering questions during a PhD viva). Unfortunately, this heuristic does not very accurately capture the research process as it is often experienced for at least four different reasons. First, it implies a far more individualized view of research than is typically the case. Any study is likely to involve many people throughout its duration – as participants or co-researchers, mentors or supervisors, and many others besides – and will be situated in a whole host of wider academic, social and political contexts (see Box 3.1). Gaining access to a community for fieldwork, for example, might require a long period of negotiation and trust-building with community leaders before this can even begin (Wiebe 2013). Isolating the researcher and their work from these contexts and relations therefore offers a very partial understanding of any research (Jarvis 2013).

Second, this model emphasizes the intellectual aspects of research above other – equally significant – issues. While the intellectual drivers of any project are, clearly, crucial, pragmatic considerations over access to resources (finances, contacts, time, and so on), and emotions experienced by the researcher(s) (fear, anxiety, excitement, determination) are equally significant in the decision to embark upon (and continue with) any piece of work (D'Aoust 2013). Löwenheim's **autoethnographic** account of growing up in the Palestinian/Israeli conflict, for instance, situates his autobiographical experience as a major factor – if not strictly a cause – in his subsequent efforts to understand violent conflict:

> # Box 3.1 Research communities
>
> Here is a list of people that contributed to a research project conducted by one of the authors. This was a relatively small project on anti-terrorism powers that used a focus group method, based in one country, and had a data collection 'stage' that lasted for less than a year:
>
> - Two researchers.
> - Administrative staff who helped secure funding for, and manage, the research.
> - Participants in the project's 14 focus groups.
> - Participants in the project's 2 pilot groups.
> - Contacts or 'gatekeepers' within non-governmental organizations who arranged several of the focus groups.
> - Other researchers and contacts who organized focus groups for the project team.
> - (Professional) transcribers who typed up the conversations.
> - Authors of related work whose ideas influenced the research.
> - Attendees at two workshops organized by the project, including think tank representatives.
> - Colleagues, students, friends and family who listened to, and provided feedback and encouragement on, the research as it developed.
> - Attendees at academic conferences at which the project's findings were presented.
> - Peer reviewers of articles submitted to academic journals, and their editors.
>
> The important point to take from this (no doubt, partial) list is the sheer number and diversity of individuals involved in even a small piece of research. For further information on this particular project, see http://www.esrc.ac.uk/my-esrc/Grants/RES-000-22-765/read.

I grew up with war's shadow and fear; I lost loved ones to the war system and culture; violent death was around me. In light of this, for me one of the major motivations in studying war through the lenses of IR theory is to give meaning to the terrifying reality of war. (Löwenheim 2010: 1038)

Reflecting on this further, however, Löwenheim then redescribes what at first seemed to be an (intellectual) search for meaning as something far more visceral, emotional and personal:

> On second thought, perhaps meaning is much too complex and illusive a concept. I cannot see meaning in a child's plight, in death in war, in the concept of 'friendly fire', in the dread of being torn to pieces by a suicide bomber, or in the suicide of a young soldier. The world, after all, goes on. Rather than meaning, I want theory to help me master my fear of war. (Löwenheim 2010: 1038)

Third, stages of research models do not adequately capture the multi-directionality of any project which involves considerable movement – 'backward' and 'forward' – between its diverse stages. Analysing collected data may help identify further information that is needed to 'triangulate' one's findings. Alternatively, an initial – or 'pilot' – collection of data (for example, a small number of interviews, or a trial focus group) may lead the researcher to reframe their research questions, perhaps because unexpected results emerge or because the original questions are discarded as unanswerable or redundant.

Fourth, it is also important to remember that research is an activity undertaken by a reflexive subject (the researcher). Although convenient to think of a research project as a teleological endeavour always moving toward its ultimate conclusion, in reality much of this process is characterized by the reconsideration and revision of earlier assumptions, decisions and even errors. Whether or not failure is an integral part of the academic system (Salter 2013), an active and consciously reflexive stance during research is infinitely more desirable than empirical, theoretical or methodological inertia. Reflecting on his work on counter-terrorism policy formulation, for example, Neal (2013) describes how his project evolved from its original conception as a discourse analysis, to a Foucauldian study supplemented by the works of the sociologist Bourdieu. Rather than the result of indecision or error, however, this reframing of projects and questions should be viewed as a necessary dynamic of (re)consideration, where: 'as critical scholars we have to work these things out ourselves: there are no straightforward how-to guides' (Neal 2013: 128).

As this all suggests, there is no single pathway or blueprint to doing successful or valuable security research. Any project is situated in its own tapestry of contexts, resources, emotions, relations, reflections, and decisions. For, as Alford (1998: 21) summarizes:

> No work springs out of thin air; it is a historical product, grounded in the intellectual traditions you have absorbed, in the theories of society you have learned, in the audiences for which you write. But it also reflects a series of choices, almost always made with uncertainty, because, by definition, you do not know enough to make

the right choices. Constructing an argument is an emotional as well as a cognitive process, a series of leaps of faith, sometimes grounded in hard evidence, sometimes in sheer speculation. You look about for support and for inspiration from books and articles, from colleagues and friends, from your inner resources of imagination.

Key Points

- Methodology is an orientation toward the generation of knowledge: it involves doing and thinking about research.
- Research methods are the particular techniques employed in generating knowledge.
- The research process is a complex one that exceeds the individual researcher and their intellectual concerns.

Measuring and modelling security

Until relatively recently, discussions of methodology within Security Studies were far further advanced within positivist approaches than their post-positivist counterparts. The study of International Relations in the 1980s, in particular, was dominated by what became known as the 'neo-neo debate', or – more critically – the 'neo-neo synthesis' (see Chapter 1). This was a situation in which the most recent defenders of the liberal and realist faiths – neo-liberals and neo-realists – became far more closely aligned with one another than had their forebears in these longstanding traditions. This new proximity was in part ontological: a product of an increasingly shared assumption that the international system is anarchical. It was also – and perhaps more importantly – an epistemological one: the outcome of a shared belief that the scientific study of global politics is both possible and desirable (see Wæver 1996: 160–70; and Chapter 2). With so much of the meta-theoretical space for thinking about security therefore uncontested – at least within IR's orthodoxy – the methodological question of *how* knowledge about security could be generated became ever more prominent.

Statistical models, broadly defined, are designed to investigate – and to measure – the relationships between different phenomena. One of the most common of these is regression analysis: a term for a range of techniques used to assess whether changes in one (independent) variable affect another (dependent) variable. Gartzke (1998), for example, uses this method to investigate claims associated with the **democratic** peace thesis, and the correlation this suggests between democratic states (independent variable) and pacific relations (dependent variable). To test his hypothesis that national preferences might explain this relationship – as much as the various institutional or cultural factors that are prioritized in democratic peace arguments – Gartzke studies voting patterns in the UN General Assembly as a proxy variable for the extent of similarity between nations' preferences. Building on earlier statistical studies (see Oneal *et al.* 1996; Maoz and Russett 1993), Gartzke (1998: 20) argues that 'the more two nations' preferences diverge, the more likely it is that they will engage in a militarized dispute'. While circumspect about the limits of his findings, this study demonstrates that regression analysis can be used to investigate empirical relationships as a mechanism for theory testing and refinement.

In a more recent study, Choi (2012) applies a similar research methodology to investigate the stability of different types of wartime coalitions. The focus in this analysis is specifically the empirical question of whether democracies are more likely to be committed to their allies than non-democratic regimes during war. Drawing on data from the **Correlates of War (CoW)** project, Choi found that – as she had hypothesized – this was indeed the case. In addition, she also found that 'the longer the war lasts, the smaller the chance of victory a state anticipates, and the larger the size of coalition, the more likely a state will leave the war before it ends. [Moreover] The United States is particularly effective in maintaining wartime commitment amongst coalition members' (Choi 2012: 649).

To conduct this analysis, Choi needed to make a number of methodological decisions. These included selecting the appropriate variables to investigate, and deciding how to code the data she was using to measure these. This included attributing values to the level of 'democracy' in each of the states in her sample, measuring the capabilities of the 47 wartime coalitions she studied, and identifying whether or not the US was a participant in the coalition. The latter is an example of a **nominal variable**, in that the possible 'yes' or 'no' answers have no mathematical value themselves and are only coded numerically (1 or 0) for the purposes of the analysis. The former – the level of democracy – in contrast, is an **ordinal variable** which posits a scale of increasing and decreasing values (countries can be more or less democratic than one another). Decisions such as these – on variable selection, definitions and coding – are fundamental to the quality of any statistical analysis. Indeed, one of the major debates around the democratic peace thesis has been the appropriateness of different measures of 'democracy'. Another, of equal importance, relates to the sample size from which this thesis has been inferred, given that, (i) democracy, and (ii) war between any two given countries, are both historically rare phenomena (Layne 1994).

Given the dominance of positivist approaches within Security Studies, and given the association of these approaches with quantitative research methods, there are a vast number of studies applying regression techniques and related methods to different cases and contexts. These have included, *inter alia*, analyses of the relationship between religion and civil war (for example, Toft 2007), debates over the number and type of casualty during warfare, and whether this is changing over time (for example, Lacina *et al.* 2006), the reasons for declining levels of violence in particular wars – such as the post-2003 conflict in Iraq – (Biddle *et al.* 2012), and studies of the impact of interdependence on conflict between states (McMillan 1997: 43–6).

Despite their prominence, and despite the value they hold for their advocates, there are caveats to the value of statistical approaches within the field of security. First, as is widely and frequently noted, regression analyses are only capable of demonstrating correlation, not causation. While it may be possible to demonstrate that changes in one variable are associated with changes in another, more is needed to demonstrate that changes in the former are responsible for, or directly *cause*, changes in the latter. In other words, some kind of theoretical and explanatory apparatus is needed to account for the relationship that seems to exist between democracy and the lack of war. Second, statistical methods are only as useful as the data being explored. If there are problems in the collection or coding of data this will, inevitably, affect the **reliability** of any findings and their analysis. Missing variables, errors in calculation, and poorly conceived variables or indicators may all have a negative impact upon statistical findings (see Box 3.2).

An alternative mathematical method used within Security Studies is formal modelling. This method is associated with rationalist social science approaches (such as rational choice and **game theory**) which have had a major impact on prominent IR theories, especially neo-realism (see Chapter 2). Rationalist traditions tend to approach research as a 'top-down' enterprise that applies **deductive** reasoning to initial theoretical assumptions about the world. The statistical models considered above, in contrast, tend to be associated with empiricist epistemologies and 'bottom-up', **inductive**, approaches to knowledge that make inferences from the available evidence (compare Walt 1999 and Martin 1999 on the value of modelling). Formal models, which are often underpinned by considerable mathematical sophistication, provide stylized explanations for the likelihood of particular outcomes under certain conditions. They have value, for their advocates, because they offer:

Box 3.2 Economic growth and debt

An academic research paper from 2010 – 'Growth in a Time of Debt' – found a significant statistical relationship between the economic growth of a country and the size of its debt. According to its authors, when a country's debt rises above 90% of a country's GDP, its economic growth slows down dramatically. This finding received considerable attention at a time of global financial crisis, and was widely discussed to legitimize the austerity programmes that countries such as the UK were instituting in their efforts to reduce national debt. Unfortunately, the finding was later found – by a PhD student – to be based on significant methodological errors, including the omission of important data from the spreadsheet from which the article was drawn. Once these methodological errors were addressed, the relationship between debt and economic growth appeared far less dramatic than it had previously.

Source: Alexander (2013).

a deductive, logically coherent method for relating assumptions and hypotheses to each other. It forces researchers to make their assumptions explicit, and provides a tool for understanding the extent to which hypotheses are robust or highly sensitive to particular assumptions. It exposes logical flaws in more informal arguments that can degrade their ability to generate coherent complexes of insights. (Martin 1999: 76)

Modelling issues of international security was a widespread exercise in Cold War era debates around nuclear deterrence and the prospects of international cooperation. As outlined in Chapter 1, this was a time in which the field was dominated by the militaristic concerns of **Strategic Studies** (for example, Achen and Snidal 1989; Langlois 1989). They have also, however, been applied to a range of other hypothetical contexts more recently, including efforts to assess the possibility of conflict between the world's two current major powers – China and the United States (Goldstein 2013), the dynamics of alliance formation (Garfinkel 2004), the threat of terrorism, including suicide attacks and cyberterrorism (Caplan 2006; Giacomello 2004), and climate change (Ward 1996).

Criticisms that have been levelled at mathematical modelling within Security Studies (although see Powell, 1999), include, first, the argument that these approaches are overly parsimonious and unable to account for the complexity of real world situations. As Hollis and Smith (1991: 138) argue of foreign policy: 'decisions are often the unintended consequences of group interactions whose conduct is not suited to Game Theory. Decisions can result from group pressures or bureaucratic politics. Individuals may have restricted world views and not be susceptible to incoming information.' Second, and partly following the first, sophisticated modelling may have limited policy relevance: the complexity of such models is better, perhaps, at explaining rather helping to make decisions in an uncertain environment. Third, rational choice models, in particular, rely upon fairly questionable ontological assumptions about social actors, whether presidents or terrorists. Not least amongst these is the assumption that these people are rational and act in their self-interest, unencumbered by broader institutional, political or material constraints. Fourth, the level of mathematical sophistication within these approaches – and the specialized language that is often used to describe work of this sort – has been criticized for rendering them impenetrable to outsiders lacking the requisite training in this area. Although criticisms of this sort are regularly targeted at a range of approaches by outsiders, especially post-structuralism (see Østerud 1996), there are questions to be asked about the value of a method that is inaccessible to many students and researchers working in a shared discipline. As Walt (1999: 20) put it:

> Some of the inaccessibility arises from the use of more sophisticated mathematics, but an equally serious barrier is the tendency for many formal theorists to present their ideas in an overly complex and impenetrable manner. In general, formal theorists rely heavily on a specialized jargon and what Donald McCloskey has termed a 'scientistic' style, in which formal proofs, lemmas, and propositions are deployed to lend a quasi-scientific patina to otherwise simple ideas.

Although mathematical methods – whether statistical or formal – tend to be favoured by researchers working within traditional and positivist approaches to security this is neither completely, nor necessarily, the case. For example, perhaps we are normatively inspired to challenge the securitization of an ethnic minority population as a threat to a majority population. One strategy for doing this would be to generate statistical information on the actual threat posed by the minority, and then to use this information to critique the minority's portrayal as a threat (Roe 2004: 285–6). Although this – objectivist – approach to desecuritization assumes that security is real, and can be measured, it may be useful for challenging the seeming exceptionality or significance of particular fears. Mueller (2005: 488), for instance, does this in a discussion of the threat posed by terrorism:

Even with the September 11 attacks included in the count, however, the number of Americans killed by international terrorism since the late 1960s (which is when the US State Department began its accounting) is about the same as the number killed over the same period by lightning – or by accident-causing deer or by severe allergic reactions to peanuts. In almost all years the total number of people worldwide who die at the hands of international terrorists is not much more than the number who drown in bathtubs in the United States.

Although Mueller's argument draws on statistical probabilities, it is obviously a long way short of the complex mathematical modelling in which game theorists or those employing regression analysis engage. Whilst a useful demonstration of how quantitative data might be put to use for political or normative purposes, the variety of (broadly sympathetic) responses that Mueller's argument received demonstrated how such engagements will always be open to alternative 'objectivist' arguments drawing on different data or examples (Byman 2005), or to the claim that it 'misses the point' given that the future may not be like the past (Betts 2005). The important issue, though – as Sjoberg and Horowitz (2013: 105) argue - is that 'there is nothing inherent in the use of mathematical methods that assumes the existence of objective knowledge, discrete variables, or the appropriateness of dominant discourses of epistemology and ontology'. As they continue, 'quantitative methods can be used to examine normative questions, to explore discursive and performative relationships, and to increase the creativity and depth of critical theorizing' (Sjoberg and Horowitz 2013: 105).

Key Points

- The dominant research methods employed within Security Studies remain mathematical which include statistical and formal approaches.
- Although associated with positivist and 'problem-solving' research, these methods can also be used by critically inspired scholars.
- One use is in critiquing claims about the reality of particular security threats via the documentation of statistical evidence.

Words, images and practices

The attention to methodological issues within positivist approaches to security has not, historically, been matched by those sceptical of their scientific aspirations. This is true across the social sciences, where a number of authors have reflected upon the 'methodological deficit' of interpretivist and post-structuralist scholarship in particular (see, for example, Milliken 1999; Howarth 2005: 316–19). This 'deficit' has, often, been a deliberate choice rather than an omission or exclusion: a result of the priority given to ontological issues within these traditions (see Howarth 2004: 266–8; Laclau 2004: 321). It is also, however, tied to a frustration with the detailed discussions of method that accompanied the development of rationalist and empiricist traditions. For critics, those traditions have often conducted research projects because of the methods that are available to them, rather than because of problems or questions they might have. Put more provocatively, they have tended to study what can be counted, rather than what counts. This resistance to 'methodological fetishism' is entirely understandable given the contrasting epistemological positions of positivist and post-positivist approaches (see Chapter 2). It may, however, have contributed to the latter's marginalization within some areas of security research, and a corresponding lack of dialogue between those finding themselves on different sides of IR's 'third debate' (see Milliken 1999: 228; and Chapter 2).

Fortunately, in our view, things have begun to change in recent years. Several important new books have now been published detailing the diversity of research methods available to critical scholars of security (Shepherd 2013; Salter and Mutlu 2013). New research initiatives have also been established to facilitate the development of methodological ideas on security, especially amongst those inclined toward critique (see further resources below). It is also, importantly, far more common now to encounter detailed engagement with research methods in articles and academic monographs on security by authors working beyond the mainstream, positivist approaches.

One important driver of this shift was the emergence of feminist security studies. Feminism was central in bringing methodologies from other disciplines into the study of IR, in part because it has tended to be driven by different questions and assumptions to the mainstream approaches (Tickner 1997: 620). These included some of the methods explored in more detail below such as discourse analysis and 'bottom up' ethnographic research (Tickner 2004: 46). A second reason is that critical security studies has now begun to reach something of a level of theoretical maturity. This opened space for greater reflection on methodology to complement and develop the earlier meta-theoretical debates around what security is and what we can know of it between critics and the mainstream (the subject matter of Chapters 1 and 2). Third, there are also institutional factors at work here, where academic funding bodies such as the UK's Research Councils put a great deal of emphasis on methodological sophistication in decisions over whether a particular research project will secure funding. And, fourth, the training provision in methods and study skills for postgraduate students has improved dramatically in recent years within universities. This has no doubt contributed to the enhanced interest and sophistication in this area amongst early career researchers. While there is still much to be done (for example, Newman 2010), the range and sophistication of methodological tools available today is unarguably far greater than it was when 'critical security studies' was first explicitly discussed in the mid-1990s.

One of the most widely used research strategies within critical security studies is that of discourse analysis. Although the term incorporates a range of approaches – partly because there are differing views of what discourse is – these all share an effort to explore the ways in which the world and its contents are given meaning – or constructed in particular ways – via language or other meaningful practices (see Box 3.3). In one of its 'thinnest' or narrowest variants, this type of approach can be found within securitization studies (see Buzan *et al.* 1998). Proponents of this framework explore the ways in which privileged actors use the language of security to turn a public policy issue into a security concern (see Balzacq 2011). And, by attributing no objective or predetermined content to security (see Chapter 1), the approach is sufficiently flexible to be applied to a range of quite different issues, as diverse as (but by no means limited to) cybersecurity (Hansen and Nissenbaum 2009), asylum seekers (McDonald 2005), the environment (Floyd 2010) and recreational drugs (Crick 2012).

A similar approach that is related to, but separable from, securitization studies is that of critical discourse analysis. Critical discourse

---

Box 3.3 Doing discourse analysis

The linguist James Paul Gee (2005) identifies seven different questions that can be asked about any text in the conduct of a discourse analysis. These are:

1. How are things being made significant or not in this text?
2. What activities is this text being used to enact?
3. What identities is this text being used to enact?
4. What relationships is this text enacting with others?
5. What political values are communicated in the text?
6. How does the text connect or disconnect things?
7. How does this text privilege or disprivilege sign systems?

analysis mobilizes an explicitly normative desire to reveal the relations between language and power, drawing inspiration from the writings of social theorists such as Michel Foucault, Karl Marx and the Frankfurt School of **Critical Theory** (Wodak 2001). As one of its proponents, van Dijk (2001: 96), puts it, CDA, 'is, so to speak, discourse analysis "with an attitude". It focuses on social problems, and especially on the role of discourse in the production and reproduction of power abuse or domination. Wherever possible, it does so from a perspective that is consistent with the best interests of dominated groups.'

CDA's interest in exposing and challenging how power relations work through language has obvious potential for the critical study of security. Constructions of danger, threat, risk and enemies, and the practices that these constructions make possible, are integral to contemporary governance processes, as well as being implicated in the domination and abuse of individuals and groups (e.g. Jackson 2007). One useful example is Richard Jackson's (2005b) exploration of the war on terrorism discourse of George W. Bush's administration. In this, he analyses over one hundred speeches, broadcasts, interviews and reports to explore how this conflict was constructed and justified by the American political establishment. Box 3.4 contains the questions Jackson applied to each of the texts he used in his analysis. Other studies have applied the method to a range of disparate issues – often in conjunction with notions of securitization – including the 'othering' of migrant communities (Baker-Beall 2009; Teo 2000), fears around energy security and potential resource crises (Rogers-Hayden *et al.* 2011), and the foreign policy fears of states in periods of transition (Mäksoo 2006).

Discourse analytic approaches such as those above have undergone two important transitions in recent years. The first follows the development and growth of Computer-Assisted Qualitative Data Analysis Software (CAQDAS) packages such as NVivo which allow researchers to collect, code, search, analyse and visualize vast quantities of texts that would previously have been unmanageable (Hassan 2013). Hassan's (2012) analysis of George W. Bush's 'Freedom Agenda' in the Middle East used CAQDAS to provide a thematically driven, but empirically rich, account of this paradigm as well as changes therein (Hassan 2013: 177). A second important development is the application of discourse analytic methods to non-linguistic forms of representation such as cartoons, photographs, paintings, diagrams and film. In part, this was a response to critiques of the 'linguistic reductionism' of approaches such as securitization in their earliest formulation. As Williams (2003: 525) argues, the emphasis on 'speech acts' within securitization studies, 'stands in contrast to a communicative environment

Box 3.4 A critical discourse analysis of the war on terrorism

Jackson (2005b: 25) applied the following ten questions to each of his sources in his analysis of the war on terrorism discourse:

1. What assumptions, beliefs and values underlie the language in the text?
2. How does the grammar, syntax and sentence construction reinforce the meanings and effects of the discursive constructions contained in the text?
3. What are the histories and embedded meanings of the important words in the text?
4. What meanings are implied by the context of the text, and in turn, how does the context alter the meaning of the words?
5. What patterns can be observed in the language, and how do different parts of the text relate to each other?
6. How stable and internally consistent are the discursive constructions within the text?
7. How is the language in the text reinforced or affected by discursive actions?
8. What knowledge or practices are normalized by the language in the text?
9. What are the political or power functions of the discursive constructions?
10. How does the language create, reinforce, or challenge power relations in society?

ever more structured by televisual media and by the importance of images'. As he continues:

> nightly images of shadowy figures attempting to jump on trains through the Channel Tunnel between France and the UK, for example, or of lines of 'asylum seekers' waiting to be picked up for a day's illicit labor (both common on UK television), have whatever the voiceover an impact that must be assessed in their own terms, constituting as they do a key element of the experience of many people on the issue of immigration and its status as a 'threat'. (Williams 2003: 526)

Vuori's (2010) discussion of the 'Doomsday Clock' used by The Atomic Scientists to visualize the likelihood of a global catastrophe offers an interesting attempt to apply securitization to a non-linguistic symbol. 'Reading' the clock through an aesthetics lens, Vuori argues that the image of a clock not only implies scientific precision, but that it also evokes 'all of the crucial ingredients involved in a securitization "plot": the lateness of the hour (urgency) and impending doom (existential threat), as well as the possibility to reverse course by moving the hands of time far away from midnight (way out)' (Vuori 2010: 264).

At the post-structuralist end of discursive research, distinctions between linguistic and non-linguistic aspects of social reality are frequently rejected. Lene Hansen's (2006: 64) overview of different intertextual research models for the study of foreign policy, for instance, includes film, computer games, comics, paintings, pamphlets and websites as potential research objects depending on the analytical focus of a project. This approach chimes with a number of contemporary studies of security and popular culture, which have focused on texts including video games (Sisler 2008; Robinson 2012), tourism guidebooks and practices (Lisle 2008, 2013), cartoons (Hansen 2011), television (Weldes 1999a; Buus 2009; Rowley and Weldes 2012; Dixit 2012), film (Shaheen 2003), commemorative projects (Edkins 2003; Zehfuss 2009) and websites (Jarvis 2010, 2011). Analyses of this type have connections to **semiotic** approaches, which study how meaning is conveyed through signs and their social contexts.

An alternative approach that first emerged within (social) anthropology is ethnography. Ethnographic research involves the researcher immersing themselves in the context they are studying (whether a factory, a Balinese village, or a university research institute) to try to develop an 'insider's' account of the meaning of the various practices, relationships, identities and so forth therein (see Geertz 2003). A very famous example is Carol Cohn's (1987) description of the year she spent as a participant observer at a university centre on defence technology and arms control. This immersion in her research context gave Cohn the opportunity to learn the highly specialized (albeit frequently metaphorical) language – or 'technostrategic discourse' – of these nuclear security experts, and to explore its role in normalizing the violences associated with arms racing, deterrence strategies and so forth. This familiarization with strategic discourses, she argues, opened up important opportunities for deconstructing this discourse, its assumptions and functions.

In a very different context, Megoran (2005: 557) describes his encounter with communities located on either side of the Kyrgyzstan/Uzbekistan border at a time of escalating crisis in the region. His recounting of the different reception he experienced with each of these communities demonstrates the value of the personal encounter that typifies this type of participatory research:

I first went to a mountainous pasture on the Kyrgyzstani side of the border that was highly susceptible to guerrilla attack and had been evacuated the previous year. Yet, when I visited, I encountered no security forces and roused no suspicion on the part of those camped out tending flocks. People extended hospitality, and even joked about the impending invasion, hoping the attackers would pay good money for live-stock. A few days later I visited the Uzbekistani side of the boundary. However, on this occasion,my reception could not have been more different: I was mistaken for a 'terrorist' by local farmers, who rapidly mobilised an army detachment to apprehend me. The arrival of the soldiers was welcome as the large crowd of terrified residents, who refused to believe that my (British) passport and letter from the local police chief were genuine, were angrily accusing me of being a 'Wahabi' terrorist, concealing weapons in the sand, and hypnotising them.

Interviews offer another common research method for studying security and insecurity. Depending on the research problem, these might be with members of political or other elites, or, alternatively, with the subjects or objects of security practices. Peters and Richards (1998), for example, use this method to powerful effect in their exploration of the motivations that led young combatants – 'child soldiers' – to join the Sierra Leone civil war that began in March 1991. In the published account of their findings, they note: 'The purpose of the present article is to let young combatants explain themselves direct[ly]…The reader is left to decide whether they are the dupes and demons sometimes supposed' (Peters and Richards 1998: 184). This demonstrates the normative as well as the intellectual impetus underpinning a research project.

There are a range of different interview strategies available to researchers. It is common to differentiate between structured, semi-structured and unstructured interviews. Where the former employs identical questions asked in the same order to all interviewees, the latter two are more flexible with increasing latitude afforded to the interviewer to respond to the answers provided by the interviewee (see Blakeley 2013). Pragmatic considerations to consider when employing interviews include: how to access one's interviewees – is this via 'snow-balling' from others or 'cold-calling'; how to conduct the interview – in person, via telephone, Skype, or email, and so on; and, whether to record the conversation or to rely on note-taking alone. There is, of course, no 'best practice' here. One's decisions will depend on the research problem, as well as methodological and ethical considerations. Johnson (2013: 69), for example, decided *not* to record her interviews with people living in refugee camps, because:

The daily experience of the migrants I was speaking with meant that I was not comfortable recording our conversations at risk of increasing their vulnerability. This was true particularly because we were speaking directly about their strategies and plans for further attempts to illegally cross borders. In addition to my concerns about vulnerability, a recording device would have negatively impacted an already cautious and fragile trust relationship, which was of greater concern to me than word for word recall.

Another method that has more recently attracted the interest of researchers working on security is focus group research. Focus groups enjoy the same face-to-face interaction as the interview, but differ because they involve a researcher working with a small group of (typically) four to ten participants. The researcher's role, in this type of project, is to stimulate conversation between the participants, usually through a series of open-ended questions. As with a university seminar tutor, their job is to guide and facilitate discussion. The advantages of this method are several (see Morgan 1996, 1997; Kitzinger and Barbour, 1999). First, because participants in a focus group discuss the topic with one another, group dynamics emerge that are not present in interview research. These interactions offer the researcher an extra dimension to analyse when compared with one-to-one interviews. Second, focus groups offer an opportunity to explore the flexibility or rigidity of a person's views on a particular topic, especially when they are challenged or contested by other members in a group. Third, the method is also useful for revealing shared ideas or sources of knowledge that members of a community might turn to in order to justify or make sense of their opinion. These might include localized anecdotes that a group feels are relevant to the discussion, shared cultural resources such as books or films that resonate across the group, or (inter)national developments or events of which all members of the group are aware or interested.

Jarvis and Lister (2013a, b, c) employed the focus group method to investigate the ways in which different publics across the UK talk about and conceptualize the contested term 'security' in their daily lives. In fourteen focus groups, they identified six distinct understandings of security, relating to survival, belonging, hospitality, equality, freedom, and insecurity, respectively (see Table 3.1). Exploring vernacular discussions of this sort is important, they argue, first, because it sheds light on the extent to which academic perspectives on security such as those explored in this book adequately capture 'everyday' concerns and experiences. And, second, because public experiences may throw up conceptions and uses of the language of (in)security that academics are yet to consider. Vaughan-Williams and Stevens (2012) employed a similar method in their research into public articulations of security threats. Their work drew upon twenty 'mini-focus groups' of three individuals, thus combining the individual depth of a one-to-one interview with the group dynamics of focus group research. This was triangulated with survey research to produce a 'mixed methods' analysis. Jackson and Hall (2012), similarly, conducted a study of fourteen focus groups to investigate how elite discourses on terrorism had been received by different publics. As they argue:

> this approach allows for, among other things: the analysis of individual knowledge and beliefs in vernacular conversation as opposed to survey research language; the analysis of flexibility, variation and dissonance in the discursive construction of beliefs and knowledge; the identification of shared sources of knowledge, collective narratives, cultural frames and rhetorical commonplaces employed to aid interpretation; the identification of key words, metaphors, assumptions, repertoires, grammatical forms and other shared forms of speech; the exploration of the social actions individuals undertake in speaking, such as assigning blame, praise, justification and the like; the ways in which individuals self-censor, justify or reflexively adjust their opinions on the basis of what they believe others think; and the broader kinds of meaning created in social interaction. (Jackson and Hall 2012: 6–7)

As the above demonstrates, there are a range of non-mathematical or 'qualitative' research methods available for studying of security, many of which have been applied in a diversity of contexts and research agendas. Despite their value for creating new and different types of insight into how security dynamics work, we conclude this section by identifying two possible concerns with their usage. These concerns derive, in part, from the 'unscientific' status often ascribed to these methods. As such, they follow on from the epistemological issues explored in Chapter 2.

First, many of the methods explored in this section are unlikely to generate statistically representative results. That is, a focus group study of public views on whether climate change constitutes a security threat is unlikely to sample a sufficient proportion of a national population to generate a reliable claim to 'public opinion' on this issue. This is in contrast to the large-scale survey or questionnaire studies employed by some academics, opinion polling organizations and the like, which do attempt to generate an accurate representation of a wider population than the people that are polled. In traditional social scientific language,

Table 3.1 *Focus groups and conceptions of security*

Security	Example
Survival	'Security means…to protect your life.'
Belonging	'Security means feeling happy where you are, feeling that, you know, there's no one to threaten you…you're not feeling like, oh I can't [go] there…I don't belong there.'
Hospitality	'I think if we feel welcome [here] we'd probably feel more secure.'
Equality	'Security is equality, to have all the same rights…There shouldn't be any difference between the black, white, foreigner…This is the meaning of security.'
Freedom	'I equate [security]…to freedom, really; to feeling that you can do what you want and be where you want within the confines of the law…without fear.'
Insecurity	'Well, that's security to me, it's an affiliation with military, martial law. That's instantly what I believe [when] they say we're going to increase security. I think of martial law.'

Note: Table 3.1 offers examples of the six distinct conceptions of security identified in Jarvis and Lister's focus group research (see Jarvis and Lister 2013c).

this is a question of reliability: in other words, do the findings accurately convey what they are supposed to?

Second, is the question of the **researcher effect**. This refers to the impact of a researcher on the situation, people or context which is being researched. Factors such as how an interviewer interacts with their interviewee and the physical space in which an interview takes places are likely to have a major influence on the types of data that is generated in the research (Blakeley 2013). Similarly, the very presence of an ethnographic researcher within a community is likely to change the behaviours of people within it: perhaps even permanently. Because the social world is amenable to change, and because human agents are reflexive, it is necessary in this kind of work to sacrifice **ceteris paribus** assumptions, and to accept that research findings will be less than objective; less than perfect. In traditional social scientific language this is a problem of **replicability**. So, where two statisticians running the same regression analysis on the same data should find the same results, this will not be the case for two ethnographers embedded in and interacting with the same context.

Because of issues such as these, it is obviously imperative that the security researcher thinks carefully about their research question, design, and the types of claim they are interested in making when analysing and disseminating their findings. In some senses, concerns around reliability and replicability rely upon a rather outdated understanding of the generation of 'scientific' (or academic) knowledge. From our point of view, 'data' or knowledge on the politics of security is not out there waiting to be discovered. Instead, it is actively constructed by the researcher and participants in the process of doing a project. If I am interviewing you to find out what makes you secure, it is likely that your thoughts and views will form, develop and change in the context of that interview (as will, likely, mine). Moreover, as outlined in the opening section, this always takes place in the context of specific conventions (academic and social), paradigms (of theoretical knowledge or methodological practices), and pragmatic constraints and opportunities. None of these are rigid or uncontestable, but they do help to shape what can and cannot be known about the types of security question explored in this book.

Key Points

- Recent years have seen a dramatic rise of interest in methodology and research methods amongst non- or post-positivist scholars.
- A range of qualitative or non-mathematical models are now used in research on security, including discourse analysis, ethnography, and focus group research.
- These methods require us to rethink traditional positivist research aspirations including validity and replicability.

Conclusion

As this chapter has argued, the attention afforded to research methodology and methods within Security Studies has risen dramatically in recent years. The traditional positivist interest in how knowledge is generated has been taken up by non-positivist approaches using methods that until recently had no place within the major debates on security. The emergence of these new methodologies – and the debate surrounding them – is important, in part, because it helps to challenge the association of positivism with methodological rigour. The standards by which research is to be assessed may need pluralizing as a result of this, but this should not be seen as a lowering of standards. Ultimately, a chapter such as this can only introduce the range of methods that are now available. It is up to the researcher to throw oneself into research projects and contexts in order to explore – and develop – appropriate ways for studying the practices and politics of (in)security. To conclude this discussion, then, let us now outline five different reasons why this methodological attention is a positive development.

First, the more attention afforded to methodological matters, the better constructed a research project will be. Thinking about how knowledge of climate change, poverty or refugeeism is acquired is, we think, at least as important as any ontological debate on what climate change, poverty, or refugeeism refer to. Second, greater attention to methodology is likely to lend itself to greater explicitness and reflexivity around the process of doing research. It is important, we suggest, to be as clear as possible on what one is and is not doing in a research project, for as Fairclough (2003: 14) notes: 'in any analysis, we choose to ask certain questions about social events and texts, and not other questions'.

Third, the emergence of new techniques such as ethnographic methods has rendered Security Studies a far more interesting discipline than it was before its pluralization. New types of analysis have been made possible with these developments and new types of 'data' have been rendered amenable to analysis (words, images, practices and so forth). Thus, not only is Security Studies more diverse now than it has ever been, and therefore less subject to the tyranny of methodological monolithism, it is also capable of exploring, understanding, interpreting, describing, explaining, analysing, and critiquing far more than it was in the past. Fourth, the emergence of non-traditional techniques has also helped foster interdisciplinary connections with a spread of other academic disciplines beyond the traditional home of Security Studies in International Relations. Just as the emergence of formal modelling techniques engendered connections between Strategic Studies, Political Science and Economics, so the development of new methodological approaches has fostered new connections with Anthropology, Gender Studies, Sociology, Geography, and beyond. This, we argue, makes the study of security a far more dynamic and engaging activity than if it were left to the hegemony of orthodox or traditional methodologies and methods.

Finally, thinking more carefully about *how* security knowledge is generated also leaves researchers better equipped to assess claims that are made about security threats and how best to respond to these (see Chapters 4 and 5). All designations of threat – whether risk assessments by government departments, speeches by political executives or activists, or academic models and debates – rely upon methodological choices. Understanding how these are made, and how findings are presented, therefore helps critically-minded researchers to engage with, evaluate, and perhaps contest securitizations and the practices they make possible.

Further Reading

Although not focused on security specifically, Halperin and Heath (2012) is an extremely useful introduction to research methods and their value for exploring political dynamics. Milliken (1999) provides one of the earliest – and still most helpful – engagements with the methodological issues involved in studying discourses within international politics. Salter and Mutlu (2013) is a very engaging collection of short reflections on methodology from researchers currently active in critical security studies, including many early career researchers; and Shepherd (2013) provides a very helpful overview of contemporary theoretical approaches within critical security studies and the methodological techniques that are associated with these.

Internet Resources

ICCM (2014) is home to the International Collaboratory on Critical Methods in Security Studies. This is an ESRC-funded project whose website includes discussions of critical research methods as well as blogs and academic articles that can be downloaded by visitors. Morgan Centre (2014) is the Morgan Centre for Research into Everyday Lives at the University of Manchester. Their website hosts a range of resources and 'tool kits' on various research methods including interviews and participatory approaches.

Chapter 4

Security for Whom or for What?

Chapter Overview

This chapter introduces debates over the referent object of security, asking to whom or to what are we referring when we speak about security? It begins by focusing on the state which has long been viewed as the dominant referent within the disciplines of Security Studies and International Relations. After exploring the reasons for this dominance, we introduce a number of its limitations. Here, we: outline the heterogeneity of states; question the importance of agency for security's referent; and destabilize the hyphen in 'nation-state'. The chapter's second section then introduces the state's major contender in these debates: the individual human. The benefits of a 'human security' approach are outlined with reference to debates on emancipation, gender and everyday life, before outlining some of the criticisms such understandings of security face. These include the potential for state co-option of 'human security' discourses, and the limited utility of these discourses for policy impact. Third, the chapter considers alternative referents, beyond states and people, evident within discussions of 'societal security' and 'ecological security'. The chapter concludes by arguing that designations of threat and insecurity are central to the production and reproduction of all of these referent objects. The 'whom' or 'what' of this chapter's title is actively created in security practices and discourse, rather than pre-existing these.

Chapter Contents

Introduction: security referents

This chapter introduces readers to debates over the referent object(s) of security. Bluntly, it asks to whom or to what are we – or should we be – referring when we invoke the language of security. In this section we outline what we mean by the term 'referent object' and what is at stake in determining and contesting the referent object of security. We argue that disagreements over security's referent have important political implications for thinking about responsibility within international and domestic arenas. This argument is made with reference to contemporary debates on R2P (responsibility to protect) in Afghanistan (see Boxes 4.1 and 4.2). This case study highlights that the referent object of security matters in real and political ways. What then do we mean by the term 'referent object' and does security really need one?

Perhaps the most famous and explicit linking of the terms 'security' and 'referent object' has taken place within the debates of the

---

Box 4.1 R2P – Responsibility to Protect

The norm of 'responsibility to protect' suggests that the rulers of states have responsibilities to the population they govern. Three pillars govern international society's interpretation of this norm:

1. The state carries the primary responsibility for protecting populations from genocide, war crimes, crimes against humanity and ethnic cleansing, and their incitement.
2. The international community has a responsibility to encourage and assist states in fulfilling this responsibility.
3. The international community has a responsibility to use appropriate diplomatic, humanitarian and other means to protect populations from these crimes. If a state is manifestly failing to protect its populations, the international community must be prepared to take collective action to protect populations, in accordance with the Charter of the United Nations.

Together, these mean that 'Sovereignty no longer exclusively protects States from foreign interference; it is a charge of responsibility that holds States accountable for the welfare of their people' (UN 2014). Unfortunately, as Figure 4.1 shows, this norm emerges out of the repeated failure of state leaders to realize this responsibility.

Source: United Nation, Office of the Special Adviser on the Prevention of Genocide (2014).

Copenhagen School (see Introduction). Their framework is one in which something only counts as a 'security issue' when it is presented as 'posing an existential threat to a designated referent object' (Buzan *et al.* 1998: 21). Traditionally, the referent object identified in discussions of security has been 'the state', and, more specifically, powerful states. Yet, with the impact of Peace Research in the 1970s, a growing human rights movement concerned with R2P, and more recent critical interjections in these debates, we have seen a contemporary return to the original association of security with the individual (Rothschild 1995; Glasius 2008: 31). Discourses of 'human security', for example, seek to displace the dominance of 'state security', and in so doing to mitigate the harm done to individuals by this traditional preoccupation (see Chapter 2). This effort to 'open up' and politicize the question of security's referent object is important because it has also made it possible for other scholars to consider further referents that are neither states nor people. In recent years, some have sought to locate collectivities – societies or communities – as security's appropriate referent, for example in debates around **societal security**. Others, associated with **environmental security** approaches (Epstein 2008; McDonald 2011b) have focused on the biosphere and the requirements of planetary existence, asking not 'whose security?', but 'what' is required for life (human and non-human) to continue.

In different ways, all of the above approaches recognize and codify a longstanding tendency within Security Studies and International Relations to view security as the potential *absence of threat* to something or someone. As Chapter 1 illustrated, however, conceptualizing security as threat, fear, or its elimination (see Burke 2001) is contentious and potentially problematic. So too is the argument that security is about threats *to someone or something*. The implication of such an assertion is that security – understood as a condition characterized by the removal of threat and its fear – can ultimately be achieved. Yet, the possibility of such a condition – of security's realization – is something that the authors of this text would deny. This impossibility is made clear in the final section of this chapter, discussing security's intimate imbrication within identity, and in Chapter 7 which considers the nature of the necessarily incomplete condition of (in)security.

The process of identifying the person, collectivity or thing that is having its security threatened is itself a deeply political act, with important political consequences. Within Security Studies, no author has more directly acknowledged the politics of security's referent than Ken Booth within Critical Security Studies (CSS). The question that Booth (1991) explicitly asks is 'whose security?'. Asked at a time

Box 4.2 Security's referents and the 2001 Afghanistan War

The political nature of security's referent object becomes clear when considering contemporary military interventions. The 2001 US-led operation in Afghanistan stands as a useful example.

First and foremost this was an intervention, following 11 September 2001, to re-establish *American* security. Here, the state emerges as the primary referent object. There was, however, an important disconnect evident in the secondary aims of the intervention. On the eve of the intervention, Bush insisted that 'as we strike military targets, we'll also drop food, medicine and supplies to the starving and suffering men and women and children of Afghanistan' (Bush 2001). These secondary aims made use of various referents, couched in humanitarian language, which were, interchangeably: individual Afghans; Afghans oppressed by the ruling Taliban regime; and/or the 'women and children' of Afghanistan. The third identifiable referent that emerged in the lead up to intervention took form through portrayals of Afghanistan itself as a failed state, in which Afghan society as a whole needed external assistance to achieve security.

The three referents produced different and sometimes contradictory political imperatives that would govern the possible policies of intervention. American security required a counter-terrorism operation, focused on finding and destroying Al Qaeda. The security of Afghan individuals required a humanitarian effort, with priorities such as famine relief, medical supplies and, in many instances, provision of shelter. Taking Afghan society as security's referent object shifted the emphasis away from the 'major combat operations' of Operation Enduring Freedom, towards the concerns of nation-building, counter-insurgency, and medium-to-long term development post-stabilization. NATO's ISAF

→

when Security Studies was dominated by often unspoken assumptions about the importance of the state and national security this was a question designed to disturb the reader. In other words, it forced them to confront tacit ontological assumptions about the way the world works and what matters within it, as well as implicit epistemological concerns about particular types of existing knowledge (see Chapters 1 and 2). Booth's question is certainly not asked neutrally; rather, his intention is to force a rethinking, away from the prevalent, the commonsensical and the dominant. It is a question that finds its articulation through an engagement with the Critical Theory tradition in social theory and its younger, reworked variants of critical

→
mission continues to attempt to fulfil the political and ethical commitments presented by this referent.

It is telling that this ordering of state, human, and societal security mirrors the hierarchy of official US priorities after 9/11. The outcomes and successes of intervention have replicated this prioritization, with Al Qaeda in the AfPak region shattered, humanitarian aid delivered inconsistently, and the challenges of stabilization and nation-building ongoing despite the looming drawdown of NATO troops. Claims from the Bush Administration that divergent security objectives, related to multiple referents, could be simultaneously achieved have come under attack from NGOs charged with delivering humanitarian assistance (HPG 2011). In 2001, Bush claimed that the United States was 'holding the Taliban government accountable, [and simultaneously] also feeding Afghan people' (2001). The Humanitarian Policy Group (HPG) of the Overseas Development Institute (ODI), however, refuted these claims, as well as the possibility that such mutual aims could ever be met. Experience on the ground has led the HPG to argue that counter-terrorism in the name of state security, and humanitarian intervention in the name of human security, work to undermine each other. This is, in part, because: 'Counter-terrorism laws and other measures have increased operating costs, slowed down administrative functions and operational response, curtailed funding and undermined humanitarian partnerships. They have also prevented access and altered the quality and coordination of assistance' (HPG 2011). The case study of Afghanistan, then, shows that security's referent matters in determining policy priorities and the possibility of their success. The competing referents of Operation Enduring Freedom, humanitarian assistance and NATO's ISAF mission have therefore contributed to undermining the possibility of delivering state, human, or societal security.

scholarship in International Relations. Most directly, Booth's question is inspired by Robert Cox's (1981) argument that knowledge is always for someone and for some purpose. For Booth – and for many other critics – the established, traditional ways of knowing and doing security support existing power structures (Booth 2005b: 7, 2007: 36; Mutimer 2007: 63–4; also Chapter 2). The question, 'whose security?', is intended, then, to unmask these operations of power, creating a space for considering alternative referent objects, towards whose security we might work. For, as Box 4.2 demonstrates, any security issue or framework is capable of supporting a number of quite distinct referents.

Key Points

- Security's referent object is a political choice, not objective fact, which has important ethical implications.
- The Copenhagen School has most directly illustrated the contingency of constructions of referent objects within the language of security.
- The Welsh School of Critical Security Studies has most explicitly theorized the political underpinnings and implications of these constructions.
- Beneath these different approaches, however, is a prevalent, but problematic, assumption that security involves threat – to someone or something – and its alleviation.

The state as referent

This section introduces the state as the political unit most frequently employed as security's referent. In it, we trace a number of justifications for focusing on matters of 'national security', including: the state's continuing dominance of military capabilities; assumptions that agency resides with states in the global system; the significance of national identities within 'ordinary' understandings of the social and political world; and the statist organization of the international system. The section concludes by exploring a number of important limits to this particular, and still dominant, state-centric approach. These include: ontological concerns over the diversity of states; normative concerns around the role of the state as security's guarantor; arguments that agency should not be included as a criterion for decisions about referents; and challenges to the conflation of state and nation implicit in discussions of national security.

If security is by necessity a 'hyphenated concept', attached to a particular referent object, the most frequent accompanying concepts have been 'national', 'state' and 'international' (Buzan and Hansen 2009: 10). All three have been used, confusingly and misleadingly, to mean the same thing. Thus, within academia, studying security has traditionally involved finding ways to promote and realize 'national security'. While the term 'national security' is actually itself a misnomer – 'state security' would be a more accurate term – let us ask how this particular understanding came to dominate academic and policymaker communities, beginning with historical factors.

Following the 1947 US National Security Act, security came to be understood as (and conflated with) the security of the state, closely tied to the idea of the national interest. The Act developed the ideas at the heart of the **Treaty of Westphalia**, imagining a world of competing states. In order to prosper, within this model of world politics, states were expected to vigorously defend their national interest, the first and foremost component of which was national security. National security was seen as the precondition for the achievement of further elements of the national interest (such as growth and the pursuit of power). Definitions of 'state/national security' are plentiful, contested and evolving, but nonetheless centre on: (i) the physical (geographical/territorial) protection and integrity of the state, primarily through military means; and (ii) the maintenance of economic and political structures; as well as (at times) (iii) the avoidance or elimination of threats to shared values.

The 1947 National Security Act created the contemporary architecture of American national security, including the National Security Council (NSC), CIA and Department of Defense (National Military Establishment). The context of the creation of this security architecture centred on the United States' role as victor of World War II and its emergence as a leading superpower on the international stage. In this moment, following the slaughter of the war, it was clear that military capability lay almost exclusively in the hands of states. And, the technological developments of the Cold War, manifested in arms races, nuclear weapons capabilities and **national missile defence**, ensured that military capability would remain the near-exclusive preserve of the nation-state throughout the twentieth century. It is this dominance of

---

Box 4.3 Military spending – PMCs and the 2003 Iraq War

Military spending during the 2003 War in Iraq reached unprecedented levels. US military expenditure hit US$550 billion annually, with an additional US$150 billion earmarked for overseas contingency operations. The War in Iraq is also noted for the increased role played by Private Military Companies (PMCs) for the provision of security. Consider, for example, that, in 2009, Lockheed Martin received over US$7 billion, and thirteen companies received over US$2 billion. While this outsourcing of security to private companies appears dramatic it does not mark a decrease in the dominance of the state's role in military issues. These statistics reflect spending on contract work by the US Department of Defense.

Source: Isenberg (2012).

military capability above all else that accounts for the conflation and synonymy of the phrase 'national security'. The military capabilities of other agents remain dwarfed by that of states in the contemporary international system. And, this asymmetry of military capability, alongside the belief that the state is the principal guarantor of (internal state) security, has meant that security, for many, simply *is* national security. In this sense, the statist and militaristic study of 'security' is very much a product of its Cold War origins.

If the dominance of military capability is the first reason for the prevalence of the 'state/security' conflation, the second lies in a related assumption that agency resides principally with the state in the international system. Associated with variants of political realism (see Introduction), this is an argument that other agents are relatively incapable of effecting change on the world stage. Again, military capability is important here. The composition of the UN Security Council, for example, alludes to an underlying military logic: victory in **Great Power War** coupled with the possession of nuclear weapons. However, the agency of the state extends beyond relative material capabilities. Even those states with minimal capabilities are taken seriously on the world stage by virtue of their recognition as states. This element of Westphalian sovereignty – the external, legal recognition of the state (see Krasner 1999) – ensures that states are granted a voice in international political dialogue that is denied to other actors and potential security referents. Consider, for example, the importance of statehood to agency as manifest in the 'observer status' the United Nations affords to Palestine (Box 4.4), or the more limited roles played by international non-governmental organizations (INGOs).

A third explanation for the state's dominance in debates on security can be found in the continued prominence of the *national* (i.e. state) identity. The state remains by far the most common form of collective identity: people, as citizens, statespersons, security analysts and so forth, still frequently view the world through this lens. Consider that even when contested or compromised, challengers still frequently define themselves through (or occasionally in opposition to) national identities. The recent constructs of 'British Asian' and 'British Muslim', for example, retain and reinforce the dominance of state identification (Croft 2007), as have labels such as 'African American' over a longer period. While an American national identity dates back only two centuries and a British identity arguably only gained resonance three or four centuries ago, the current era is dominated by a desire to identify, often quite personally, with the state. As Cohen (1996: 803) argues, national identity is an expression of self-

Box 4.4 Palestinian statehood

The importance of statehood within the international system can be seen within Palestinian efforts to secure it, and the debates surrounding this. In 2011, President of the Palestinian Assembly, Mahmoud Abbas, addressed the UN General Assembly, asserting the right of statehood for the Palestinian population. In it, he argued, 'Enough, enough, enough. It is time for the Palestinian people to gain their freedom and independence.' Israel's President, Benjamin Netanyahu, responded by arguing that statehood was conditional upon behaviour and adherence to international norms: 'The Palestinians must first make peace with Israel, and only then get their state.' Hamas, in contrast, argued that statehood is something achieved rather than bestowed by other actors: 'The Palestinian people do not beg the world for a state, and the state can't be created through decisions and initiatives. States liberate their land first and then the political body can be established.'

Source: Adams (2011).

identity: 'It is to say, "I am Scottish", when Scottishness means everything that I am; I substantiate the otherwise vacuous national label in terms of my own experience, my reading of history, my perception of landscape, and my reading of ... literature and music, so that when I "see" the nation, I am looking at myself.' The resonance of national identities remains a powerful explanation of the state's dominance as security's referent. It is an explanation that moves us from realist-premised arguments on national interests and relative material capability, towards a more constructivist account of international relations (e.g. Wendt 1992).

Realism, as embodied in legislation such as the 1947 National Security Act and the growing influence of George Kennan's thinking, unabashedly presents a state-centric view of the world. This assumption provided Security Studies with a useful, parsimonious starting point, from which to develop powerful and 'elegant' explanatory theories (Waltz 1979). It is, moreover, an assumption that has even infiltrated approaches formulated in opposition to realism. For instance, digging beneath the surface of constructivist literature, we find that this ontological starting point for security analysis is tacitly supported, rather than challenged and rejected. As Buzan and Hansen (2009: 196) argue, 'Constructivists comply analytically with state-centrism', pushing 'to the background the normative implications of accepting the state as the referent object and the state as the privileged realm' (see also Campbell 1998b). Take, for example,

Alexander Wendt's now infamous argument that 'anarchy is what states make of it' or Peter Katzenstein's seminal work, 'the culture of national security'. Both Katzenstein and Wendt reflect a conventional constructivist tendency to analyse the social construction of specific things, by the state, that may lead to or avert conflict. The Copenhagen School, too, reproduces a state-centric approach to security given its emphasis on well-positioned 'securitizing actors'. In Booth's (2007: 166) critique:

> Securitization studies therefore suffer from being elitist. What matters above all for the school is 'top leaders', 'states', 'threatened elites' and 'audiences' with agenda-making power. Those without discourse-making power are disenfranchised, unable to join the securitization game.

Within all of these approaches, then, security remains understood as, and concerned with, the military affairs of the state. To explore the limits of this ontological starting point for security's referent, we must venture beyond realism and constructivism, to the insights of post-colonialism and post-structuralism.

One of the central tenets of realist and especially neo-realist thought is the 'functional equivalence' of states, as they co-exist under/within a condition of anarchy (an international system lacking world government, see Waltz 1979). Post-colonialism has raised two important concerns about this approach to security. First, post-colonialism highlights the heterogeneity of states, which are arguably not 'functionally equivalent' and do not share universal features, from which a single state security approach can be sustained. The history of post-colonial states has frequently been very different from previously colonial states, leading to very different experiences of security. When combined with post-structural insights on relational identity formation, state security for colonial states can be seen to come at the expense of post-colonial states, with post-colonial identities constituted in negative, anti-Western terms. The post-colonial cause with regards to security then promotes new epistemologies and methodologies that might better account for this diversity of experiences and heterogeneity of states more generally (see also Chapter 2; and Buzan and Hansen 2009: 201–2).

Second, a state-centric conceptualization of international relations offers little in the way of an analytical or normative starting point, 'from which to identify the threats that regimes may pose to their own citizens' (Buzan and Hansen 2009: 201). Post-colonialism has highlighted that the state is itself no guarantor of the security of its

Figure 4.1 *Selected instances of state violence*

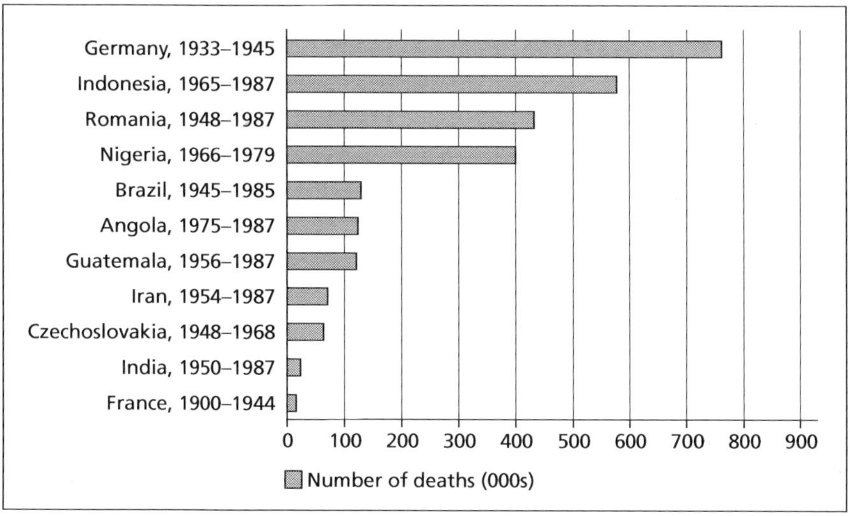

Source: Data from Scully (1997).

citizens, and on many occasions has actually been the primary threat to the security of individuals or communities (see Figure 4.1). It is only necessary to consider the recent human rights atrocities in Libya and Syria that have come at the hands of the governing regimes (as well as rebel groups). In Libya, NATO intervention was launched to prevent an imminent massacre in Benghazi. In Syria, the UN reported that over 100,000 citizens had lost their lives by July 2013 in ongoing clampdowns on protestors, which have been reported to include the use of chemical weapons and systematic starvation of rebel-held Damascus suburbs. In both instances, insecurity had arisen at the hands of the state. Far from being security's guarantor, state sovereignty has actually reduced the possibility of security for many. This creation of insecurity by the state has had both internal and external dimensions, with the rule of law eroding beneath state claims to a monopoly on the legitimate use of violence at home, and a corresponding decrease in legitimacy in the eyes of the international community. The drive towards a 'doctrine of international community' over the last decade has rendered sovereignty contingent and meant that a state's inability to provide for the security of citizens has warranted a lack of international legitimacy and enabled the possibility of military intervention (e.g. Blair 1999).

The decreased ability of states such as Libya and Syria to provide for citizens at home and demand recognition abroad raises an important point about agency. The ability of the state to act and affect change in the world has been central to its position as security's dominant referent. However, taking agency as an implicit precondition for a referent object is a deeply problematic move, highlighted by the plight of so-called failed and failing states, as well as alternative referent objects. While an individual's agency relative to that of a state might be minimal (measured in terms of influence on the international system), this does not constitute an ethical argument to rule out human security approaches in favour of national security pursuits. Likewise, linking security's referent to agency, without justifying this linkage, would seemingly rule out entities such as the biosphere from consideration, on the basis of its inability to consciously affect change in the world. Such logic also works to exclude those unable to articulate their own insecurities to the world because of their marginalized position in social, cultural or political structures (e.g. Hansen 2000). Because of this, some human security and CSS approaches argue explicitly that, for analytical *and* normative reasons, we should instead begin our analyses by focusing upon those least able to exercise agency in articulating and achieving security.

Finally, it is also important to note that, as a constructed category, the state arguably lacks agency itself, but is instead represented through the collective agency of its constituent parts (e.g. Wendt 1992). Once we recognize this, we can then begin also to interrogate the conflation of the term nation-state, which enables the synonymy of international security, state security and national security. International Relations has long acknowledged that 'state' and 'nation' are frequently not coterminous, despite the illusions of the protean neologism: 'nation-state'. Failing to acknowledge this has had devastating consequences in recent years. For instance, the Coalition of the Willing acknowledged a lack of post-war planning and a failure to understand the situation on the ground, prior to the launch of Operation Infinite Justice in Iraq in March 2003. Iraq is a multi-ethnic and arguably multi-national state, with Sunni and Shia Muslims predominant in the south, and Kurds forming the majority in the north. Pulling these diverse groups together, in the absence of a dictatorial leader, has proven problematic. After years of repression, Kurds, who have long been denied a nation of 'Kurdistan', are keen to be represented in the new Iraqi government, as are Shia Muslims who were marginalized under the rule of the Sunni Ba'ath Party.

> ### Key Points
>
> - Since the 1947 US National Security Act, the state and 'national security' have remained the dominant unit of analysis and aim of Security Studies.
> - Although this dominance is particularly pronounced within the realist tradition, a number of contemporary critical alternatives replicate this assumption.
> - Reasons for privileging this security referent include the state's military power, its association with agency, and the significance of national identities.
> - Limits to this approach include: the diversity of states; examples of states causing insecurity; arguments that agency should not be included in decisions about referents; and challenges to the conflation of state and nation implicit in discussions of national security.

People as referents

In this section we introduce the human individual as an alternative answer to the question: security for what or for whom? This is most prominent in debates over human security, some feminist approaches, and in Critical Security Studies' (CSS) focus on emancipation. In exploring these approaches, we chart the different justifications for focusing on the individual made by each. Linking back to Chapter 2, we argue that human security and CSS arguments derive their strength from a normative concern with the everyday lives of people and the variety of harms they encounter. The section also charts the increasing use of 'human security' rhetoric by important middle-power states in the world system (including Norway, Canada and Japan), and concludes with a range of pragmatic and conceptual criticisms levelled at these approaches. These include their risk of co-option by state actors, and their potentialities for concrete policymaking.

'Human security' is a term and an approach that has faced much critical interrogation since its emergence in the UNDP's 1994 'Human Development Report'. The report explicitly attempted to broaden the logic of security by shifting the referent object away from the state and associated concerns to 'people'. With people as referent, security becomes detached from traditional discussions of the national interest and military capabilities, and is instead 'concerned with how people live and breathe in a society, how freely they exercise their many choices, how much access they have to market and social opportunities

– and whether they live in conflict or in peace' (UNDP 1994: 23). This refocusing of security's referent precipitated a radical broadening of the security agenda, opening it up to include the environment and food, as well as health and economics more broadly, alongside political, personal and community security. The report argued that these components are *interdependent* within a *universal* struggle to achieve human security (UNDP 1994: 22). The idea of 'human security', the report suggested, has the power to transform the politics of the twenty-first century. The report's message resonated powerfully with the Wilsonian moment of 1990s world politics (Suhrke 1999), appealing, as it did, for a radical rethinking of how security was thought and 'done':

> In the final analysis, human security is a child who did not die, a disease that did not spread, a job that was not cut, an ethnic tension that did not explode in violence, a dissident who was not silenced. Human security is not a concern with weapons – it is a concern with human life and dignity. (UNDP 1994: 22)

At its heart, the UNDP report recognized that the most pressing issues faced by the majority of the world's people are not the result of major international crises. Rather, for many, insecurity is a constant experience within everyday life and the challenges this throws up:

> For most people, a feeling of insecurity arises more from worries about daily life than from the dread of a cataclysmic world event. Will they and their families have enough to eat? Will they lose their jobs? Will their streets and neighbourhoods be safe from crime? (UNDP 1994: 22)

This is a realization that 'human security', feminist and Critical Security Studies approaches share (albeit, as we will see, one that remains contested). However, all three approaches conceptualize and prioritize their shared referent of 'people' in different ways. Drawing on post-colonial thought and Peace Research, Critical Security Studies (the Welsh School) argues that 'individual humans are the ultimate referent' of security because states are unreliable guarantors of security and too heterogeneous to serve as the foundation of a universal theory of security (e.g. Booth 1991: 319; Buzan and Hansen 2009: 206). These are salient points, in response to which CSS attempts to emancipate those individuals whose security (as the freedom to act as they would choose) has been impinged upon by the conditions of the current world order. Individual and global security are, therefore, connected, in that the oppressive effects of an unjust world order impinge upon individual security. These are aims with which feminist approaches sympathize but sometimes divert from.

Feminist understandings of and approaches to security remain relatively overlooked despite their growing prominence. Indeed, one study found fewer than forty of over five thousand articles published in the top five security studies journals over a twenty year period addressing gender issues (Sjoberg 2009: 184–5). This marginalization is due to the continued dominance of traditional, militaristic and state-centric approaches within Security and Strategic Studies. Feminist approaches themselves are fractured and multiple. However, they frequently share with CSS an epistemology based upon experience and situated knowledge, and a desire to replace the state as security's referent with 'people' and particularly 'women'. Feminist approaches to security also share with CSS a desire to emancipate individuals from conditions of oppression and insecurity. They do this, however, in a way that feels more bottom-up than their CSS colleagues, embracing (for instance) story-telling methodologies from anthropology (for example, Tickner 1997, 2004; also Sylvester 2013). While numerous criticisms remain, major claims have been persuasively made concerning the importance of everyday female experience and the centrality of banal, routine forms of insecurity. If feminist approaches have advocated recognizing that the personal is political, they have also revealed the centrality and importance of experience to politics and security.

The progress made by human security, CSS and feminist approaches was reflected in the development of the UNDP's (1994) Human Development Report. The report and developments in Security Studies were both driver of and response to the increasing prominence afforded to 'human security' by some middle-power states. While some differences were evident, the 1990s saw countries such as Canada, Japan and Norway all begin to speak the language of 'human security'. Canada, in particular, as an affluent state, arguably isolated from more traditional security concerns, provided global leadership on emerging human security issues such as the International Campaign to Ban Landmines. Strong support from Canadian Foreign Minister Lloyd Axworthy gave state backing to a coordinated transnational campaign driven by INGOs and civil society actors. The 1997 Ottawa process, culminating in the Ottawa Treaty banning the use of landmines by 158 signatory states, was lauded as a success for proponents of human security and as evidence of the beginning of a new era of security oriented around a human referent. Norway's role in various peace processes and Australia's 1999 intervention in East Timor, inspired by public outrage at human rights abuses, all seemed to support this thesis. However, by

2004, Suhrke (amongst others) was expressing scepticism at the degree to which a new agenda had been realized.

Suhrke's (2004) critique of human security contains two particularly important points – its relation to national security and its potential for practical realization by states – which encompass five more specific limitations of the emerging human security agenda. First, Suhrke notes the limited take-up of the agenda beyond core states such as Canada and Norway. Second, this is compounded by the growing disinterest in human security issues amongst those original core states. Most recently, for instance, Canada has reverted to a national security imperative in opting out of the Kyoto Protocol. Third, states tend to support a human security agenda when it suits them, or when national security is a lower imperative. For example, after East Timor in 1999, Australia intervened in the Solomon Islands in 2003 due to the perception that Australia's national interest was threatened, not principally because of a desire to achieve the security of Solomon Islanders. Fourth, although approaches to security that take the human as their referent are located within a long, broadly liberal, Kantian tradition, there remains considerable susceptibility to abuse from the demands of *Realpolitik*. Human security rhetoric has frequently been used as window dressing to gain support for policies designed to pursue the national (state) interest. While a clear hierarchy of interests may be evident, as with intervention in Iraq in 2003, the lower priority of tearing down Saddam Hussein's 'apparatus of terror' was nonetheless an extremely useful justification, in that it helped to silence dissent and achieve acquiescence for foreign and security policies formulated with the state as referent (Krebs and Lobasz 2007; Krebs and Jackson 2007; Holland 2013a; McDonald and Merefield 2010). Fifth, a persistent critique of human security has been the limited scope for policy formulation offered by such a broad approach (see Chapter 2). Since the state continues to dominate international relations, those tasked with working for and representing the state are necessarily beholden first and foremost to the concerns of national security.

These are important critiques, which have garnered responses from various strands of human security literature. They have also inspired a set of related academic critiques of human security, which pertain to the definition and nature of human security, as well as resultant implications for the study and possibility of security. Within human security approaches, two distinct trends are evident, the commensurability of which is the topic of ongoing debate (e.g. Kerr 2007). These trends can be thought of around competing attempts to define human security in narrow or broad terms. 'Human security' approaches have, for instance, been concerned (broadly) with 'generalized poverty' (underdevelopment) and its avoidance, as well as (more narrowly) conflict and its consequences (political violence). On one hand, approaches adopting 'people' as security's referent have focused on identifying core, universal human rights and advocating for their protection. On the other hand, a broader focus exists, which marries a desire to protect fundamental human rights with a desire to promote social justice and human fulfilment. It is this latter variant that most explicitly connects security to everyday life, but that also potentially derails the possibility of security and its analysis. The 'academic', definitional critique of 'human security' approaches has tended to coalesce around two major points of concern. First, if security is defined so broadly as to encompass everything, critics of human security approaches would contend that it comes to mean and be capable of delivering nothing. Second, broadening an understanding of security's referent too far can lead to an inability to prioritize sources of harm, to separate out key variables within human suffering, and to subsequently establish and understand relations of causality between these (see, for instance, Mack 2005; also cited in Hampson 2008: 231).

Key Points

- The 1994 UNDP 'Human Development Report' questioned the centrality of the state to issues of security and put 'human security' on the international agenda.
- The term 'human security' is used in different ways by different approaches and has faced intense critical interrogation since its emergence.
- Concerns over the term 'human security' include that it can be invoked by states pursuing self-interested aims and that it is hard to realize a security agenda concerned with the plethora of harms which impact on the everyday life of people around the world.

Beyond states and people?

In this section we identify a range of other referent objects posited within contemporary security studies. These include efforts to broaden the field still further by taking the biosphere as security's referent in discussions of ecological security, on the one hand. And, on the other hand, Copenhagen School discussions of societal security with an emphasis on collective identities.

As the Cold War drew to a close, multiple approaches were already noting the limitations of a state-centric Security Studies, preoccupied with the military, territory and national interests. Two strands of thought in particular have been at the forefront of moving Security Studies beyond states and people: societal and environmental security. Barry Buzan's (1991) *People, States and Fear* first introduced the term 'societal security', building on work in the previous decade that had begun to argue that Security Studies should be widened beyond the narrow confines of the realist paradigm. Buzan's work responded to this challenge by arguing that security could be rethought around different 'sectors': military, economic, political, environmental and societal. While Buzan's formulation continued to prioritize the military and focus upon the state (which societal insecurity could threaten), it nonetheless helped to open the scope for Security Studies to consider alternative referents, beyond states and people. In the case of societal security, the primary referent is the survival of collective identities other than the state. These might include ethnic groups, religious communities or other types of 'we' within global political life.

The above example of the aftermath of the 2003 Iraq intervention offers a useful case study on societal versus state security. As American forces withdrew at the end of 2011 and start of 2012, Iraqis reported as a whole that they felt worse off than before the intervention (Gharib 2011). However, that figure belied a sharp divide between societies within Iraq. Sixty per cent of Kurds expressed that they felt better off after the intervention, compared to twenty-nine per cent of Shia and fifteen percent of Sunni communities. The 'we' of the 'Iraqi people', therefore, actually camouflages several smaller 'imagined communities' (Waever 1993; Anderson 1991), with very different identities, and therefore experiences of security. For the Kurdish community, the invasion offered an opportunity to move beyond a history of repression they had suffered in Iraq and elsewhere. And, more optimistically, a potential opportunity for realizing the establishment of a state of Kurdistan.

Societal security is brought into focus most clearly when perceived threats to collective identity manifest. Three recent European examples are illuminating. First, contemporary French legislation to ban the wearing of religious clothing – notably the Islamic veil and headscarf – could be read through a societal security lens. These overt symbols of religion were widely seen as presenting a challenge to the traditional separation of church and state in France and therefore the continuation of this 'way of life'. Second, similar dynamics have been evident in Swiss attempts to limit the construction of minarets, as a Christian 'we' has perceived a threat to their collective identity from an Islamic 'they'. While neither state has sought to exclude the possibility of a shared national identity, the idea that there are clearly competing Christian,

Box 4.5 Societal insecurities

Unfortunately, in Italy and across Europe, insecurity has remained a persistent feature of everyday life for the Roma community for centuries. Under the policies of the Third Reich such insecurities reached their pinnacle, as they did for Jewish, homosexual, disabled and black communities. While the Holocaust stands at the abhorrent zenith of societal security concerns, there are numerous other, equally troubling if less widespread, threats to the survival and identity of societies. Catholics in Northern Ireland, Hungarians in Transylvania and Muslims in the former Yugoslavia have all, to varying degrees and in different ways, been depicted as a security threat, because of their identity as Catholics, Hungarians or Muslims. Whether forcible assimilation, institutionalized discrimination, or the targeting of markers of cultural identity, threats to the identity of societies have been a pervasive feature of contemporary political tensions in Europe and beyond. In Australia, fears over the arrival of undocumented immigrants – so-called 'boat people' – have been met with a strong, militaristic response, backed by the promise of a 'frank, open and honest' debate, which served to legitimize those voices who might portray asylum seekers as an existential threat to the cultural identity of Australia as a Western nation (see McDonald 2011a).

Islamic and secular identities has dominated these debates and their emphasis on particular values at risk of erosion. A third contemporary case study in Europe has seen the growing suspicion of the Roma community in Italy (see Box 4.5). This decreasing respect for Roma life came to a tragic culmination, in 2011, with the deaths of two young Roma children, whose bodies were left unaccounted for on a beach following their drowning. What was most remarkable was that normal Italian life carried on around their covered bodies; local people continued to sunbathe, picnic and enjoy the beach. While this lowered regard for Roma life has been fuelled by perceived threats *from* the Roma community, it is abundantly obvious that the Roma community is itself threatened in the response from the Italian state.

Societal security then (may) help to move us beyond the state by thinking about the security of collective identities, although it usually finds its voice with reference to the state. A more wholesale challenge to the notion of the state as security's referent has developed out of environmental science and green politics literatures. Environmental security seeks to push the subdiscipline of Security Studies beyond the state. It also seeks to move security's referent beyond people. Taking the biosphere as security's referent, environmental security is concerned with environmental change as a threat to the biosphere; a threat to that relatively thin band of interlinked ecosystems that encompasses planet Earth, containing and enabling all life.

Although environmental concerns surfaced in the 1960s, they only really emerged as an issue for discussion within Security Studies in the 1980s, as the Soviet Union crumbled. Robert Kaplan's *The Coming Anarchy* popularized the potential linkage between environmental change and (national) security. And in the 1990s politicians such as Al Gore pushed for greater environmentally focused policy. While the Clinton Administration, like Robert Kaplan, focused upon the impact of environmental change on nation-states, alternative 'green agendas' also took hold. Ecological security – as opposed to environmental approaches which, for example, attempted to secure the state from nature – instead prioritized focusing on the totality of ecology contained within the biosphere. They offered a complex approach to the study of security, drawing on Green Philosophy, as opposed to parsimonious Malthusian warnings of overshoot and inevitable collapse. The argument that is proffered is not only that people are only secure *within* their environment (Dalby 2002; McDonald 2011a), but also that we should be wary of prioritizing people above other aspects and life forms of that environment. In this sense the more pertinent question may not be how can we protect humans from natural disasters. Rather, how can we protect the natural environment from humans which are only one part of it?

Unfortunately, the complexity of an interlinked ontological starting point, informed by a specialized scientific and radical philosophical literature, has meant that ecological security has had limited, if increasing, policy impact. It is also an approach that is quickly overlooked in times of prominent national (state) security concerns. As it was during the Cold War, environmental security has once again been overlooked and marginalized during the 'War on Terror'.

Key Points

- The end of the Cold War and Barry Buzan's (1991) *People, States and Fear* helped to put different issues and referent objects on to the agenda for Security Studies.
- Particularly important within this were notions of societal and environmental security.
- Immigration and climate change are recent examples of societal and environmental concerns respectively that have been spoken of as 'security' issues.

Security and identity

Building upon these discussions of security's referent leads us into the chapter's final section which offers a more detailed overview of the relationship between security and identity. Here, we argue that these two phenomena may be analytically, yet not ontologically separated. In other words, claims to security and insecurity are integral to the construction of referent objects at all levels of analysis, while claims to identity are complicit in the identification and management of security issues.

To suggest that security and its referent can be separated is misleading. What security *is* – what it is about, seeks and prioritizes – depends on the referent object that is being invoked. Equally, a referent object is, in significant part, brought into being through logics of (in)security that help to construct its identity and fix the borders of its internal Self and external Other. Security and identity are intimately connected due to the social, cultural and discursive construction of both, as well as the linked, relational and often binary nature of both security and identity.

Within Security Studies, these arguments have been made, in particular, by those drawing on critical constructivist and post-structuralist ideas. In this vein, David Campbell (1998b, see also Buzan and Hansen 2009: 218, Der Derian and Shapiro 1989) explored the relational nature of security and identity for the United States during the Cold War, concluding that states *need* enemies – constructed and imagined Others – to maintain their own self-identity. In the case of Cold War America, this 'Other' was the Evil Empire of the Soviet Union. Previously, American identity had been forged in opposition to Native American, Spanish, African and European Others, as well as less obvious antitheses such as witchcraft (Campbell 1998b: 115). At the onset of the War on Terror, Campbell (2001) suggested that time appeared to be broken, as we witnessed the inevitable return of the security *and* identity logics that had defined and enabled the Cold War.

Architectures of security then are not only supported by the discursive and cultural architectures of amity and enmity that attempt to fix identities. Rather, their very existence is made possible through them. At its crux, the social construction of particular identities enables security policies that reconstitute those identities. Recent American (and Western) concerns about the possible development of an Iranian nuclear weapon are founded upon an (often tacit) assumption that nuclear weapons cannot and should not be held by Iran. This assumption is based upon knowledge gleaned from a variety of sources, the two most important of which are the Enlightenment and **Orientalism**.

The former privileges rational thought as the marker of modernity and civilization and an obvious prerequisite for the ownership of the ultimate weapon of modernity. The latter denies this quality to Middle Eastern subjects, who are seen to be mired in irrational, less-than-civilized, ways of life. It is only within this intertextual, discursive framework that US policies of sanctions and increasingly overt military posturing become possible, and seen as necessary. Iran's identity is constructed – as irrational 'rogue' rule-breaker, rather than rational actor attempting to balance Israeli and Saudi power in the region – through the logic of (in)security. This occurs in a range of places including the speech acts from authorized American voices, repeated referrals to the UN, as well as a cascade of media punditry and academic analysis on the implications of Iran's (assumed) policy. And yet Iran's identity is itself central to the possibility of this particular security policy; they are co-constitutive, vital to each other and only analytically separable. This helps to explain why Obama's recent efforts to, first, 'extend the hand of friendship' to Tehran, and, second, to thaw relations with Rouhani, have failed to resonate with many Americans.

Security, then, is as much about 'who we are' as it is about 'survival'. It is a part and parcel of processes of meaning-making that construct the borders of a moral community (Pettmann 2005). Attempts to redefine national identity are an obvious example of this dynamic. They also highlight an essential, if occasionally overlooked, component of a discursively attuned approach, recognizing the mutually constitutive relationship of security and identity: the importance of strategic agency. If identity construction enables security policy, and security policy reinforces identity construction, we are potentially left trapped within a logic of security from which escape is unlikely. Fortunately, security, identity and their relationship is not structurally determined; as Chapter 1 argued, both context and conduct matter. It is in this relationship between structure and agency that issues of change and continuity are resolved. Consider, for example, that former Australian Prime Minister Paul Keating's attempts to 'regionalize' the Australian national identity met resistance and were reversed by his successor, John Howard. Longstanding tensions and an antagonistic imagining of the neighbouring region proved too deeply engrained to wholly overturn, as Howard's Hobbesian portrayal of the region resonated. Directly linked to the question of whether Australia was a 'Western' or 'Asian' nation was the logic of a policy response that would either see Australia attempt to achieve security *from* or *within* the Asia-Pacific region. Questions of Australian identity were linked directly to Australian security policy. Their resolution depended upon both the strategic agency of politicians and the wider, underlying Australian cultural context.

It is not just the state, however, that illustrates the imbrication of security and identity. As has been shown, shifting consciousness of societal identities can alter security's referent and with it the apparent nature of security. The demands of security shift with the identity of its referent; calls for basic nutrition and health provision for a displaced minority population stand in stark contrast to the often elite interests driving state security policy. The ethical and moral questions that shift in line with changing personal pronoun use lay at the heart of questions and logics of security. However, how identity is formulated and the implications of these insights for Security Studies remain contested.

Broadly, the role that identity plays in security is controversial. Traditional approaches deny its relevance altogether, while middle-ground constructivist positions might acknowledge its importance but reduce identity to another 'explanatory variable', which is treated as a fixed, immutable given. While we argue that identity is a crucial component of security, ontologically inseparable from it, we also acknowledge that identity is still not fully understood or agreed upon. Drawing on Derrida, Foucault and Laclau and Mouffe, post-structural social science has long suggested that identity is derived through difference. Self-understanding is achieved in opposition to something that the Self is not. However, whether identity is binary is up for dispute. To what extent must identity be formed through juxtapositional or antagonistic differences? Is identity always a process of inverses and opposites? Ole Waever (1993) has argued that the case of Europe shows how a polar attraction can generate a fading gradation of nuanced identity construction, in contrast to (for instance) Campbell's (1998b) or Jackson's (2005b) insights on the Manichean identity constructions that enable United States security policy. Nevertheless, contra Wæver, it remains feasible to argue that a Kantian, enlightened and peaceful European identity is still widely constructed in contrast to a more Hobbesian, brutish United States (Kagan 2003) and a less civilized non-European identity (e.g. Said 1979).

Despite these ongoing debates, recognizing the mutual construction of identity and security pushes Security Studies in particular and important directions. Discourse and culture become necessary fields of enquiry, alongside and perhaps even in place of the 'hard power' measures of relative military capability. Discursive analyses of security have been increasingly prevalent since the end of Cold War, with a spectrum of approaches from a pseudo-rationalist Copenhagen School, through Critical Security Studies, to Bourdieu-inspired work in the Paris School and within International Political Sociology. These studies have shed new light on environmental security (Epstein 2008; McDonald 2011b) and state security (Jackson 2005b). However, taking seriously the claim that identity and security are co-constitutive raises the fundamental and inexorable question of security's possibility, to which we turn in Chapter 7.

Key Points

- What security is – what it is about, seeks and prioritizes – depends on how we define its referent object.
- Security and identity are co-constitutive. They create and sustain each other. This makes the study of identity and ideas, as well as language, culture and discourse, just as important as the study of guns, tanks and missiles.
- An important question for Critical Security Studies is: how does identity form and is it always binary?

Conclusion

This chapter began by asking: security for what or for whom? The answer has implications for both the nature of security itself and the pertinence of particular security threats and challenges: the themes of Chapters 5 and 6. Recognizing that the identification of security's referent is a *political* act highlights the need to rethink security. This chapter has shown that national (state) security has a long history of dominating the study of security, to the point where security and state security have become almost synonymous. The end of the Cold War and the reduction of existential fears for both superpowers created space to consider alternative sites of security. Human security, taking people as its referent, predates IR preoccupations with the nation-state and potentially offers a route to overcome some of the implications of a state-centric discipline. Limitations, however, remain. Hence, in the last two decades, Security Studies has increasingly looked beyond states and people, considering alternative sectors and referent objects such as collective identities and the environment.

At its crux this chapter has suggested that the question of security's referent is central to conceptualizing the nature, possibilities and potential policies of security. Additionally, the question of security's referent helps to determine the equally contestable and political question: what qualifies as a security issue? The question 'security from whom or from what?' guides Chapters 5 and 6. First, the traditional dominance of state security, the national interest and military strategy ensures that it is necessary to consider the changing of war. Second, a host of new security challenges are discussed, in light of recent empirical developments and concomitant contemporary trends in Security Studies. As we shall see, debates about the threat of new security issues are always inevitably interlaced with contestations and assumptions about security's referent.

Further Reading

Booth (2007) provides a book-length overview written by the main figure within the 'Welsh School' of Critical Security Studies. In it, he outlines his approach to security and its relation to emancipation and community. Buzan *et al.* (1998) provide a similar statement in relation to the Copenhagen School's approach and its account of securitization and security sectors. Buzan (1991) was an important moment in the initial broadening out of security studies, as was Krause and Williams (1997), which is an edited collection of essays from feminist, post-colonial and other 'non-traditional' thinkers.

Internet Resources

UNDP (1994) is the Human Development Report which helped catapult the concept of 'human security' into the international arena. SIPRI (2014) contains lots of useful data, maps and other resources relating to global military expenditure, arms transfers and the like. SIPRI is an acronym of the Stockholm International Peace Research Institute. The Humanitarian Policy Group (2011) explores the impact of counter-terrorism powers on humanitarian action and funding.

Chapter 5

Security from Whom or from What? The Changing Nature of War

Chapter Overview

This chapter considers a particular, but very prominent, security issue within the Security Studies literature: military violence. It begins by reflecting on the nature of warfare as a form of organized violence, exploring the psychological, social, political and international factors that help explain inter-state war, as well as war's human, economic, domestic and international consequences. These arguments are made with reference to issues of structure and agency and illustrated through the case studies of World War II and the post-2003 conflict in Iraq. The chapter's second section then investigates the changing nature of warfare, considering in turn: the likelihood and potential obsolescence of major war; the changing geography of war; new practices and types of warfare; and the privatization of contemporary war. Examples explored in this discussion include the continuing conflict in Uganda and the 1990–91 Gulf War. The chapter's third section turns to the role of weapons in the international system, introducing: debates over nuclear weapons in the Cold War and contemporary eras; concerns over other forms of Weapons of Mass Destruction (WMD); and the use of small arms globally. The chapter's fourth section offers a study of international terrorism, sketching the use of this tactic by a diverse range of groups – including states – the scale of the terrorist threat, and the consequences of different counter-terrorism strategies. The chapter concludes by returning to broader questions about the purposes of Security Studies in view of the changing nature of war. Returning to the complexity/parsimony debate, we contrast claims that a narrow focus on military force introduces coherence and focus into this subdiscipline, with more expansive readings of Security Studies that emphasize the important role played by alternative forms of violence such as those considered in Chapter 6.

Chapter Contents

Introduction

An enhanced (and, for many, belated) recognition of the importance of non-traditional security challenges was one of the major stimuli behind the widening of Security Studies toward the end of the twentieth century. In this and the following chapter we explore these debates, encouraging readers to reflect on the most significant contemporary threats to security for the different referents sketched in Chapter 4. The chapters are organized by types of threat: military and non-military. In this chapter, we focus on military threats, considering: the causes and consequences of war; the changing nature of armed conflict; the evolving role of different types of weapons in the international system; and contemporary terrorism.

While clearly an important topic, it is certainly not an obvious, natural, or even apolitical decision to focus exclusively on military threats in this chapter. Indeed, such a decision risks contributing to a discourse and practice that couples security to military power, which we would rather work against and overcome. Our concern centres upon the fact that thinking about security in predominantly militaristic terms can have pernicious consequences. Official congressional reports have noted that the military interventions of the War on Terror have cost the United States alone an estimated US$1.3 trillion (Belasco 2011), with some suggesting that figure actually sits closer to US$5 trillion (Thompson 2011). Annual US defence spending sits at around $700 billion (ibid.). And, each detainee at Guantanamo Bay – four years after President Obama signed an Executive Order promising the facility's closure – continues to cost

American taxpayers three-quarters of a million dollars annually (Van Veeren 2012). Arguably, this gargantuan financial expenditure – not to mention the colossal loss of life that the '9/11 wars' (Burke 2011) have caused – is entirely disproportionate when measured against the empirical fact that, statistically, terrorism remains an almost non-existent irrelevance (Zulaika 2009: 147; Jackson *et al.* 2011). Why then are military options and solutions so often prioritized in contemporary international relations? And why would we choose to focus in this chapter first, and exclusively, on military threats to security, in that this might further legitimize a worrying preoccupation with '**hard power**' (Nye 2005)?

As the previous chapter outlined, Security Studies has long been preoccupied with the security of the state and the pursuit of the national interest centred upon the use and the threat of military power. This preoccupation rapidly became a deeply engrained conflation – whereby security *was* national security – as the two were welded together in the heat of the Cold War's intermittent crises. The thawing of the Cold War did, to an extent, create an environment conducive to new ways of thinking about security, both in terms of security's referent and security threats. Climate change, development and self-determination, for example, were all pushed up the international agenda, in lieu of existential nuclear concerns that characterized the Cold War. However, even these 'new security issues' (see Chapter 6) were frequently read through the lens of the state and its military options. And, as this chapter will demonstrate, the events of 11 September 2001 returned issues of military security firmly to the forefront of policymaking and Security Studies (see also Chapter 1). War, intervention and armed conflict remain some of the most significant and prevalent threats to security in the world today, despite the fact that military measures are usually seen as the mechanism through which security can be achieved and ensured. It is a perverse irony then that policymakers' preoccupation with achieving security through military means frequently generates a condition of insecurity, which warrants our initial and exclusive focus on this particular type of threat here. It is an irony that we attempt actively to highlight and ultimately undermine.

Military threats to security are not and certainly should not be treated as exceptional. However, they are dominant, both in the minds of practitioners, charged with delivering security, and of researchers charged with understanding security. This is especially true of realist approaches to Security Studies, as Stephen Walt (1991: 212) famously argued:

Security Studies may be defined as *the study of the threat, use and control of military force*. It explores the conditions that make the use of force more likely, the ways that the use of force affects individuals, states and societies, and the specific policies that states adopt in order to prepare for, prevent, or engage in war.

For many twentieth-century scholars sympathetic to Walt's characterization of Security Studies, the use of military force of primary interest was Great Power Wars. However, military threats also encompass other important forms of conflict beyond the clashes of well-armed states (see Figure 5.1). Changing technologies, politics and tactics have led to the increasing importance of specific weapons, asymmetric conflicts and terrorism. It is only narrow and arbitrary prioritizations in the discipline of International Relations that have traditionally relegated these issues to secondary concerns. Specifically, it is the dominance of realism and its variants within IR that ensured inter-state war and in particular great power conflict have been prioritized for study due to their impact on **international order** (see, for example, Henderson and Singer 2002: 171). Moving chronologically with the changing nature of warfare and resultant intellectual shifts in Security Studies, this chapter explores the causes and consequences of inter-state war, before considering some of the relatively recent changes that are taking place on the battlefield and which have redefined it.

Figure 5.1 *Types of war in the international system, 1816–2007*

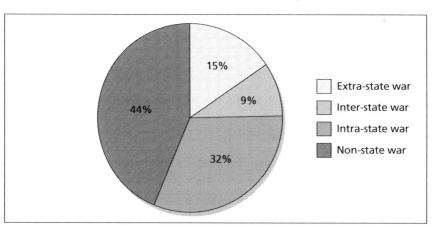

Note: This figure demonstrates the comparative rarity of inter-state wars in relation to other types of military conflict. It is worth noting the difficulty of defining these categories and distinguishing between them, as well as the statistical problems that might logically follow. Data from Correlates of War Project.

Key Points

- Military threats to security have long dominated the academic study of security.
- Thinking about these threats as exceptional – as different to non-military threats – reinforces this dominant, and dangerous, coupling of security and the military.
- The type and spread of military security threats are historically variable: with new types of actor, weaponry and conflict prominent areas of change.

Inter-state war: causes and consequences

In this section we explore the psychological, social, institutional, political and international factors that help explain inter-state war. These factors are tied to the issue of structure and agency which debates whether it is the behaviour of actors (agents) or the constraints and opportunities of social and political contexts (structure) which determines what happens in any situation. We begin, in the first half of the section, at the highest level of explanation, considering the role played by the structure of the international system. We then move to progressively lower levels and smaller scales of explanation, considering national, elite and individual causes of war. The section then reflects on the difficulties of studying the causes of war as well as the inherent biases researchers might face. Finally, we consider the consequences of war at different levels of analysis including human, economic, domestic and international.

From its recognized emergence in the early twentieth century, International Relations developed as an academic discipline with a particularly noble aim: to prevent the re-occurrence of the futile horrors that had characterized World War I. The huge expense of human life, for minimal apparent gain, was sufficiently ghastly to inspire a new field of enquiry with the principal normative aim of understanding the causes of conflict so as to attempt to avoid its appalling consequences. This was not in itself a new venture, as attempts to understand the causes of war were certainly not exclusive to International Relations. Psychology, sociology, history and philosophy all have longer traditions of assessing conflict's contributory factors. International Relations has, however, focused to an unusual degree on systemic level explanations, shifting the root causes of war away from the failings of men's minds, to the level of the specific form of state interaction apparent since the Treaty of Westphalia enshrined the state as the highest form of political organization.

The (neo-)realist story is now very familiar to scholars and students of International Relations. The story tells us that the condition of anarchy – the absence of world government or a Leviathan – is responsible, above all else, for the risk, and frequent outbreak, of inter-state war (for example, Waltz 1979). This structural condition – which is populated by competing states, which replicate each others' functions – is sufficient to ensure that war is endemic within the international system. World War II is one of the best examples of this anarchical logic playing out its inevitable **security dilemma** (Herz 1951; Waltz 1979). Scepticism of the intentions of other states, the story goes, is sufficient to ensure that states stockpile weapons in preparation for the playing out of a worst-case scenario. Game Theory can show how the lack of a world government to arbitrate disagreements and ensure compliance with international treaties and other conflict avoidance measures means that arming one's own state appears to be the only logical, rational and prudent course of action. The trouble arises in that, while a state's intentions in arming may be purely defensive – an attempt to prevent and avoid conflict – they can never, logically, be interpreted as such by another state, which must also assume the worst in order to prepare to survive. The rational response in the second state is therefore to implement a policy of building up armaments to counter and hopefully nullify the first state's initial stockpiling. Inevitably and tragically, the first state is compelled to respond in kind, as we descend into a(n **in**)security spiral** of ever-increasing military capabilities, rapidly escalating suspicions and heightened international tension (see Box 5.1).

The neo-realist story then posits a structural, systemic cause of inter-state war, heavily reliant upon notions of (a very particular conceptualization of) rationality. Rationality is seen to ensure the suspicion of other states and the pursuit of the national interest through a policy of arming the state. But where exactly the source of this rationality might lie is an important question. Is it in the state itself, the politician who leads it, or the bureaucratic processes that comprise its governance? Asking this question flags up two further important questions to ask of the neo-realist story. First, what is rationality and can it be assumed (see also Chapter 2)? Second, at what level of analysis should we focus to explain military conflict: the international system, the state, the government, political parties, society, or the individual? International Relations, dominated in recent decades by neo-realism, has tended to rely on an Enlightenment understanding of rationality, whereby actors make cost–benefit calculations in their own interests. This particular understanding of rationality enables structural-level explanations of

Box 5.1 Security spirals and World War I

On the one hand, it is possible to envision the world as a large game of 'chicken', whereby deterrence and diplomacy keep war at bay, through fear of the potential repercussions that would follow. On the other hand, international relations can be understood through the 'security dilemma' and the spirals of (in)security it can generate, as states seek to arm themselves in response to the actions of others (e.g. Jervis 1978). This latter explanation of international conflict can be fruitfully, if not uncontroversially, applied to World War I.

Fears over the behaviour of neighbouring states arguably inspired the actions that led to World War I. First, alliances were pursued to increase the individual security of states. However, as a new state was added to each alliance, a zero-sum view of security suggests that it also detracted instantly from the security of those states in the opposing alliance, as they confronted a greater counter-alliance. Second, German fears of fighting a war on two fronts helped to inspire the development of the Shlieffen Plan, which proposed an accelerated military operation to crush adversaries in the West and East. The rapidity of this proposal inspired greater concerns amongst those potential adversaries, whose actions were accelerated and accentuated in turn. Third, as states perceived increasing threats in the immediate geographical and strategic environment, they responded by developing their military capabilities accordingly. Whether for defensive or offensive reasons, the close geographical proximity of states on the European continent ensured that intentions were often perceived as offensive and therefore posed a threat. Together, these arguments can lead to the claim that war broke out, quite logically, despite its undesirability on the part of all concerned parties: World War I, by this logic, is the outcome of an intractable security dilemma that governs the behaviour of states.

conflict and other global dynamics, as individuals and states alike become mere vectors of logical decisions and subsequent actions, inspired by exogenous events which are dispassionately and accurately interpreted (see Hay 2004). Other disciplines and approaches have focused to a greater extent on the role of individuals and sub-state groups, taking seriously the misinformation, bias and emotion that can contribute to the outbreak of inter-state war.

Anger and frustration have both been suggested as emotional causes of war (e.g. Saurette 2006). German resentment at the perceived harshness of the conditions imposed upon it at the Treaty of Versailles, for example, can be seen as a contributing factor to the outbreak of World War II. The bias and drive of ideology – such as that of National

Socialism – can likewise be seen to inspire governments, leaders and their states to war. And misinformation can similarly initiate conflict. Britain has twice been either victim of underestimation or guilty of emitting the wrong signals, as Hitler in 1939 and Galtieri in 1982 each concluded that the United Kingdom would not commit forces to war when faced with German military might or in pursuit of a cause as distant and inconsequential as the Falkland Islands. The divide between misinformation and ideology is often blurred. Did Galtieri misread the intentions of the British government because of inaccurate information? Or, alternatively, was Galtieri's perception coloured by a particular ideological commitment to the Malvinas that shaped his judgement?

Within **Foreign Policy Analysis** (FPA), the concept of **groupthink** has been particularly useful in accounting for how a particular idea can take hold and go on to dominate clusters of key decision-makers, often excluding alternative ways of thinking. This explanation of collective mentality as a cause of war, developed from psychology, argues that the 'crowd psychology' of key groups, devoid of dissonant voices (that are weeded out or silenced), can create its own perpetuating logic. The hostage rescue mission of the British government during the Falklands campaign (Janis 1982; Heller 1983) and the decision to intervene in Iraq in 2003 (Badie 2010), for example, can both be explained with recourse to the very particular ways of thinking that were evident within top level policymaking circles at those particular moments. Infamously, on the latter, politics and intelligence became perilously intertwined, as the British government acted on the 'fact' that Saddam Hussein's Iraq was pursuing a WMD programme.

At the lowest level of analysis – the individual and their genetic and moral composition – work in biology and philosophy has posited that the causes of war might lie in the way people are 'wired'. In International Relations, Thomas Hobbes is most famously associated with the apparent selfishness of humans. Life, as IR undergraduates are taught, is nasty, brutish and short, precisely because humans are hardwired to look after number one. For Hobbes, individualistic behaviour, which comes at the expense of others' well-being, is an intractable feature of the human condition. In IR, this belief has served as the bedrock of classical realism (e.g. Morgenthau 1978). While an unpleasant and unnerving thought for a discipline which emerged around the study of war in order to achieve its abolition, those sharing this view do not necessarily believe societies should simply accept these basic human traits (Garnett 2007). Cooperation can be incentivized, encouraged and taught, through norms and institutions, as well as through mechanisms that might deter defection and ensure tacit and formal agreements are adhered to. But the hypothesis remains: we go to war because of what we are, and if we are to avoid conflict we have to work hard to overcome our more basic instincts.

Positing human nature as the cause of war does not necessarily imply volition and conscious choice. If war is in our genes (our 'selfish gene' as Dawkins suggests), its inevitability lets us off of the hook; we are merely the victims of our own selfish nature (e.g. Hay 2002). What though if humans choose to fight, exclusive of the structural determinants of an anarchic international system or the biological impulses of human nature? What if inter-state war is an option that humans contemplate, decide upon and pursue? **Clausewitz** has provided students of war with a framework suggesting just that (Beier 2008). Following his seminal *On War*, Clausewitz's dictum that conflict is the continuation of politics by other means has informed the thinking of military personnel for over one and a half centuries. In Clausewitzian logic, war is seen as the instrumental pursuit of the national interest, when other options have failed or are less effective. It is an explanation and philosophy that shares little in common with more ideological, eschatological and cataclysmic understandings of war (Rapoport 1968; Williams 2008); and it is therefore a model that better explains, for example, resource than holy wars. It is also a model that lends itself to particularly agentic explanations, but is prone to ignore the complex ways in which people's conduct interweaves with the contexts in which they act (Hay 2002).

There are two further important points to note of efforts in IR to establish the *causes* of *inter-state* war. First, accurately identifying the causes of any war is a challenging and potentially impossible task. The colossal undertaking of the Correlates of War project within International Relations pays testament to the plethora and complexity of potential variables involved. This project has established a data set that political scientists can analyse to establish which variables correlate with instances of inter-state conflict. The word correlate is significant here precisely because the coincidence of different variables (whether authoritarian rule, nationalism, shared geographical borders, and so on) might lack explanatory significance (see Chapter 2). Establishing causation is extremely difficult given the complexity of war and the multitude of its influencing factors. It requires theory building as well as the observation of empirical regularities. Outside of IR, this difficulty has been recognized and embraced, as rather than attempting to establish universal laws based on statistically significant data, disciplines such as History have instead explored the rich complexity of conflict, for example by delivering detailed case studies of individual conflicts. These divergent methodologies reflect deeper, underlying differences within the social sciences, which pertain to the parsimony/complexity trade-off.

Second, the relative lack of concern for *intra-state* war that IR has historically demonstrated is testament to the importance of the question posed in the previous chapter: in whose security are we interested? As Beier (2008) points out, the relevant question here becomes: whose bodies are piling up? Intra-state war remains a deadly and ever-present feature of our world, but one that is afforded only a fraction of the funding and focus that scholars have invested in understanding the causes and consequences of inter-state war. The location of those scholars and the Anglo-American dominance of the discipline they represent goes much of the way to explaining the lower priority of intra-state conflicts, given the overwhelming concentration of such conflicts outside the global north. This normative and ethnocentric bias in our dominant subject matter is reinforced, moreover, by a less troubling but equally artificial exclusion. Intra-state war is deemed as insufficiently significant for IR, since its consequences tend to be limited to the domestic structure of the state and its governance, rather than impacting directly on state interaction and higher level questions of international order.

The idea that war, and in particular inter-state war, might serve a purpose is controversial but enduring. Garnett (2007: 21) cites Hegel and Treischke who suggest that war is a remedy for failing nations and an insurance in the preservation of the ethical health of nations (also George 2005). At the outset of the discipline, paraphrasing Karl Marx, E.H. Carr wrote of war as 'the midwife of change': in that, wars 'break up and sweep away the half-rotted structures of an old social and political structure' (1942: 3, cited in Garnett 2007: 21). For International Relations and realism, war's ability to alter the international order and reshape power distributions is precisely what makes inter-state conflict so crucial. The transitions from multipolarity to bipolarity and unipolarity were achieved in significant part through the ruptures and redistributions that inter-state war brought. It remains to be seen whether American decline and the rise of the **BRICs** will play out as violently as **hegemonic transition theory** predicts, or whether other factors will lead to a more peaceful transition in the distribution of relative material capability. Either way, realism can look back and pinpoint the moments of 1945 and 1989 for their significance in reshaping the international order; they marked the end of the British Empire and the conformation of unchallenged American hegemony respectively.

Beyond the preoccupations of realist IR with international order, the impacts of war are keenly felt at human and economic levels, although these have tended to be neglected within Security Studies. As argued in this chapter's introduction, the dynamics motivating the birth of the discipline after World War I remain relevant today. Some blunt statistics make the case for the importance of studying war very persuasively. In World War I an estimated 21 million people died. During World War II an estimated 25 million soldiers were killed, alongside approximately 75 million citizens. And, following the 2003 intervention in and subsequent occupation of Iraq, four and a half thousand American soldiers were killed, with estimates of civilian casualties varying by a factor of ten. Former Commander of US Central Command, General Tommy Franks, infamously observed that the United States does 'not do body counts'. This alarming view has contributed to the difficulty in documenting the human costs of this war. It is approximated that between one hundred thousand and one million Iraqis lost their lives between 2003 and 2012 as a result of the conflict (see, for example, Iraq Body Count). Clearly, there remain very good analytical, normative and empirical reasons for Security Studies to analyse military threats and inter-state wars. Less clear, however, is the justification for continuing to prioritize such threats to the exclusion of other equally valid, dangerous and significant threats (see Chapter 6).

Key Points

- The preoccupation of Security Studies with inter-state war is traceable, in part, to International Relations' emergence in the aftermath of World War I.
- The dominant approach to security today – neo-realism – prioritizes systemic explanations of international conflicts.
- Alternative perspectives, from approaches including foreign policy analysis, prioritize individual or bureaucratic explanations of war.
- Identifying causality (as opposed to correlation) in war is a notoriously challenging task.

The changing nature of war

This section investigates the changing nature of warfare. It is organized around four themes. First, transformations in the likelihood of military conflict, in which debates over the obsolescence of major war are explored. Second, changes in the geographies of war, and the importance of intra-state or 'new' wars. Third, changes in the practice of warfare in which we discuss the **Revolution in Military Affairs** (RMA). And, fourth, the privatization of contemporary war with a discussion of Private Military Companies (PMCs). Examples explored in this discussion include, child soldiers and the Kony 2012 campaign, the 1990–1991 Gulf War and the use of drone technology in the **AfPak** border region.

The changing nature of war has been a common refrain within International Relations and Security Studies for several decades now. Following the end of the Cold War, some of the strands that comprised a fairly disaggregated literature on this theme coalesced. The term 'Revolution in Military Affairs' came to capture the technological and organization changes in the structure of (primarily the US) military. This 'revolution' came amidst broader changes as the military responded to a diverse array of new and evolving features in the practice of organized political violence. Here, we attempt to isolate and interrogate some of the principal aspects of these perceived changes.

The first and most important of these new features is particularly dramatic: arguably war (or at least some types of war) is, for some, closer to becoming obsolete today than at any point in human history. While the claim may appear nonsensical at first, not least against the recent backdrop of a prolonged War on Terror, there are two arguments in particular that help us to understand the grounds on which such arguments can be constructed.

First, technological developments in war have meant that the destructive potential of **total war** is greater than ever; certainly far greater than at the time of Clausewitz's ruminations on 'absolute war'. This potential, however, has not yet been realized and, fortunately, remains unlikely, given the current conditions of the social and political world. The Cold War, for example, was not fought as a total war in the manner of the two World Wars, during which the entire resources of competing states were invested in winning a conflict that threatened to determine their very existence. Rather, the Cold War was fought as a series of limited 'proxy' wars elsewhere around the globe. And, crucially, even when total wars have been fought, making use of every resource of the state, some measures have remained deliberately avoided. For instance, even during the existential conflicts of the World Wars, important limitations on the use of force existed, such as those governing the use of mustard gas. As we will see in the following section, norms concerning the appropriateness of particular weapons placed important limits on the use of force in both World and Cold Wars. In Vietnam, for example, the United States clearly possessed a weapon capable of defeating their enemy, but opted not to use nuclear weapons due to tacitly recognized norms of acceptable conduct. Christopher Coker (2001) has placed such tendencies within a broader trajectory towards 'humane war', whereby states go out of their way to justify conflicts around socially constructed and accepted standards, subsequently fighting in a manner (broadly) consistent with their logic.

Second, McInnes (2002) has argued that – beyond listening to politicians' justifications of war – for the majority of people in the world and especially the Western world, war is neither participated in as combatant nor experienced as victim. War, put bluntly, is something that happens elsewhere. This is part of the reason that the events of 11 September 2001 – interpreted and framed as acts of war – were so shocking for American citizens, who expected violence to belong to American history or well away from American shores (Holland 2009, 2013a, 2013b; Holland and Jarvis 2014). For McInnes (2002 and Mann 1988) then, war has become something of a spectator sport, the outcome of which is far less fundamental to our own personal well-being than in decades and centuries past. In both likelihood and geography, war is less relevant than it once was. For most people, political violence has become a matter of choice rather than necessity. The **Uppsala Conflict Data Programme** (UCDP) has attempted to empirically trace this trend. They have found that inter-state war has decreased dramatically since the start of the 1990s due to the end of colonialism and the Cold War, as well as the rise of international activism, spearheaded by the UN. Within these decreasing wars, fewer people are losing their lives, with death-per-conflict figures halving over the last five decades.

The historical picture is more nuanced than pure decline, however, as the UCDP report also demonstrates increases in non-state (intra-state) war and a shift in the geographical distribution of organized political violence. Particularly in the 1990s, this shifting regional focus of conflict became increasingly concentrated on Sub-Saharan Africa. In addition, there have also been concomitant rises in the number of child soldiers and fatalities, as well as civilian deaths. The question of 'who fights and who dies?' then certainly has a different answer today than previously, but it does not appear that war is either obsolete or unimportant. If the tendencies underpinning the transition to 'humane war' can better be harnessed to influence the increases in intra-state, high casualty wars, in which child soldiers are amongst the combatants, it is possible that they will appear less obsolete to the Western spectator. The recent success of the 'Kony 2012' campaign attempted this fusion of morality and awareness to achieve political and normative aims. For Mary Kaldor (2007) **'new wars'**, such as that which Kony's Lord's Resistance Army have waged in Uganda, South Sudan, the Democratic Republic of Congo and Central African Republic, are fundamentally distinct from earlier forms of armed conflict. The 'new wars thesis' argues that intra-state conflicts – characterized by the role of identity politics, rather than the national interest – are increasingly prevalent in contemporary international relations.

Kaldor (2007) argues that the political economy of war has altered, driving a new decentralization of organized political violence, out of the hands and control of the state. The term 'new wars' does not stand as an antonym to 'conventional war'; rather, it denotes a new type of low-intensity conflict, untied to the resolution of disputes that arise from competing national interests. Guerrilla armies, the police, criminals and gangs are more likely to fight these post-modern wars than the armies of the territorial nation-state. In Kaldor's own words:

> An 'old war' was a war between states. The war was fought by opposing uniformed armed forces, and the decisive encounters of the war were battles between those forces. Soldiers were clearly distinct from civilians. No war conformed completely to that model, of course, but the model is drawn from the experience of twentieth century wars and from the cold war, which kept that model alive in our imagination.
>
> A 'new war' is fought by combinations of state and non-state actors, and is usually fought not for reasons of state or ideology, but for identity. Battle is rare and most violence is directed against civilians – that is absolutely central to understanding new wars.
>
> Old wars simply became too destructive to be fought. Does that mean there was now nothing to be gained by using violence? Well, there is nothing to be gained by using violence against a similarly armed opponent. But there is definitely something to be gained against an unarmed opponent – and that is a central characteristic of new wars. (Kaldor, interviewed in Johnson 2007: 16)

New wars then have different actors, causes and consequences. They are also fought in distinct ways and using different weapons. The small arms and light weapons that sustain these conflicts are funded by a variety of practices more irregular than the systems of taxation on which states rely. These can include extortion, kidnap, drug trafficking, and money laundering, as well as development aid. Alongside producing these weapons, Western states' principal involvement in new wars, for Kaldor, has been in the provision of peacekeeping forces.

When and where Western states do continue to fight so-called 'conventional wars', the most notable shifts have been witnessed in their war-fighting style, driven by both economics and the capabilities of new technologies. Since 2005, perhaps no weapon has better embodied these shifts than the predator drone. The sight and sound of drones in Afghan skies has become the symbolic quintessence of the American campaign in the AfPak region. Flown remotely, there is zero risk to soldiers piloting **unmanned aerial vehicles (UAVs)**. This is the latest in a long line of technological developments marked by moments of accelerated transition and development, punctuated by periods of relative stasis. It was the First Gulf War that really inspired an interest and uptake of the RMA agenda. The speed and ease of the American victory – broadcast for the first time through the embedded journalism of 24-hour news coverage – signified a shift in how states would fight and win war. This increasingly 'post-modern' or **fourth generation warfare** (4GW) (Gray 1996; Der Derian 2001) was characterized by flexibility, mobility and high-end technological prowess. Over-whelming aerial superiority reinforces speed and adaptation on the ground. It was a revolution symbolized by Donald Rumsfeld's tenure as Secretary of State for Defense in both George W. Bush Administrations.

Rumsfeld was central in accelerating the pace of change in US war-fighting capabilities and tactics during both wars in Iraq. With the Soviet Union no longer threatening American primacy, advocates of 4GW sought to increase the flexibility and speed of America's armed forces in line with the new security threat and new types of conflict that characterized the 1990s. This was coupled with a reliance on technological innovation and associated precision, which allowed wars to be fought at a distance, potentially with far fewer troops committed on the ground. The speed of American advancement in the Gulf War encapsulated these advances and the changes in war-fighting style that would accompany the end of the Cold War (see Baudrillard 1995). The inglorious failure to stay the course in Somalia in 1993, however, set out some of the limitations to such an approach. Public expectations of minimal American casualties have been heightened as a result of the possibility of fighting in this way. Opinion has been sensitized to the kind of images that were broadcast from Mogadishu – later dramatized in the movie *Black Hawk Down* – and which led to eventual American withdrawal. Nonetheless, airpower and mobility, aided by elite forces on the ground, working in concert with indigenous forces, has become a stable model of American and Western military interventions since the end of Cold War. The role of Apache helicopters in Afghanistan, 'Shock and Awe' in Iraq, and the NATO bombing in Libya, can all be read as evidence of the changing nature of war, the revolution in military affairs, and the fact that for most people war has become a spectator sport, fought (by others) through choice rather than necessity.

Box 5.2 Private military companies

In Chapter 4, we introduced levels of military spending during the 2003 war in Iraq to highlight the continued pre-eminence of the state in the military realm. We also noted, however, that during the war in Iraq Private Military Companies played an increasingly important role in the provision of security. This involvement raises important political, legal and ethical questions. To whom are PMCs accountable? Here, to highlight the size of this feature of contemporary war, we list the top five PMC recipients of funding (contracts and the like) from the US Department of Defense in 2009 (alone):

1. Lockheed Martin 7,040 (all values in millions of US dollars)
2. Northgrop Gumman 6,050
3. KBR 4,660
4. L3 Communications 3,710
5. Humana 3,460.

Source: Isenberg (2012).

Recent conflicts such as these have also revealed the increasing role played by private military companies (PMCs) (see Box 5.2). While the hiring of mercenaries has a long history in armed conflict, the role played by PMCs has become more important in recent wars. Indeed, as one analyst (Leander 2005) has noted, the private contractor/ soldier ratio was 1/60 in the 1991 Gulf War; 1/10 in Bosnia; 1/2 in Kosovo; and perhaps even higher in the post-2003 war in Iraq. In these conflicts, PMCs are frequently employed by governments effectively as a way of outsourcing significant elements of organized political violence. For instance, Academi – previously Blackwater – is the largest of three PMCs used by the US Defense Department. They have a 250 million dollar contract, awarded by the Obama Administration to work with US forces in providing security in Afghanistan. At the same time, PMCs such as Academi are faced with the demands of making money for stakeholders. Their services can be paid for by wealthy elites who require the provision of security in areas affected by conflict. The reliance on the provision of security from private contractors – by government personnel as well as wealthy elites – has raised important questions about the rules of armed conflict, not least on those occasions when Blackwater employees have been accused of killing Iraqi citizens in Baghdad. During the War on Terror, the cost-effectiveness of contractors was arguably prioritized over the blurring of the rules of engagement.

Key Points

- War is increasingly obsolete for many people, especially those living in the West for whom conflict is experienced primarily as a spectator.
- Inter-state war is declining but intra-state war is increasing, with a higher percentage of child soldiers and civilian casualties.
- Technological developments have led to a revolution in military affairs, which in theory brings greater precision and fewer risks to soldiers.
- Although war and security have a long history of being contracted out to private forces, PMCs are an increasingly prominent actor in contemporary conflicts.

Weapons in the international system

Here, we investigate the significance of weapons in the international system. We begin by introducing debates over nuclear weapons in the Cold War era and their role in contemporary global politics. We then investigate concerns over other forms of Weapons of Mass Destruction (WMD), highlighting difficulties involved in their acquisition and deployment. These are tied to contemporary fears over **'rogue states'** and 'failed states'. The section concludes by exploring the manufacture, distribution and use of small arms around the world.

Mutually Assured Destruction (with the apt and terrifying acronym 'MAD') was and remains the centrepiece of academic and policy-makers' explanations of why the Cold War never had nor would escalate beyond the use of conventional weapons. The ludicrousness of the acronym reflects the fact that nuclear capabilities 'introduce galactic scale forces into a terrestrial environment' (Wirtz 2007: 273). While these fears of impending nuclear apocalypse may have eased following the end of the Cold War, significant concerns do still remain. For many neo-realists, it was not that a norm of appropriateness or legitimacy prevented the use of nuclear weapons. Rather that their usage was irrational at the time, for fear of the inevitable reprisal that a **second strike capability** ensured. As Kenneth Waltz (1990: 743) argued, to strike first – under this logic – made little sense, as it would be the final act of a state dooming itself to oblivion:

> Nuclear weapons dissuade states from going to war more surely than conventional weapons do. In a conventional world, states going to war can at once believe that they may win, and that, should they lose, the price of defeat will be bearable.

Nuclear weapons then, it has been argued, ensured the peace by inhibiting their own use. The knowledge of certain reprisal ensured that no sane political leader would ever be the first to launch a nuclear weapon. This condition arguably supported an indefinite status quo and perpetuated a condition of bipolarity, with two rival, nuclear-armed, superpower states both rationally avoiding the use of nuclear weapons in view of the certain consequences such an act would precipitate. Today, however, the nature of the principal actors and issues involved in nuclear security has altered.

For the United States, and other countries, issues of proliferation, rogue states and non-state actors have replaced deterrence as the principal nuclear concern. Presidents Bush Snr and Clinton both recognized the shifting nature of the nuclear threat in their dealings with Russia, as the risk from the former superpower's ageing stock of nuclear warheads shifted from first and second strike capability to the potential for fissile material to fall into the hands of a third party. During and since the Cold War, in other words, proliferation has altered the role that nuclear weapons play in the international system. Although a few scholars have suggested that 'more may be better' (Waltz 1981), the issue of horizontal proliferation (more actors acquiring nuclear weapon capabilities) has been viewed as a significant security threat by most Western policymakers. To begin with, given the unwelcome attention that a policy of nuclear acquisition often receives, let us consider why it might be that states go to great lengths to pursue what appears to be an essentially unusable weapon?

First, the acquisition of nuclear weapons offers prestige in the realm of international affairs. For example, all five members of the UN Security Council have acquired the ultimate deterrent. Second, following the logic of deterrence, the acquisition of nuclear weapons is still seen to increase security. The security that nuclear capability affords is frequently deemed to outweigh the inconveniences of penalizing mechanisms, such as sanctions, designed to make their acquisition more difficult. If Iran, for example, were to attempt to build a nuclear weapon it would be possible to understand that decision in relation to recent American interventions in Afghanistan and Iraq – Iran's immediate neighbours to the east and west – and the lack of US military engagement with the North Korean regime. It is the same pursuit of security that has driven Israel to build nuclear warheads. Third, the acquisition of nuclear weapons can also offset domestic difficulties for governing regimes. North Korea, unable to provide food security for its people, has invested considerable sums of money in establishing (limited) nuclear security capabilities instead. The prestige of nuclear weapons and the sense of security that they inspire can, therefore, help to placate domestic populations and quell opposition to governing regimes.

Fortunately, while a desire to possess nuclear weapons might be driven by the logics of prestige and security in the international system, acquiring nuclear weapons remains a significant challenge, despite the fact that seventy years have passed since 'Little Boy' was dropped on Hiroshima. Only nine states currently possess nuclear weapons, with the biggest limits to developing the devices being the production of fissile material, rather than mastering the technology of the warhead (Wirtz 2007). Highly enriched uranium and plutonium are extremely difficult to acquire. Moreover, the international community have developed a number of mechanisms designed to prevent the spread of nuclear weapons. First, the **International Atomic Energy Agency (IAEA)** is charged with monitoring the production and storage of nuclear material, as well as the behaviour of both declared and undeclared **nuclear weapons states** themselves (Wirtz 2007). Second, the **Nuclear Non-Proliferation Treaty (NPT)** attempts to prevent the proliferation of nuclear technology, in exchange for the reduction in nuclear states' stockpiles and the accepted use of nuclear technology to meet energy requirements. As Table 5.1 shows, although 190 states have now joined the NPT, it has failed to prevent several regional powers – including Pakistan – from acquiring nuclear weapons. It has also failed to force nuclear weapons states to reduce and ultimately eliminate their own stockpiles. However, there have been some successes in preventing the development of nuclear weapons by states deemed to be a threat to the international community. In 2003, Colonel Gaddafi declared that Libya would abandon its nuclear weapons programme. South Africa also disassembled its six warheads in the 1990s, while Belarus, Ukraine and Kazakhstan all gave up their nuclear arsenals at the end of the Cold War.

Table 5.1 *Nuclear weapons and the NPT*

Country	Fission Device	Fusion Device	Declared	NPT Signatory
United States	1945	1952	Yes	Yes
Soviet Union	1949	1953	Yes	Yes
Great Britain	1952	1957	Yes	Yes
France	1960	1966	Yes	Yes
PR China	1964	1967	Yes	Yes
Israel	1967	1973	No	No
India	1974	1998	Yes	No
Pakistan	1998	1998	Yes	No
North Korea	2002	–	Yes	Withdrawn

Sources: J. Wirtz (2013) 'Weapons of Mass Destruction', in A. Collins (ed.), *Contemporary Security Studies* (Oxford University Press), p. 259; and www.sipri.org site.

The US – as the world's sole superpower, the first state to develop nuclear weapons, and the only state to have deployed them in conflict – has often been at the forefront of attempts to regulate their development, storage and spread. Frequently, American efforts have centred on the possibility of nuclear weapons and other WMD falling into the hands of rogue states or non-state actors. The United States has not historically opposed the spread of nuclear technology to all states. Close cooperation with the United Kingdom and tacit approval of Israeli nuclear policy has shown that perceptions of threat remain closely tied to particular understandings of identity. The recent US policy of economic sanctions on Iran has centred on a particular and contentious view that an Iranian nuclear weapon would pose a threat to the region and the US national interest. This belief centres on Iran's identity, within American political culture, as a rogue state (see Chapter 4). In 2002, Iran was declared part of the 'axis of evil' in George W. Bush's State of the Union Address. These concerns revolve around the nature of the regime and associated assumptions about rationality. Former President Ahmedinejad, for example, was frequently portrayed in political discourse, media coverage and popular culture as an evil, irrational despot. Policymakers fear that the lack of a true democratic structure will prevent the will of the public from being realized through an established chain of command, exacerbating the

---

Box 5.3 A rogue by any other name

The term 'rogue state' is a contentious one that came to prominence in the early 1980s. Although it initially referred to states engaged in the repression of their own populations, it is now typically applied to those states seen to pose a threat to regional or international security. Three criteria, in particular, are used in applications of this label. First, is the facilitation, sponsorship or active engagement in international terrorism. Second, is the development or active pursuit of weapons of mass destruction. Third, and more controversially, is the defiance of international laws, norms, rules or conventions. Critics of the term argue, first, that it is applied inconsistently, often determined by prevailing political interests. Second, that it overexaggerates the threat of those states to whom it is applied. And, third, that designating states 'rogue' helps to legitimize responses that can cause considerable harm to their populations, such as the use of economic sanctions against Iraq and North Korea.

Sources: Bilgin and Morton (2002, 2004); Bleiker (2003); Hoyt (2000); Caprioli and Trumbore (2003).

risks of having unpredictable personalities at the heart of the Iranian regime. In short, 'rogue' states are perceived as a threat because they are seen to lack the rational decision-making process of an established democracy (see Box 5.3). Within this understanding, rogue states cannot be trusted with nuclear weapons, and nor indeed with any other type of WMD. Again, we see that this can help to explain popular resistance to the 'softer', diplomatic policy stance that Presidents Obama and Rouhani have recently adopted.

There is no readily identifiable definition of what constitutes a weapon of 'mass destruction'. The term tends to be used in order to make a qualitative distinction based on a weapon's potential to cause levels of damage that can be deemed 'catastrophic'. As a consequence, WMDs vary hugely in type and destructive capability but can be put into three principal (non-nuclear) categories: chemical, biological and radiological. Just as the NPT has attempted to regulate nuclear weapons, the Chemical and Biological Weapons Conventions seek likewise in relation to chemical and biological WMD (see Box 5.4). Chemical weapons have a long history, but were first used to significant effect on the battlefields of World War I, where chlorine and mustard gas blinded, choked and blistered troops. Saddam Hussein's Iraq employed them in the 1980s against Iranian forces and Iraqi Kurds; while sarin gas was also used in the August 2013 attack to the east of Damascus, Syria. Non-state actors have also employed sarin in attacks against civilians, most notably the Japanese group Aum Shinrikyo in their 1995 attack on the Tokyo subway. In contrast to chemical weapons, biological weapons make use of living organisms and toxins to sicken and kill people, plants and animals (Wirtz 2007). One of their most infamous uses came in 2001 when, shortly after 9/11, Bruce Edwards Ivins sent a series of letters to politicians and news media offices, which contained anthrax spores. At the time, it was assumed that these attacks comprised part of the wider War on Terror and were launched by external enemies, hostile to the United States and sympathetic to Al Qaeda. This assumption was inaccurate, but played an important role in helping to cement the emerging discourse of the War on Terror (see Jackson 2005b).

The War on Terror was noteworthy for the worst-case scenario thinking that dominated policy-making (Mueller 2006). The 1% doctrine dictated that elected officials had a duty to imagine and prepare for the worst, working to prevent its realization. At the apex of these nightmare scenarios was the potential for a WMD-terror nexus whereby a rogue state provided a terrorist group with WMD capability (see Box 5.5). This threat was invoked regularly within American, British and Australian foreign policy in the lead up to intervention in

Box 5.4 Regulating weapons of mass destruction

The Nuclear Non-Proliferation Treaty (NPT)
The NPT came into force in 1970 and aims to prevent the spread of nuclear weapons and nuclear weapons technology. The 'deal' at the treaty's heart divides nuclear weapons states and non-nuclear weapons states, seeking to temporarily retain the division (as nuclear weapons states work towards disarmament), by assisting with the development of nuclear technology for peaceful means such as energy. Non-proliferation, disarmament and peaceful use are therefore the 'three pillars' of the NPT. Although key states have reneged on and withdrawn from the NPT – by developing or attempting to develop nuclear weapons, or by failing to disarm – it remains the central international treaty governing nuclear weapons and nuclear technology.

Chemical Weapons Convention (CWC)
The CWC came into force in 1997 and aims to outlaw the use, stockpiling and development of chemical weapons. With 190 signatory states and over two-thirds of the world's chemical stockpiles destroyed, the treaty has had considerable success, most recently in Syria. One notable absence is Israel, which has yet to ratify the treaty.

Biological Weapons Convention (BWC)
The BWC came into force in 1975 and aims to outlaw the use, stockpiling and development of biological weapons. With 170 signatories and in absence of formal verification measures the treaty has seen less success than the CWC.

Iraq in 2003 (Holland 2013a, 2013b). The emergence – or construction – of terrorist networks as a threat comparable to rogue states altered the focus of American foreign policy after 9/11. And, the potential for rogue states and terrorists to work together was an underlying concern throughout the War on Terror. However, before we turn to the role that terrorism has had on re-orienting the focus of security efforts and changing the nature of war, it is imperative to remember that WMD attacks have actually demonstrated remarkably low casualty figures in the modern era. They are certainly dwarfed by the continued threat to human life posed by conventional weapons and small arms. That is to say nothing of the threat posed by the structural violences of poverty, disease, famine, and so forth (see Chapter 6).

Whilst (logically) terrifying, the 1995 sarin attack on the Tokyo subway killed only twelve people, although many more suffered serious harm. And despite widespread media coverage, the 2001 anthrax

Box 5.5 Proliferation and Pakistan

Concerns over nuclear proliferation and Pakistan take two forms. The first pertains to the intentional provision of nuclear technology and expertise by Pakistani scientists and officials to other states. The second to Pakistan's internal instabilities and perceived inability to secure its nuclear arsenal.

In 2004, former Pakistani scientist Abdul Qadeer Khan revealed that he had provided unauthorized technical assistance to Iran amidst revelations that he may also have provided information on gas centrifuges – used in the enrichment process – to Libya, Iraq, Syria and North Korea. Having played a key role in Pakistan's development of nuclear weapons, he remains a revered and protected figure, despite the US continuing to regard him as a threat of proliferation. The concern for the United States and their allies is that other states may have been, or could in the future be, provided with further assistance of this sort. While Pakistan is not the only country on which such concerns centre (reports have also highlighted possible Chinese assistance to North Korea), the case of AQ Khan remains unique in the history of nuclear proliferation.

In 2011, President Obama authorized a successful operation to find, identify and kill Osama bin Laden, whom the CIA had ascertained with some certainty was living in Abbottabad, Pakistan. Graham Allison (2012) has noted the impact this raid poses for US policy options and Pakistani security concerns, relating to Pakistan's nuclear weapons. The ability of American Special Forces to launch an unannounced and undetected raid in Abbottabad (also a nuclear weapons site) highlighted the potential vulnerability of Pakistani nuclear weapons. This vulnerability comes in a variety of forms. First, with Pakistani intelligence seemingly unaware of Osama bin Laden's whereabouts, there are concerns over the state's ability to monitor and secure nuclear weapons from third parties. Second, both US and Pakistani officials will be increasingly aware of the logical follow up question to the raid on bin Laden's compound: could a similar operation be authorized in order to seize Pakistani nuclear weapons?

attacks killed only five people. Sixty per cent of the world's **Small and Light Weapons (SALW)** stockpiles are owned by civilians, with around thirty-eight per cent in the hands of uniformed, traditional military forces (Hartung 2008). There are around 900 million SALW in the world today, with up to 100 million AK47s alone. In 2003, the fall of Saddam Hussein indicated the scale of the small arms trade as it precipitated the transfer of around 4 million small arms from uniformed soldiers of the state to citizens and guerrilla fighters (ibid). Non-traditional forces also often acquire small arms legally. In Colombia and

---

Box 5.6 Small arms and the conflict in Congo

It is possible that you might not even be aware of one of the most deadly wars on the planet in recent years. The death toll from the conflict in Congo – the First, Second and ongoing wars – is estimated to exceed 7 million people, with far greater numbers injured and displaced. The conflict is also noted for its extensive involvement of child soldiers. The Second Congo War began in 1998, involving nine states and twenty distinct military groups. Competing interests regarding the region's abundant natural resources, in part, inspired the conflict. And the conflict was sustained, beyond the 1999 disbanding of militia groups, by the proliferation of small arms throughout central and southern Africa.

Mexico efforts to quell sub-state actors have been hindered by their ability to easily purchase weapons in the United States. And, in Afghanistan in 2001, the US found themselves fighting against an enemy they had spent $2 billion arming during the 1980s. The scale of the small arms trade indicates that, despite the spectacular nature of WMD, it is in fact SALW – symbolized by the AK47 – that remain the most dangerous weapons in the world (see Box 5.6). It is with small arms that most conflicts are currently sustained, and it is small arms that continue to kill more people than any other type of weapon, despite the recent focus of Western governments on WMD and contemporary terrorism.

Key Points

- Mutually Assured Destruction is used to explain how nuclear weapons keep the peace.
- Despite nuclear deterrence and the efforts of the NPT, nuclear weapons are still desired by some states for prestige and security.
- In recent years, terrorism has increased concerns about non-nuclear WMD.
- SALW, however, continue to kill far more people than WMD.

Contemporary terrorism

This section explores the significance of international terrorism as a contemporary security issue. We begin with a brief sketch of the use of this tactic by a diverse range of groups with distinct motives. The section then explores the scale of the terrorist threat and the consequences of different counter-terrorism strategies. We conclude this part of the discussion by reflecting on state terrorism and the contribution of scholars in the emerging subfield of Critical Terrorism Studies.

Following the events of 11 September 2001, the issue of terrorism has dominated international relations. In April 2012, however, the world was reminded that Islamic terrorism does not have a stranglehold on this particular form of violence. The trial and prosecution of Anders Breivik for the murder of seventy-seven people in Norway gave him a platform to account for his actions. This he did calmly and candidly in the language of societal security (see Chapter 4), explaining the threat that he saw from Norwegian immigration policy and multiculturalism. In combining the bombing of government offices in Oslo (killing eight) with the shooting of sixty-nine young people gathered on the island of Utoya, Breivik claimed that he had perpetrated the most sophisticated act of violence that Europe had witnessed since the end of World War II. Breivik's words and actions serve as a reminder of two things. First, the wide variety of types of terrorism that exist, and, second, the plethora of motivating factors that inspire them.

Also at the start of 2012, shortly before Anders Breivik was paraded for the world in a Norwegian courtroom, the Home Affairs Select Committee of the UK Government issued a report on British counter-terrorism strategy. The report – titled 'Roots of Violent Radicalisation' – acknowledged the *diversity* of processes of radicalization, which was nonetheless still seen to be a pre-requisite for terrorism. Explicitly, the report dismissed some of the central claims upon which British counter-terrorism (CONTEST) and counter-radicalization policy (PREVENT) had been constructed after 9/11 and 7/7. Amongst these was the claim that particular forums – universities, mosques and prisons – were especially important sites of radicalization. Likewise, in direct response to Breivik's actions in Norway, 'Roots of Violent Radicalisation' reiterated that a preoccupation with Islamic terrorism was not only in error but moreover also counter-productive. This preoccupation meant that other 'sources' of terrorist violence had been overlooked – such as historical grievances concerning Northern Ireland and the risk posed by so-called right-wing or nationalist terrorism. The report made two telling contributions, which have sadly not yet been fully followed up. First, terrorism is not a significant security threat at least numerically, relative to that posed from other sources. And, second, a sense of grievance is the *only* single uniting factor that can be identified in processes of radicalization that lead to terrorism.

First then, let us consider the threat posed by contemporary terrorism. Zulaika (2009) has argued that statistically the terror threat is irrelevant at worst and non-existent at best. As John Mueller (2005:

488) notes, even if we include the outlier that was 9/11, the number of Americans killed by international terrorism since the 1960s is about the same as those killed by allergic reactions to peanuts (also Jackson 2005b; Jackson *et al.* 2011). In the United States it remains true that for African-Americans under the age of forty-four the most likely cause of death is homicide: that there are eighty-five guns for every one hundred Americans in the United States may help to explain this. Likewise, every fifteen minutes, an American is killed in a road traffic accident, adding up to half a million traffic fatalities over the last decade. Contrast this with the death toll on 11 September 2001 of just under three thousand. Statistics such as these illustrate the divergent reactions to risk that different threats generate. Within this context, it is easy to see how Mueller (2006) has been able to argue that Western counter-terrorism strategies approximate a form of self-flagellation. The costs – in both blood and treasure – of counter-terrorism measures far outweigh those of the terrorist attack in the first place.

Second, let us consider the types of response to terrorism that states initiate. State responses to terrorism can be broadly divided into three principal, overlapping categories, dealing with policing, the military, and the context of terrorism (Rogers 2008). The first of these – policing – takes as its principal focus the role of intelligence, security and non-military security personnel in preventing terrorist attacks, ideally intercepting terrorists before they have had a chance to action their plans. The second type of counter-terrorism policy involves 'direct military action against paramilitary organisations' (Rogers 2008: 175). This response is more likely under (and sometimes reliant upon) partic-ular conditions, such as the fixed location of terrorist groups and the perception of a threat to the state itself. The third response takes greater consideration of the underlying and facilitating conditions that sustain terrorism in the first place. It takes seriously the motivations inspiring political violence and attempts to address that one issue that unites all terrorists: a sense of political grievance.

Usually counter-terrorism efforts combine elements of all three responses (see also Crelinsten 2009; Jackson *et al.* 2011). All three can be effective or counter-productive. Policing efforts were largely suc-cessful in Germany in the 1970s as the state tackled the Red Army Faction (RAF). In Northern Ireland, however, significant mistakes were made in the counter-terrorism effort, as Operation Demetrius saw large numbers of suspected terrorists arrested and interned without trial, further fuelling the sense of grievance that helped to ignite and sustain the conflict. A mix of all three state responses has clearly been in evi-dence after 9/11, although the War on Terror has also revealed the lim-itations of a military response. Early hubristic declaration of mission accomplished and jubilation at the destruction of the Al Qaeda network cannot obscure the fact that Afghanistan is likely to suffer a security vacuum following the 2014 withdrawal of NATO forces. This is likely, moreover, to threaten to return the country to a position akin to that which inspired military intervention in the first place. Likewise, attempts to tackle the context of terrorism have been poorly handled. Despite repeated emphasis on the positive role played by most people who share the Islamic faith, Muslims across Western states have suffered the consequences of becoming a 'suspect community' (Hillyard 1993), as state leaders have focused disproportionately on the role played by 'radical Islam' (see Spalek and Imtoual 2007; Spalek and Lambert 2008; Jarvis and Lister 2013a, 2013c).

These issues have been widely discussed in International Relations and Security Studies since 9/11. They have even helped to inspire the creation of a new subdiscipline known as **Critical Terrorism Studies (CTS)** (compare Gunning 2007; Jackson *et al.* 2009; Jarvis 2009a; Heath-Kelly 2010; Jackson *et al.* 2011). CTS attempts to critique and change social practices surrounding terrorism and counter-terrorism, taking inspiration from Critical Theory and post-structuralist approaches, as well as Critical Security Studies and the Welsh School (e.g. Jackson *et al.* 2011: 30). One of the defining features of CTS has been to contest the exclusive association of terrorism with non-state actors, which is seen to serve a particular political purpose in legitimizing state violence. CTS therefore incorporates a greater focus on the role of state terrorism in general and violence in Western foreign policy in particular (ibid: 32). For CTS scholars, terrorism and counter-terrorism are equally forms of political violence; the fact that one is pursued by a government does not make it inherently legitimate. State terrorism should therefore be rigorously interrogated, denaturalized and challenged, in the same way as the political violence of non-state actors.

There is no shortage of examples of state terrorism. The British and American bombing of Dresden is often held up as an example during World War II (for example, Garrett 2004). With around twenty-five thousand civilians killed in three days, it is possible to argue that the bombing of Dresden was conducted under the rubric of revenge rather than strategic gains. In more recent times, instances of state terrorism are also plentiful. During the past few years, an unknown number of Iranian nuclear scientists have been assassinated. Reports suggest that these assassinations are likely ordered and conducted by the Israeli state, which continues to wage a secret and likely illegal war, aiming to prevent the construction of an Iranian nuclear weapon (e.g. Meikle 2012). They are the latest in a long line of targeted killings. In a letter to the UN Security Council, Iran has argued that those killed were the victims of a 'foreign terror' campaign (Nasseri and Gaoueette 2012). Ironically enough, such state-backed terror campaigns were exactly that nightmare scenario which motivated the policies of the War on Terror in the first place.

Key Points

- Terrorism takes a number of forms, including that of the radical right and Islamic fundamentalism.
- Definitions of terrorism are difficult, often problematic and always political. Definitions often (arbitrarily) ignore, exclude and legitimize state terrorism.
- During the War on Terror the risk posed by terrorism has often been inflated.
- Counter-terrorism takes three main forms: policing, military and attempts to address the contexts of radicalization.

Conclusion

In this chapter we have focused on military threats to security. This focus poses broader questions concerning the purpose(s) of Security Studies. Returning to the complexity/parsimony distinction, we refute claims that Security Studies should adopt a narrow focus on military force for reasons of intellectual coherence. The value of this assumed coherence and focus for the subdiscipline does not offset the loss of completeness, scope and an ability to analyse a range of pressing contemporary issues. Instead we argue that a more expansive reading of Security Studies should emphasize the importance of a range of security issues including alternative forms of violence. That is not to suggest that Security Studies should downplay the role of military threats to security. This chapter has shown how important such threats are, both empirically in the real world of international relations and theoretically for debates within Security Studies. Military threats remain a pervasive and significant threat, impinging on the security of many states and people around the world today. However, this chapter has also shown that the nature of military threats is changing and that Security Studies is following an intellectual evolution in line with these alterations.

Two related themes have emerged here, which build on the arguments developed in previous chapters. First, there is no longer any reason to privilege the state as a unit of analysis for the study of security, beyond its position as a particularly dominant form of political organization. There is no intrinsic or intellectual reason the state should be prioritized at the exclusion of other actors or referents. The trends in political violence discussed here reveal the increasing heterogeneity of conflict. Terrorism, asymmetric war and the shift from inter-state to intra-state conflict all indicate that the nation-state has been challenged as the principal agent involved in the creation of military (in)security.

Second and by extension, there is no reason to privilege the military at the expense of other security threats. While military threats, like the state, have long dominated IR and Security Studies, these priorities no longer – if they ever did – reflect the lived experience of (in)security for many of the world's inhabitants. As has been argued, even in the United States issues such as gun ownership, traffic safety and obesity pose greater risks to life than terrorism and war. Indeed the biggest military risk to American life arises through the *choice* to join the armed forces. In many other parts of the world, disease, climate change and nutrition remain far more immediate and fundamental security concerns than Great Power War (see Chapter 6). While their plight may have little impact on the nature of international order, this is certainly not a legitimate reason to relegate and devalue the *security* issues that affect a majority of the world's citizens, who experience considerable insecurity in their everyday lives, which is far divorced from traditional geopolitical rivalries.

These twin legacies of realism then are being undone by empirical changes and theoretical innovations. Such alterations, we argue, do not undermine the intellectual coherence of Security Studies, but rather enrich its ability to analyse a diverse range of issues of increasing importance for the study, pursuit and operations of security. Military threats and state security should remain at the heart of Security Studies, but they should be contested and denaturalized, in order to create space for the study of security beyond the state and national interest, such that other pressing contemporary issues can also occupy security scholars, despite their labelling as non-mainstream. Since the purpose of Security Studies is no longer intimately tied to the demands of the state and the achievement of its military security, it follows that the discipline can break free from preoccupations that were imposed through the biases of funding, institutionalization, politics and geography. And that is why the following chapter turns to consider equally pressing and important non-military threats to security.

Further Reading

Clausewitz (1968) is often seen as one of the most important contributions to Strategic Studies. In it, Clausewitz draws out his understanding of war and warfare, providing a range of key concepts including the trinity, fog of war, and friction which remain widely used today. Rapoport's introduction to this edition is especially worth reading. Der Derian (2001) provides a post-modern view of contemporary warfare, and the ways in which military power is connected now to media and entertainment industries. Freedman (1994) is a reader on war, with excerpts from major texts on this phenomenon, and Kaldor (1999/2007) outlines her 'new wars' thesis with respect to the conflicts in Bosnia-Herzegovina and Iraq (post-2003). Jackson *et al.* (2011), finally, provide a critical introduction to terrorism and counter-terrorism, including chapters on state terrorism, terrorism and culture, and gender.

Internet Resources

The Correlates of War project (2014) has been ongoing since 1963. It attempts to bring together data related to war and conflict between states. It is an invaluable resource for quantitative approaches seeking to explore and analyse the conditions and causes of war. Iraq Body Count (2014) is a research project that has been active since the outbreak of the Iraq War in 2003. It attempts to bring together data on the casualties of the conflict. The data shows how difficult it is to estimate Iraqi civilian casualties, with large variations between documented and undocumented deaths. UCDP (2014) is home to the Uppsala Conflict Data Programme. This project has been ongoing since the 1970s and houses data on conflicts between and within states. The site also uses an internationally recognized classificatory system, which serves as the basis from which to assess the changing nature of war.

Chapter 6

Security from Whom or from What? New Security Challenges

Chapter Overview

This chapter builds on and extends the discussion of security threats introduced in Chapter 5. Following a brief introduction, it begins by encouraging readers to think more carefully about the nature and meaning of violence. This emphasizes the importance of Peace Studies debates of the 1960s and 1970s in helping scholars and activists move beyond a restrictive focus on direct, observable, somatic forms of harm. Accounts of structural and cultural violence are introduced here, alongside a discussion of the potential of these concepts to shed light on social practices that are frequently more pervasive and harmful than the militaristic security threats explored in Chapter 5. The chapter's second section then introduces a range of contemporary non-military security threats and their consequences, including climate change, famine, poverty and organized crime. Feminist discussions of gendered violence are also explored in this section to illustrate the particularity of certain security challenges. The chapter's final section then ties the range of issues explored in Chapters 5 and 6 to debates over the measurement of threat. Here, we point, first, to the significance of interpretation in the identification of dangers; second, to the difficulties associated with calculating future occurrences; and, third, to the contemporary interest in notions of 'risk' across Security Studies and related disciplines including Sociology. To illustrate, we discuss the United Kingdom's National Risk Register of civil emergencies, which maps risks according to their relative likelihood and impacts.

Chapter Contents

Introduction

Since 1989, the number of people dying as a result of armed conflict has been falling. During the same period, the number of people perishing as a result of malnutrition, disease and inadequate access to clean drinking water has been rising. And yet, even during the Cold War – the centrepiece of national security thinking – the estimated number of total casualties (outside of China and the USSR) stood 'only' at 15 million. Compare this with the summer of 2012, where in the Sahel region of West Africa alone 18 million people faced starvation as the result of famine. In this chapter we will explore the significance of quantitative or total numbers such as these, asking how much they tell us about contemporary insecurities. We will also point to a range of less dramatic sources of harm that impact upon the quality of life – upon the conditions of everyday existence – without posing immediate, catastrophic or fatal risk. We will argue that such harms can, indeed, usefully and coherently be thought of as security threats (Amoore 2013). They are, in other words, not only worthy of discussion, but moreover their inclusion within the remit of Security Studies is imperative.

Phrases such as 'new security challenges', 'new security issues' and the 'new security agenda' have become increasingly prominent within Security Studies over the last two decades. The irony of this is that it is the subdiscipline, rather than the nature of such threats, which has undergone a period of change. Many of the issues included under this heading are some of human history's most enduring threats. Food and health security – nutrition and disease – for example, have always impacted humanity's struggle for survival and an improved existence. Readily visible security threats, such as crime, moreover, often have their roots in more insidious forms of insecurity, including inequality and discrimination. It is possible to argue that such (non-military and non-state) structural insecurities are permanent features of the human condition, given their seemingly omnipresent existence in every society.

As such, perhaps Security Studies has simply 'got over' the Cold War, returning its attention instead to the more pressing, and enduring, everyday threats that affect the lives of a majority of the world's population.

To trace this refocusing of Security Studies, it is useful to revisit earlier arguments within Peace Research from the 1960s and 1970s. Debates on the nature and meaning of violence – how violence should be defined and understood – are key to the 'widening' and 'deepening' undergone by Security Studies in recent decades. As understandings of 'security' have been deepened to include non-existential but nonetheless crucial issues, a wider 'security agenda' has concomitantly formed. In this chapter we discuss five of the most important of these misleadingly named 'new security challenges': climate change, famine, poverty, crime and gendered violence. Building on the arguments of the preceding five chapters, introducing these non-military security issues raises three questions at the heart of contemporary (Critical) Security Studies. The first question concerns the reality of security threats. Building on Chapter 1, it is important to ask questions about **threat inflation** or exaggeration. Is it possible to identify overblown or misaligned policy by pointing to the empirical reality of a security threat? The second and third questions concern the probability and temporality of security threats. What is the intellectual and policy impact of the human and scientific desire to predict the likelihood and timescale of identified future risk? Do attempts at forecasting future risk bias policymakers towards the calculable, the inevitable, the short term and the cataclysmic, leaving less dramatic and less immediate threats unconsidered? And, crucially, *how* have social scientists and practitioners gone about calculating risk and to what effect? This final question draws the chapter to a close and is picked up in Chapter 7, where we consider security's very possibility, arguing for the need to live with insecurity. We begin to lay the foundations of this argument, here, by thinking about violence.

Key Points

- In numerical terms, deaths from non-military security issues far outweigh their military counterparts.
- Descriptions of famine, disease or poverty, for example, as 'new security challenges' are misleading: these have always impacted the security of individuals and communities.

Thinking about violence

This section introduces readers to debates about the nature and meaning of violence. Here, we urge readers to think carefully about definitions and understandings of violence, as well as the intellectual and policy implications they may have. These debates require us to revisit the insights of Peace Studies, which helped to move scholars and activists away from a restrictive focus on direct and observable forms of harm which are somatic – or targeted at the body – in nature. This move, we show, enables scholars, activists and policymakers to consider other forms of structural and cultural violence, which are frequently more pervasive and harmful than the militaristic security threats explored in the preceding chapter:

> We live amidst violence. It has always been with us. Natural environments are violent places. Humankind has improved the techniques for the delivery of violence, but has not diminished the violence those techniques were ostensibly designed to protect against. Of course, most human violence is not physical. It is structural. It occurs not simply in the beatings, killings, and fear that are the daily fare of so many of our fellows. It is in the needless poverty, marginalization, and hopelessness that are always there even when the physical violence ebbs. (May 2012)

The above citation is taken from the excellent Histories of Violence project (see Further Reading), where students can watch introductory lectures on some of the most influential thinkers on topics of violence. The opening paragraph contains the idea that violence is a natural, environmental condition, inherent in beast and (wo)man. The enduring nature of violence remains today, altered primarily only in the efficiency of its delivery thanks to the technological advances of the industrial revolution and so forth. These assertions are important and informed some of the thinking behind Chapter 5. In the second paragraph, however, May (2012) argues that violence is primarily structural, not physical. It may not, in other words, necessarily involve harm to a person's body. This is an argument with which Booth concurs. Discussing the key insights of Peace Studies, Booth (2007: 68) notes that 'violence should be understood as a structural phenomenon and not simply the use of brute force'; Peace and Security Studies, therefore, should be concerned with liberating people from *all* forms of violence.

Peace Studies, like the discipline of International Relations, was forged in the fires of a normative desire to achieve a better, more peaceful world. Ending and preventing war motivated both. However, as International Relations reached the zenith of its scientific and strategic aspirations at the height of the Cold War, Peace Studies responded with a radical alternative take on the study of conflict, violence and security (see Table 6.1). Johan Galtung first coined the term 'structural violence' in an influential article, 'A Structural Theory of Imperialism'. This seminal contribution helped to steer Peace Studies away from a focus on ending war in order to bring about peace: understood traditionally as a negative concept, defined by the absence of violent conflict. Galtung's argument was that the task was to build peace in a positive sense: understood in terms of addressing avoidable harms and working toward social justice. This approach had a major influence upon the emancipatory project of Welsh School security analysts, who were inspired by this intellectual and normative move (Booth 2007: 67). For scholars such as Booth and Galtung, just as being healthy means more than being free of disease, so being secure means more than being free of any immediate risk of death (see Galtung 1985).

Some of life's most significant insecurities arise not at the barrel of a gun, but in the invisible and insidious capillaries of power that condition and shape the possibilities and potentialities of life itself even if

Table 6.1 *Competing views of violence and peace*

	Violence	Peace
Traditional View	*Direct* • By an identifiable perpetrator • Intentional • Somatic: targeted at the body • Discrete: an event	*Negative* • The absence of war or conflict • Potentially temporary • No necessary resolution of underlying hostilities or grievances
	Example: A death from stabbing	*Example: A ceasefire*
Alternative View	*Structural* • No obvious perpetrator • Not necessarily intentional or somatic • A process, rather than an event • Avoidable	*Positive* • Addresses physical and structural violences • Emphasis on social harmony and justice • Enduring
	Example: A death from smallpox today	*Example: Human rights regimes*

they cannot be seen. Many people's wellbeing and aspirations, for instance, are conditioned and often limited by widespread but entirely contestable assumptions about gender femininity and womanhood. These range from the practice of female genital mutilation (FGM) which over 125 million women and girls across the world have experienced according to UNICEF, through to the denial of education, voting rights and equal pay to many of the world's women. While FGM is clearly a form of physical violence, all of these harms are outcomes of a particular kind of structural violence: patriarchy. Patriarchy refers to embedded social patterns of gendered inequality in which female prospects and opportunities are inferior, and subordinated, to those of males.

Key Points

- Violence can take many forms. These can be direct, observable and physical, as well as indirect, unobservable and structural.
- Security Studies should be concerned with understanding and addressing all forms of violence.
- A focus on 'structural violence' in Peace Studies has inspired and demonstrates significant parallels with the emancipatory ambitions of Critical Security Studies.
- Studying structural violence enables Security Studies to consider topics such as patriarchy as security issues.

Non-military security threats

Here we introduce five non-military sets of issues that changing understandings of violence enable us to discuss under the remit of Security Studies. First, we consider climate change and the burgeoning literature on environmental security. Second, we introduce the topic of famine and the issue of 'food security'. Third, we discuss poverty, drawing on recent important insights of critical (international) political economy. Fourth, the chapter turns to consider organized crime, focusing on the recent escalation of violence between Mexican drug cartels. And, fifth, the section ends with a discussion of gendered violence, focusing on American, British and Australian case studies in turn.

Environmental security

Environmental issues achieved recognition as security problems from the 1980s onwards. This attention subsequently manifested itself in the policy responses of the Brundtland Commission which reported in 1987 and the 'Earth Summit' in Rio de Janeiro of 1992. The reasons for this interest at this time were fourfold. First, was a series of catastrophic events, including the Chernobyl nuclear reactor accident of 1986 and growing awareness of deforestation in the Amazon at the end of the 1980s. Second, climate change accelerated in pace through the twentieth century, generating more extreme weather events as the result of increasing use of natural resources and the accompanying production of greenhouses gases. Here, political concerns about the environment mirrored the growth in empirical evidence of human-induced – or **anthropogenic** – alterations in long-term climate conditions and short-term weather patterns. Third, previous concerns about environmental security had centred on the threat posed to non-Western populations at risk of famine, disease and poverty. An important change in the late 1980s was the growing political recognition that environmental security would impact the developed world as well. This was important given the concentration of global political and economic power in richer states. And, fourth, these developments also sparked new intellectual trends in the study of the environment which focused on its potential to threaten 'the self'. Previously influential literatures on Green Philosophy (see Chapter 4), which contained explicit ethical commitments to the well-being of others, lost sway amidst this growing attention to the Global North's insecurity, prominent in the writings of authors such as Robert Kaplan.

Kaplan's famous 1994 article 'The Coming Anarchy' arrived at a moment ripe for the discussion of its central ideas. With the concerns of the Cold War ended and state leaders struggling to understand the new landscape of security, Kaplan provided an easily understood narrative to fill the security void. 'It is time to understand the environment', Kaplan (1994: 58) wrote, 'for what it is: *the* national-security issue of the early twenty-first century.' Kaplan wrote in dramatic prose, with wide-reaching public and policy impact. He warned that global resource wars and extreme variations in weather and climate would be experienced globally. This experience, however, would be differentiated by individual nations' abilities to master these changes and the conflicts they would spark. Kaplan summarized his predictions succinctly: Francis Fukuyama's Last Man in the Global North would master his environment. Thomas Hobbes' First Man in the Global South, in contrast, would reap the terrible consequences of environmental insecurities. A modernist project of man mastering nature would, he predicted, ensure the developed world remained 'pampered' and 'well fed', in contrast to the 'nasty, brutish and poor' life of those in developing countries (Kaplan 1994: 60).

Kaplan's hyperbole had three principal impacts of concern to us. First, whatever its limitations, the article helped increase the environment's visibility as a potential security threat in popular, policy and academic debates. Second, the article inspired further debate on whether environmental issues should be incorporated under the label 'security'. Daniel Deudney (1999), for example, lamented the conceptual confusion that such inclusion caused. If, he argued, the environment was a security issue because it may inspire conflict, then it should be included as an additional variable in debates on the causes of war. On the other hand, if it is, of itself, a security issue, then its nature is so markedly different from military security that their conflation is unhelpful (Deudney 1999). We agree with this second critique, which leads usefully into the third impact for discussion here. Third, then, Kaplan's article inspired a more nuanced and less military-focused response in the environmental security literature, which de-centered the state as security's referent.

As we noted in Chapter 4, alternative 'green agendas' took hold in particular during the 1990s, mirroring politicians' concerns with the environment's impact on the state. 'Ecological security' took as its focus the biosphere: the narrow band of life that encompasses the planet. Inspired by Green Philosophy, this view approaches nation-states as part of the story, but refuses to view their survival, security and power as the end-goal of possible solutions; people are seen to be secure only *within* their environment (Dalby 2002; McDonald 2011b). Coupled to a 'radical' philosophical literature is a powerful and growing scientific base. In recent years, with increasing certainty it has been possible for scientists to point to extreme weather events resulting from climate change. Such events vary from the inconvenience of Britain's wettest ever summer in 2012, due to the warming of the Atlantic, to the devastation of Hurricane Katrina in 2005 and Superstorm Sandy seven years later. Such events and the science that links them incontrovertibly to man-made activities helps to ensure that environmental issues are afforded ever-more attention: as security issues. Alongside climate change, clear evidence of human activity increasing environmental insecurity is evident in the loss of life in deforestation-induced floods and landslides, the loss of livelihood from vast oil spills in the Gulf of Mexico, and the widespread loss of both experienced in the 2010 Haitian earthquake, to name only a few. For ecological security approaches, these events and their impacts are sufficient to warrant the study of the environment as a security issue, regardless of whether such instances lead to conflict (see Table 6.2). Similar concerns characterize debates on food security to which we now turn.

Table 6.2 *Major environmental disasters (selected)*

When	Where	What	Consequences
1986	Chernobyl, Ukraine	Nuclear power plant explosion	Disputed death toll, impact of cancers resulting from radiation estimated at 40,000 by 2065.
1991	Bangladesh	Cyclone	138,000 dead, 10 million homeless.
1995	Chicago, United States	Heatwave	750 deaths.
1999	Vargas, Venezuala	Flooding, mudslides	Over 15,000 deaths, buildings submerged by 3 metres of mud.
2004	Numerous countries, including Indonesia, Sri Lanka, India, Thailand, Somalia	Earthquake and tsunami	Over 250,000 deaths in 11 countries.
2005	Pakistan	Earthquake	Approximately 75,000 killed.
2011	Gulf of Mexico	Oil spill following explosion on an oil rig	11 killed, over 200 million gallons of oil pumped into the sea, huge environmental impact, with fishing and tourism impacted.
2011	Japan	Earthquake, tsunami and nuclear melt-down	Over 15,000 deaths, widespread loss of livelihoods.
2013	The Philippines	Cyclone Haiyan	Estimated 10,000 killed, with several towns suffering 80–90% destruction of buildings and collapse of infrastructure.

Food security

Famine was for a long time seen as a 'development issue' rather than a 'security issue'. Once again, the issue was often viewed as something that affected 'them' and not 'us': an issue about which it would be desirable, yet not absolutely imperative, to do something. In any discussion of food security it is important to note that famine and malnutrition occur *not* because of a lack of food, but due to an inefficiency or inadequacy in its distribution. David Campbell (2012) has effectively charted the visual, photographic logics that have assuaged Western leaders of guilt, by framing famine and starvation as the result of scarcity of food. Famine is also, usually, not the result of corruption. Rather, famine can usefully be thought of as yet another instance of structural violence. Understanding famine, therefore, requires an understanding of international political economy, alongside international security.

Access to food – clean water and adequate nutrition – is one of the few needs which most agree should be a universal human right. The 1948 UN Declaration on Human Rights enshrines this thinking, as does its 1966 reiteration in the International Covenant on Economic, Social and Cultural Rights. Yet, despite the 1974 Declaration to end Hunger and Malnutrition, and the subsequent 1996 World Food Summit which pledged to halve the number of malnourished people to 420 million, the number of malnourished people hit one billion in 2009. Astonishingly, when nutrient-deficient diets are included, that number likely doubles to account for two out of every seven of the world's people. The Food Assistance Convention – a legally binding international treaty on food aid adopted in 2012 – has been signed by the majority of states in the 'Western world'. Critics however, suggest that questions remain over the value of treaties such as these. What *new* measures will be undertaken by signatories (Clay 2012)? Do such treaties merely enshrine existing and continuing commitments? And, more fundamentally, does the focus on aid and assistance continue to indebt recipient states in a system, which, at its crux, is both deeply flawed and unjust?

This last question again raises the issue of defining the universal human 'right to food'. Rather than ensuring governments' duties to distribute food, the UN continues to understand the 'right to food' as centred on the ability of households to produce or access adequate nutrition. Aid and assistance are a secondary, also enshrined, responsibility, but one that should be necessary only in times of crisis. This distinction highlights our final reflection on food security: the necessary interlinking of technological and political solutions. While food insecurity is a structural – political and economic – problem, it is also one that has been historically addressed through technological advancement. Dwarf wheat, which does not collapse under the increased weight of higher yields, was one such remarkable breakthrough. It helped to inspire the so-called 'Green Revolution'. Between 1965 and 1970, this revolution helped to almost double wheat yields in Pakistan and India. If the UN's (2000) Millennium goal to 'eradicate extreme poverty and hunger' by 2015 is to be realized, political, economic and technological advances will be needed (see also Chapter 7).

Poverty

As Chapter 4 made clear, security's referent has been much contested in recent decades, especially with the rise of debates around human security. With half of the world's inhabitants continuing to live on under $2US per day and with this continuing to claim more lives than conflict, it is easy to see why poverty also entered the security debate in the early 1990s (Thomas 2008). However, while academics and politicians have welcomed the integration of security and development discussions, fundamental disagreement remains over the direction of future solutions to this challenge (Thomas 2008). The primary division here is whether to work within or against the prevailing system of socio-economic organization and the regime of truth that sustains it. Is development and security – through the emancipation of individuals from poverty – best achieved through economic liberalization and integration? Or, alternatively, does poverty arise precisely because of the neo-liberal system? Is poverty best conceptualized, in other words, as a structural insecurity, requiring a new way of organizing economic relations?

A burgeoning human security literature raises important questions about the definition of poverty – relative or absolute? – and the crucial need to identify *whose* security from poverty is under the microscope. For instance, while 41% of Americans residing in Reading, Pennsylvania (see also, Flint in Michigan) live below the poverty line, that line is calculated as a function of other Americans' wealth: it is a relative measure of poverty. Absolute measures of poverty are also contested – not least because of their association of poverty with income – but take a blanket approach toward the global poverty threshold. This is frequently estimated at US$1, or US$1.25 per day: with those living off less than this deemed to be living in poverty. Over one billion people fall into this category. With this in mind, it is important, first, to note the different types of security and insecurity at stake for those suffering absolute or relative poverty. Second, to remember that such sweeping definitions mask a plethora of cross-cutting security issues – health, food, crime, etc. – that have significant implications for an individual's survival, well-being and life-chances.

As with discussions of food and environmental security, the relationship – or nexus – between poverty and conflict is a recurrent concern for security scholars. Here, however, we turn to a more fundamental and important question. Development Studies has researched poverty far longer than has Security Studies. The mainstream position of both subdisciplines has traditionally coalesced around neo-liberal approaches to economic growth, centred on the **Washington Consensus**. Neo-liberal arguments of the 1970s and 1980s, predating discussions of poverty as a security issue, suggested that poverty results primarily from a lack of integration in the global economy. The role of the state, therefore, was not directly to pursue development, *per se*, but rather to facilitate the free operation of the market, by encouraging export-led growth and liberalizing the market at home. This private sector model of growth and development has met considerable challenges but remains largely intact as the dominant mode of political and socio-economic thinking today, despite the colossal financial crisis of 2008. It also remains in place despite the glaring inequalities such policies appear to have wrought, with the world's poorest losing out disproportionately in comparison to developed states. Taking seriously the topic of poverty as a security issue heightens the intensity of some of the most important debates in politics, economics and philosophy today. Is capitalism the most significant cause of insecurity in the modern world? And, would alternatives be better?

Crime

Crime may not appear a logical inclusion in a Security Studies textbook. That is the case precisely because of the arbitrary definitions of this subdiscipline throughout its infancy and subsequent Cold War maturity. Yet, for many people, in the developed and developing worlds, crime remains a far larger source of insecurity than war. Security Studies, however, continues to insist upon exclusions such as this, by way of defining apparently legitimate topics of study. Rather than assessing the role of crime, *in general*, on the dynamics of (in)security, Security Studies has, to date, focused almost exclusively on the role of crime in its *transnational* and *organized* variants. On the former, the notion of 'transnational' crime, once again, returns the state to international security's fore (see Chapter 1), revalidating preoccupations of the national interest in determining appropriate forms of response (see Chapter 4). On the latter, the insistence upon 'organized' crime excludes many forms of violence and criminal activity that clearly impinge upon group and individual security: domestic violence, for instance. For crime to be defined as 'organized', it is necessary that a perpetrating group be organized to commit a 'serious offence' for a sustained period, before, during and after the act (Picarelli 2008). The 2000 UN Convention Against Transnational Organized Crime, moreover, insists upon a financial aspect to 'organized' crime, excluding, we suggest arbitrarily, so-called 'ordinary' crimes such as rape and murder (Giraldo and Trinkunas 2008: 352). Security Studies then, since the 1990s, has concerned itself with the activities of mafias and cartels, rather than muggings and car crime.

Transnational criminal organizations (TCOs) have benefited enormously from globalization. Globalization accelerated in pace, depth and extent during the 1990s, with TCOs reaping the benefits. Porous borders, increased ease of movement, and restructured international and sub-national socio-economic organization gave TCOs obvious opportunities to exploit whilst simultaneously weakening the hand of the state to combat them. The opportunity, for example, to operate in a low-risk, weakly-governed 'home state', despite profiting from operations in wealthy states abroad, has led to the rapid increase in the activities of TCOs (see, for example, Box 6.1). The so-called 'dark side' of globalization has, for instance, been evident in post-Soviet Russia (Giraldo and Trinkunas 2008: 354) where TCOs thrived in the power vacuum left by the erosion of the USSR. Importantly for Security Studies, these TCOs also threatened the legitimacy of the fledgling Russian democracy, undermining pretensions to transparency, free markets and the rule of law. TCOs, then, can directly threaten the state, playing into the concerns of traditional approaches within Security Studies (again, see Box 6.1).

Conceptualizing the array of TCOs has proven a challenging task for academics and policymakers, as has adopting appropriate responses to these. Prevalent hierarchical, networked and market visions of TCOs, for example, have inspired alternative and competing policy responses (Giraldo and Trinkunas 2008: 358–9). Viewed hierarchically, the logical state response to TCOs is to target the head or leadership of the organization. Viewed as a network, targeting both the nodes and flows that sustain them becomes increasingly important. In the market-place conceptualization, it is not the organization itself that drives crime, rather the logics of supply and demand that licit companies obey. If this is the case, it makes little to sense to highlight the novelty of TCOs today. Rather, policy responses must continue to manage an inevitable and enduring consequence of capitalism, which is actually far less significant and lucrative than normally assumed (Giraldo and Trinkunas 2008: 358–9). Perhaps the most obvious example of a policy response to TCOs that recognizes *all* of these features is Europol. The European Police Organization was founded in the Maastricht Treaty in 1992, commencing work in 1999. Europol facilitates intelligence and information sharing, coordinating the policing activities of member states, as they respond to inherently *transnational* activities, such as drug trafficking, people smuggling and money laundering.

Gendered violence

There are as many types of feminism as there are theories of International Relations. While liberal, radical and post-modern femi-

Box 6.1 Mexican drugs cartels

Illegal drugs smuggling, people trafficking, the black (and grey) markets of the arms trade, and money laundering comprise the 'big four' variants of transnational criminal organizations (TCOs). In recent years, one of the clearest examples of TCO activities concerning illegal drug smuggling has been the escalating violence between Mexican cartels sourcing products in Central America and selling them north of the border to a relatively wealthy American market. This is certainly not a new issue. The United States' relationship with Colombia, for example, has been shaped through the lens of a 'War on Drugs' designed to curb the supply of cocaine into the US since the 1970s. Mexico, likewise, has long been a source of illegal drugs for Americans, particularly in geographically proximate southern California, with ready access to Tijuana. What has changed in recent years is the intensity of inter-cartel feuding, with frequent and intentionally visible violence an increasingly commonplace feature of the illegal Mexico–US drugs trade. The prospect of controlling areas such as Tijuana has encouraged shootings, beheadings and the display of victims as warnings to others. From January to September 2011 alone, an estimated 13,000 Mexicans were killed in drugs related violence. During the preceding six years of President Calderon's crackdown that figure is an estimated 50,000. As a result, Calderon's strategy has come under increasing strain. A policy of mobilizing the army for zero-tolerance policing duties appears to have backfired as public opinion has soured in step with escalating casualties. The largest difficulty remains the lucrative nature of the drugs business with profits over US$13 billion annually.

nism are amongst the most frequently cited, there exists, in reality, a spectrum of feminist positions, stretching from efforts to measure gendered inequality empirically and numerically, to those more concerned with contesting the gendered dominant discourses that structure power relations. As with International Relations, gender entered Security Studies late. And the terms 'gender' and 'security' remain viewed, by many, as incommensurate or even mutually exclusive. Here, rather than retrace the concerns of variants of feminism, we explore some of the recent and controversial instances where gender and security have been brought into the political limelight. First, however, it is necessary to situate these instances in their broader context, by briefly reflecting on masculinized military violence.

The historical narrative on issues of war and peace is one deeply infused with particular portrayals of gender. For many centuries, with few exceptions, war remained the exclusive realm of men. Women have historically been seen not to belong: the category 'woman' has long been viewed as incompatible with the violence of conflict. Tropes of strength, bravery, and notions of patriotic sacrifice are characteristics that have come to define societal expectations of masculinity and manliness, in opposition to their feminized antitheses of weakness and timidity. Indeed, women are still barred from certain roles in many of the world's militaries because of assumptions such as these. If, as Anthony Burke (2001) has intimated, fear is the defining feature of perceived insecurity, delivering security would fall, seemingly 'naturally', to the gender for which being afraid was never an option. This reification of apparent biological traits into the social characteristics of the genders has been at the heart of the exclusion of women from the stories of IR and Security Studies. Thus, many feminist scholars have legitimately asked, in response: 'where are the women?'

Historically women have been largely invisible in accounts of armed conflict. Even where critics may point to Boudicca, the Amazons, Condoleezza Rice or Margaret Thatcher as evidence of women's ability to play a central role in war, it remains the case that the invocation of these (often mythical) names strengthens, rather than overcomes, gendered discourses which deprive women of any place in warfare (Kennedy-Pipe 2007). In each case, these names are invoked because of their adoption of (or assimilation to) quintessentially 'male' character traits. Even though the sight of women in uniform has now become commonplace, this gendered narrative has been sufficiently enduring to continue to shape the experience and perception of women soldiers. Here, we discuss three recent examples of the contemporary relevance of gender to issues of violence, war and security: the 'rescue' of Jessica Lynch; the birth of a child at Camp Bastion; and accusations of **misogyny** (see **patriarchy**) at the top of Australian politics (see Box 6.2).

Our first example comes from April 2003, when nineteen-year-old Private Jessica Lynch became a household name following her capture and subsequent rescue in Iraq. The Pentagon released a five-minute film to the press, detailing how Army Rangers and Navy Seals had stormed the hospital where she was held captive. It was the first successful rescue of an American prisoner of war since World War II, and the first ever of a female soldier. The video portrayed an intense and dramatic firefight, with American troops displaying overwhelming bravery and determination. Reports of her condition stated that she had suffered bullet and stab wounds. Lynch and her rescuers were portrayed as American heroes. Both had fulfilled the identities expected of them, re-animating longstanding narratives around the night-time rescue of women by firefighters in the nineteenth century (see, for example, Faludi 2008). However, it did not take long for the story and its supporting narratives to begin to unravel. Reporters quickly discovered inconsistencies in the Pentagon's story-telling, with hospital workers recalling a far less dramatic turn of events, with Lynch suffering only the injuries of a road traffic accident and being well cared for. There are two important and related points to note from this apparent paradox. First, the media strategy at the Pentagon was noteworthy for its eagerness to create a myth of heroism and rescue, centred on traditional gender stereotypes. Second, this myth was exceptionally resonant and was seized upon by both the American media and general public. America(ns) wanted heroic men and rescued women, not female combatants. And the American military knew that.

Our second example comes from September 2012, when an unnamed Royal Artillery Gunner gave birth at Camp Bastion in Afghanistan. A British soldier, originally from Fiji, the mother was unaware that she was pregnant and had even passed strenuous physical exercise tests. This was the first time a British Serviceperson had ever given birth on the front line. Media and public reports focused on the

Box 6.2 Gender in Australian politics and culture

Our third example of gender issues entering the political limelight also comes from September 2012, when Australian Prime Minister Julia Gillard accused the Leader of the Opposition, Tony Abbott, of 'sexism and misogyny' (Wright and Holland 2014). The speech won her plaudits from many commentators and (in large part) came as a response to the, often thinly-veiled, gendered language used to attack her political positions. For instance, Tony Abbott had previously insisted Gillard 'politically speaking, make an honest woman of herself'. He had also associated himself with campaigns to 'Ditch the Witch'. In response, Gillard's powerful speech went viral on social media:

'I hope the Leader of the Opposition has a piece of paper and he is writing out his resignation, because if he wants to know what misogyny looks like in modern Australia he does not need a motion in the House of Representatives; he needs a mirror. I was offended when the Leader of the Opposition went outside the front of parliament and stood next to a sign that said 'Ditch the Witch'. I was offended when the Leader of the Opposition stood next to a sign that described me as a 'man's bitch'. I was offended by those things. It is misogyny, sexism, every day from this Leader of the Opposition ... the Leader of the Opposition should be ashamed of his performance in the parliament and the sexism he brings with it.'

'surprising, unbelievable and even inappropriate nature of the event'. What seemed 'to baffle most commentators [was] the need to reconcile the image of the soldier, as life taker, with that of the mother, as life giver' (Guerrina 2012). The response to the incident revealed the incompatibility of mothering and soldiering within dominant discourses of military masculinity. These discourses sustain the idea that the armed forces are an inherently male institution. Within military and media reports, pregnancy was frequently discussed and described as a 'medical condition'. As Guerrina (2012) points out 'it should be unsurprising that the military – the most masculine of all state institutions – should seek to frame pregnancy/maternity using what is often deemed to be the only suitable male comparator, illness'; to be pregnant is to have something 'wrong', requiring 'remedy'. What Guerrina usefully highlights, then, is not the importance of the rarity of this incident; but, rather, its power to reveal the assumptions and power structures that shaped reporting on it within the British press.

Key Points

- New security issues such as climate change have frequently entered Security Studies debates due to their implications for national security.
- Poverty and famine continue to affect over one-third of the world's people: a far higher number than those affected by violent conflict.
- New security challenges often highlight the role of a state-centric ontology in creating insecurity. For instance, combating the effects of climate change or economic inequality may require a different prioritization of referent objects.
- Gender and security have long been viewed as unconnected. However, in recent years, this arbitrary bracketing has been challenged in academic literature and through substantive political developments.

Measuring threats: inroads and challenges

This section ties the range of issues explored in Chapters 5 and 6 to debates over the measurement and calculation of threat. Here, we point, first, to the significance of interpretation in the identification of dangers; second, to the difficulties associated with calculating future occurrences; and, third, to the contemporary interest in notions of 'risk' across Security Studies and related disciplines. To illustrate, we discuss the United Kingdom's National Risk Register of civil emergencies, which maps risks according to their relative likelihood and impact.

Buzan and Hansen (2009) have traced the evolution of critical constructivism, in its various strands, during the 1990s. Two of those strands take direct influence from Peace Research. The first, associated with authors such as Emmanuel Adler (1997), considered the bottom-up formation of **security communities**, as part of the peace-building process. The second, associated with authors such as Jutta Weldes (1996), focused on the linguistic dimension of foreign policy, considering how key concepts in International Relations, such as the national interest for instance, are discursively constituted. This second strand of critical constructivism is of particular interest to us here. It takes considerable inspiration from, and indeed overlaps with, post-structuralism. For post-structuralists and critical constructivists alike, the construction of identities, within discourse or through language games, lies at the heart of International Relations and foreign policy (for example, Hansen 2006). Both approaches emphasize that appeals to notions such as the 'national interest' actually rely upon and contribute to the construction of commonplace understandings about what that term actually means. Both, then, share a focus on revealing the constructed nature of international relations, foreign policy and international security, with a view to challenging and denaturalizing those elements that are seen to be inconsistent, troubling or even dangerous. While many of these concerns are shared by the two approaches, slight but important differences emerge in, for instance, the degree of agency that actors are afforded, as well as (for example) the degree of control the state is thought to have over the construction of its own identity. One prominent critique of post-structuralism has been that it falsely reduces agents to 'discoursers of discourses' (Hopf 1998: 198).

Some of the most exciting and persuasive analyses of foreign and security policy continue, perhaps unsurprisingly, to occupy the overlapping space between these approaches, such as Richard Jackson's (2005b) *Writing the War on Terrorism*. First, Jackson's work takes influence from Campbell's (1998b) post-structural deconstruction of US foreign policy, as well as Foucault's genealogy and Derrida's focus on the role of binaries in identity formation. Second, however, Jackson also takes influence from authors such as Barnett (1999) and Weldes (1996), retaining a strong sense of elite instrumentality in the deliberate creation of dominant discourses, which serve particular political agendas and vested interests. There are two important points for us to note here, regarding research such as Jackson's in the overlapping space between critical constructivism and post-structuralism.

First, security issues are not objective. Rather, threats are socially constructed. They are brought into existence through the discourses that give them meaning. A useful example of this is the case study of

HIV and AIDS. Throughout the 1980s HIV and AIDS rapidly entered political and public discourse, to be spoken of as an existential threat, in both physical and moral senses. Today, HIV and AIDS have largely returned to the status of public health – not security– issues within political and public discourse. The 'reality' of the 'threat' from HIV and AIDS was inseparable from the language used to fix its meaning. This, in turn, was inseparable from the surrounding social, political, economic and cultural issues that conditioned discussions of HIV and AIDS in the 1980s. Second, particular agents possess greater institutional capacity and power to have their words heard and accepted. One of the concerns of discourse-focused work has been to give greater voice to the voiceless, in direct opposition to the dominant discourses that those with social and institutional power can disseminate with perceived expertise and authority. For Jackson (2005b), analysing 'terrorism' must necessarily involve studying the discourses that give the term meaning, inclusive of the vested interests that inspire their production and dissemination, and the cultural context that determines their resonance. From this starting point of strategic agents (in this case, instrumental politicians) and dominant discourses (in this case, widespread narratives of 'War on Terror'), it is possible to explore their implications and work towards their destabilization, with the hope of creating space for alternative ways of thinking and acting.

One of the most important things that these discussions have added to Security Studies is an appreciation of the role of interpretation in determining political responses to security 'threats'. Taking seriously the insights of post-structuralism and critical constructivism enables us to understand how it might be that terrorism has garnered such a significant policy response, despite its relative statistical insignificance. This is in contrast to forms of structural violence – such as poverty which affects one in three people – which have consistently been relegated to the lower status of 'development' issues. Up to 5 trillion US dollars have been spent fighting a 'War on Terror' due to the dominant discourses that have constituted, at different moments, Osama bin Laden, Al Qaeda, the Taliban and Saddam Hussein's Iraq as the greatest threats to American security.

Second, practitioners of international security are required to formulate policy and strategy that considers the future. Policy decisions are taken based upon the calculation of a threat's likely future realization. Two considerations are paramount here: how likely is it that a threat will manifest, and on what timescale? The answers to both questions bring with them biases in policymaking. On the first question, since threats are constituted discursively, rather than calculated objectively, currents of thought, not rational enquiry, shape the concerns of practitioners and the public. Consider, for example, President Bill Clinton's, arguably muted, response to information on Al Qaeda at the end of the 1990s, compared to the intensity of debates on such information after 2001. The information was far clearer before 2001 and the players involved were the same. What had altered was the identity and therefore the relationship of the principal agents. On the second question, policymakers are frequently biased towards the immediate and cataclysmic, at the expense of (potentially more serious) long-term, slowly accumulating or more structural (less existential) forms of threat. Such biases explain the difficulty of speaking about climate change as a security issue, in comparison to preoccupations with the production of WMD in rogue states.

Brian Massumi (2005) has argued persuasively on the potential implications of an approach to foreign and security policy that takes the avoidance of future threat as its principal focus. Within the Bush Administration, Vice-President Dick Cheney famously argued that the biggest marker of success for Bush's presidency was the avoidance of a second 9/11. The overriding desire to avert an event that was widely interpreted as certain to occur helped to establish the conditions that would permit a particular form of emergency governance, centered on policies of **pre-emption**. For Massumi, the (affective) certainty of future attack enables an assertive pre-emptive foreign policy of military interventionism. The certainty of averting future inevitability relies upon particular foldings of a traumatic past into a present in which rapid, undeliberated decisions are required to secure the future. In Massumi's (2005: 6) own, difficult, words:

> The traditional tense of threat, the indefinite future of the what-may-come, has been translated into the future perfect: the 'will have' of the always-will-have-been-already. The French term 'futur antérieur' says it well. The future anterior is the time of certainty. It is the temporal equivalent of a tautology – which is precisely the form of governmental logic that expresses it: the foregone conclusion. A time-slip evacuates the suspended present, and with it deliberative reason. Analysis, decision, and debate are short-circuited. The baby of persuasive speech goes out with the discursively reasoning bathwater.

For Massumi, debate is short-circuited through the apparent certainty of a terrible future crisis, which must be averted at all costs. The key players in this game of altering the future are also emotionally invested in delivering tomorrow's security because they had experienced yesterday's trauma on 11 September 2001. This type of thinking has also been prominent within a second feature of attempts to predict the likelihood and timescale of future threats. Taking past knowledge and future speculation into a focus on the present, policymakers and practitioners have increasingly taken decisions via the calculation and quantification of risk. Within academia, such approaches are most closely associated with Ulrich Beck's (1992) *Risk Society*. For Anthony Giddens (1999: 3), an obsession with risk has emerged as the logical consequence of the increased political desire to deliver a safe, secure future. And, for Beck (1992), the calculation of risk – as an attempt to quantify, control and nullify threat – arises out of the conditions of modernization. Technology and a particular temporal horizon (what Massumi calls the 'present-future') have combined to create a situation in which elites rely upon the calculation of risk to define the threats of the present, based upon their likely occurrence in the immediate future.

In the UK, the National Risk Register of civil emergencies is a good example of modern approaches to security policy as a form of **risk management**. Britain's National Risk Register attempts to quantify the scale and likelihood of 'the kinds of' risks the UK 'could face in the future'. Graphic representations of identified threats are ranked relative to each other, in ways that have obvious policy implications for the prioritization of different issues. Attempting a 'dispassionate' computation of risk, the National Risk Register highlights the discrepancies evident in security policy, which has been led by dominant discourses over-playing particular threats. Calculated purely on the (i) basis of plausibility, (ii) likelihood of occurring in the next five years, and (iii) scale of impact, the report suggests that far greater emphasis should be afforded to preparing for an influenza pandemic and coastal flooding than a large-scale terrorist attack. This is a useful insight, which can be read to highlight the apparent biases of focus and funding that follow the elevation of particular threats in dominant discourses. However, significant issues remain with a risk-based approach, which the report can also highlight. First, the timescale of 'five years' is relatively arbitrary, beyond coinciding with funding cycles and the political timescale of terms of office. It clearly therefore downplays longer-term, potentially greater, risks. Second, 'impact' is calculated using five measures: the likelihood of (i) fatalities and (ii) injury or illness, as well as the scale of (iii) economic, (iv) social and (v) psychological disruption. How to measure and rank these factors, as well as the decision to exclude other potential variables, is a contestable and political decision. While we would encourage the inclusion of structural impacts, our concern would be that a risk-based approach to security de-politicizes the process by which threats are identified and confronted.

> ## Key Points
>
> - Critical constructivist and post-structuralist approaches argue that security threats are discursively constructed, rather than objectively identified.
> - This realization can help explain apparent biases in policy focus towards particular threats.
> - Policymakers have increasingly been preoccupied with securing the future and basing policies on calculations of risk.
> - Interest in the calculation of risk has had important policy implications, such as those based on the measurement of terrorist threat at any given time.

Conclusion

This chapter has considered non-military security threats, which have emerged as serious concerns for the discipline following the end of the Cold War. Their inclusion in a textbook on Security Studies has been facilitated by both this historical juncture and by the shifting intellectual concerns of a discipline coming to grips with different conceptualizations of violence. We began by revisiting these debates and their implications, suggesting that the term 'structural violence' in Peace Studies was important for moving scholars beyond the study of fatal threats to include issues that impact upon other, equally important, measures of (in)security. In Security Studies, like Peace Studies before it, a concern with 'structural violence' has enabled the study of phenomena such as climate change and poverty as security issues.

In the second section we introduced five of the most important non-military 'new security challenges' influencing security policy and debate today: the environment, food, poverty, crime and gender. What we saw is that, oftentimes, these threats have made inroads into academic debates and policy discussions because of their impact on state security. Moving beyond states and people, discussed in Chapter 4, remains an ongoing process. Crime and climate change, for instance, have frequently been discussed through the lens of national security. The states in question, sadly and inevitably, tend to remain the powerful nations of the Western world. While poverty and famine (for example) shot to prominence in the dramatic prose of Kaplan's warnings on the coming anarchy, non-military issues are, however, increasingly discussed outside of the language of the nation-state. The seriousness of these security issues has been recognized for ethical and empirical reasons, without the prerequisite that they might impinge on the security of the state. This is also a process which is beginning to take place in the study of gender and security. To date, however, where issues of gender have shot to political prominence, it has tended to be in those areas where the apparently mutually exclusive categories – gender and security – have been fused together in an unusual juxtaposition, in such a manner as to generate significant political, public and media interest.

Finally, we considered three important tendencies in contemporary international security. The first factor of note concerned the observation that threats are determined not by the reality of their objective scale and consequence, but rather come to be through the establishment of particular meanings with discourse. Threats are framed as such in language and their meanings shift in line with the political demands of the time. Second, we noted the impact that preoccupations with securing the future have on policy. In the last decade, there has been no clearer example of this than the foreign and security policy of pre-emption within the War on Terror. Third, we noted that this interest in future security has adopted a focus in the present on calculating risk. While problematic in veiling the political nature of decisions on what to base such calculations upon, risk-based analyses of security can prove to be useful counter-weights to policy and strategy formulated in response to the dominant security discourses of the moment.

Further Reading

Dalby (2002) explores the rise of environmental issues within post-Cold War debates around security, while Elbe (2006) investigates the securitization of the HIV/AIDS pandemic. Hughes and Meng (2011) is a useful reader with excerpts from articles and other publications on a range of security issues, including disease pandemics, transnational crime, migration and economic issues. Sylvester (2002) investigates the impact of feminism on the study of International Relations.

Internet Resources

Histories of Violence (2014) is a research project that brings together scholars interested in questions of political violence. The website contains numerous interviews with and lectures by leading thinkers in the field. UK Cabinet Office (2012) contains the UK's National Risk Register of civil emergencies. Kaplan (1994) was an early discussion of environmental security, exploring how 'scarcity, crime, overpopulation, tribalism, and disease' were impacting upon social and political life.

Chapter 7

Is Security Possible?

Chapter Overview

This chapter explores how, and whether, security can be achieved. The discussion begins by contrasting two very different contemporary approaches to providing security: national missile defence programmes and the United Nations Millennium Campaign. These differ, we argue, not only because they mobilize different conceptions of security's meaning and referent. But, in addition, because they mobilize different views of the likelihood and means of security's achievement. The chapter's second section then develops this example by exploring competing approaches to security's possibility from realist, liberal, and a range of contemporary, 'critical' standpoints. In the third section we argue that disagreements between these approaches are partly a result of different assumptions about the possibility and dynamics of continuity and change – assumptions about time and history – in (global) political life. The chapter's final section then explores the importance of assumptions such as these within Security Studies more broadly. It does so by discussing the swathe of recent interest in 'the new' within international politics, tracing debates around new terrorism and new wars to illustrate.

Chapter Contents

Introduction

George W. Bush was elected forty-third President of the United States of America in November 2000. In less than twelve months, the US was embroiled in costly and protracted military engagements in Afghanistan and Iraq. Concomitant with these military adventures was a shifting of US foreign policy toward unilateralism and militaralism, in which, 'the Bush administration repudiated or declined to support a whole series of international agreements' (Dumbrell 2002: 279; also compare Mazaar 2003; Nossel 2004; Gaddis 2005). This movement was perhaps most visible in the reinvigorated push for a robust national missile defense (NMD) system that would incorporate:

> an air-based laser that shoots down missiles of all ranges during their boost phase, a so-called ground-based midcourse capability against short- and medium-range threats, terminal defences against long-range ICBMs capable of reaching the US, and a system of satellites to track enemy missiles and distinguish re-entry vehicles from decoys. (Bormann 2008: 54)

The Bush administration's interest in NMD was a product, in part, of a shifting post-Cold War landscape dominated by the threat of so-called 'rogue states', some of whom had made progress toward joining the 'nuclear club' in recent years (see Chapter 5). The search for national security through such means, however, has a far longer history than this, with roots stretching back to the 1960s and 1970s (Gordon 2001; Bormann 2008: 44). Although the system's proposed target, and technological capabilities, had since evolved, George W. Bush's strategy bore more than a passing resemblance to Ronald Reagan's earlier **Strategic Defense Initiative** (**SDI**): a 'space-based missile shield' (Weitz, 2010: 101) designed to provide security from Soviet missile attacks (see Box 7.1).

Some way removed from discussions of national missile defence is the United Nations' Millennium Campaign. Building on earlier UN efforts to connect development and security (King and Murray 2001; Thomas 2001) (including, most famously, the UNDP's 1994 *Human Development Report*), this campaign centres on eight **Millennium Development Goals** (MDGs) (see Table 7.1). Through signing the declaration, leaders of 189 states committed themselves to meeting a number of deliberately ambitious targets by the year 2015. These included: halving the proportion of people with an income of less than one dollar a day, eliminating gender disparity in primary and secondary education, and halting and reversing the spread of HIV/AIDS.

Box 7.1 President Reagan on the Strategic Defense Initiative

President Reagan's announcement of the Strategic Defense Initiative (SDI) on 23 March 1983 is often regarded as a landmark moment in US national security policy. In the following excerpts, Reagan (1983) makes his case for the SDI based on a need to rethink the strategy of nuclear deterrence:

> Since the dawn of the atomic age, we've sought to reduce the risk of war by maintaining a strong deterrent and by seeking genuine arms control. 'Deterrence' means simply this: making sure any adversary who thinks about attacking the United States, or our allies, or our vital interest, concludes that the risks to him outweigh any potential gains. Once he understands that, he won't attack. We maintain the peace through our strength; weakness only invites aggression.

> This strategy of deterrence has not changed. It still works. But what it takes to maintain deterrence has changed. It took one kind of military force to deter an attack when, we had far more nuclear weapons than any other power; it takes another kind now that the Soviets, for example, have enough accurate and powerful nuclear weapons to destroy virtually all of our missiles on the ground. Now, this is not to say that the Soviet Union is planning to make war on us. Nor do I believe a war is inevitable – quite the contrary. But what must be recognized is that our security is based on being prepared to meet all threats.

> ... Let me share with you a vision of the future which offers hope. It is that we embark on a program to counter the awesome Soviet missile threat with measures that are defensive. Let us turn to the very strengths in technology that spawned our great industrial base and that have given us the quality of life we enjoy today. What if free people could live secure in the knowledge that their security did not rest upon the threat of instant U.S. retaliation to deter a Soviet attack, that we could intercept and destroy strategic ballistic missiles before they reached our own soil or that of our allies?

Source: Reagan (1983).

In a 2011 report on progress toward these goals, a number of significant successes were highlighted. Amongst these were: a reduction of global child mortality such that 12,000 fewer children were dying *per day* in 2009 compared to 1990; improved access to clean drinking

Table 7.1 *Millennium Development Goals*

Goal	Successes	Challenges
Eradicate extreme poverty and hunger	• Extreme poverty rates were halved by 2010. • 294 million workers were lifted above the poverty line of $1.25 a day by 2011.	• 1.2 billion people still live in extreme poverty. • More than 100 million children under five remain under-nourished and under-weight.
Achieve universal primary education	• Enrolment in primary education in developing regions reached 90% in 2010. • The literacy gap between young men and young women has reduced from 100: 90 to 100: 95.	• 57 million primary school age children were still out of school in 2011. • 123 million youth lack basic reading and writing skills: 61% of whom are women.
Promote gender equality and empower women	• 40% of wage-earning jobs in the non-agricultural sector were held by women in 2011. • The global share of women in parliament rose to 20% in 2012.	• Only 2 of 130 countries have achieved gender equality at all levels of education. • Women only occupy 25% of senior management positions globally.
Reduce child mortality	• Global deaths of children under the age of five declined from 12.4 million in 1990 to 6.6 million in 2012. • Since 2000, measles vaccines have averted over 10 million deaths.	• 1 in 9 children die before the age of five in Sub-Saharan Africa. • 1 in 6 children in Southern Asia die before the age of five. <div align="right">→</div>

water for over a billion people between 1990 and 2008; and a twenty per cent reduction in global deaths from malaria between 2000 and 2009 (United Nations 2011: 4). As the report also noted, however, considerable work was still to be done, with gender equality and women's empowerment representing particular causes for concern (United Nations 2011: 4–5).

The two above approaches to security could hardly be more different. Where the former prioritizes (American) national security, the latter locates the individual human as its primary referent (see Chapter 4). Second, the UN's Millennium Campaign also takes a remit extending far beyond (here, human) survival (see Chapter 1). As Table 7.1 indicates, this includes improvements in education and environmental sustainability, amongst other things. Third, the two approaches

→

Goal	Successes	Challenges
Improve maternal health	• Maternal mortality has nearly halved since 1990. • 81% of women in developing regions received antenatal care by 2011.	• Nearly 50 million babies are still delivered without specialist care. • Only 50% of women in developing regions receive the health care they need.
Combat HIV/AIDS, malaria and other diseases	• 9.7 million people were receiving life-saving medicines for HIV in 2012. • Treatment for tuberculosis averted 20 million deaths between 1995 and 2011.	• 2.5 million people are newly affected with HIV every year. • 7 million people still lacked access to HIV medicines in 2011.
Ensure environmental sustainability	• More than 2 billion people gained access to improved drinking water sources between 1990 and 2010. • Since 1990, protected areas of the earth's surface have increased in number by 58%.	• Global emissions of carbon dioxide (CO_2) have increased by more than 46 per cent since 1990. • 863 million people are estimated to be living in slums in 2012 compared to 650 million in 1990.
Develop a global partnership for development	• Official development assistance stood at $126 billion in 2012. • The developing country share of world trade rose to 44% in 2012.	• Only 26% of inhabitants in developing countries are Internet users. • Trade tariffs imposed by developed countries on products from developing countries are largely unchanged since 2004.

Note: Information taken from: http://www.un.org/millenniumgoals/global. shtml.

rely upon very different policy mechanisms for the achievement of security. Here, the former's prioritization of advanced military technologies stands in marked contrast to the broader sweep of policy instruments employed by the UN campaign, which include investments in health, education and water (UNDP 2010).

These differences are significant because they illuminate the diversity of policy apparatuses that might be used to enhance security. In this chapter we focus on the importance of such differences – as well as the assumptions from which they derive – in order to ask whether security is a realistic or achievable goal. By charting competing answers to this question offered by some of the approaches introduced in earlier chapters, we argue here that these differences exist not only because of different underpinning conceptions of security, its referent, and contemporary security threats. But, in addition, because these approaches mobilize very different understandings of the possibilities and drivers of genuine change in global political life. For these reasons, the chapter concludes by exploring the importance of claims about time and history within discussions of international security more generally. As we illustrate, to argue that the world faces a new type of terrorism is to make an argument about time as much as one about terrorism.

Key Points

- US plans for a national missile defense system offer a statist attempt to augment national security via advanced military technologies.
- The UN Millennium Development Campaign offers an example of an integrated and multi-dimensional approach to improving human security, as well as development.
- Different approaches toward the achievement of security are a product, in part, of different understandings of security, its referent, and security threats.
- These differences are also, importantly, a product of different understandings of the possibility and significance of change in global politics.

Security Studies and the possibility of security

As discussed in this book's Introduction, political realism remains the dominant intellectual paradigm for the academic study of security. Three broad assumptions within this paradigm are particularly important for thinking through the possibility of security as seen via a realist lens. First, is a belief in the existence of international anarchy (the absence of any global sovereign) as the ordering principle – or structure – of the international system. Second, a prioritization of states as the key actors in global politics. Although other actors do exist – and, indeed, do influence global outcomes – it is states, ultimately, that determine the outcomes of international relations (although, compare Ashley 1984 with Gilpin 1984). As Waltz (1979: 94) put it: 'states set the scene in which they, along with nonstate actors, stage their dramas or carry on their humdrum affairs'. For many realists, moreover, it is often acceptable (for purposes of parsimony and explanatory power) to approach states as unitary and rational actors: as singular, self-interested entities (although, see Mearsheimer 2009: 241). A third common assumption is the importance of power distributions in the international system. Profound events within the global arena can be understood, often, by continuities, and particularly changes, in these distributions (measured, typically, by material indicators). As Schmidt (2007: 43) suggests: 'Realists throughout the ages have argued that power is the decisive determinant in the relations among separate political communities and of crucial importance to understanding the dynamics of war and peace.' What, then, does all this mean for the possibility of security?

First, and most importantly, it means that the realm of international politics is a competitive, conflictual and ultimately unstable environment. The absence of any global sovereign, combined with the self-interested nature of states, means that: (i) war is perpetually possible, and perhaps even likely. It also means (ii) that no state can rely completely on any other actor (state or non-state) as a guarantor of security. For classical realists it is the human desire for power and dominance that explains this constant threat of war. As Morgenthau (1993: 4) argued at the beginning of *Politics Among Nations*: 'Political realism believes that politics, like society in general, is governed by objective laws that have their roots in human nature.' For structural realists, in contrast, it is the logic of anarchy that coerces states into acting in a self-interested way:

> With many sovereign states, with no system of law enforceable among them, with each state judging its grievances and ambitions according to the dictates of its own reason or desire – conflict, sometimes leading to war, is bound to occur. (Waltz 2001: 159)

Second, particularly within structural variants of realism, there exists a debate over the possibility of temporary stability within the international system (see, for example, Taliaferro 2000). Offensive realists, on the one hand, argue that survival is a product of the amount of power held by a state. As such, states will seek to maximize their own security by increasing their power relative to that of potential competitors. This might take place, for example, by going to war with rival states, blackmailing them, or by encouraging competitors to enter into costly and protracted wars with one another (Mearsheimer 2001). Defensive realists, on the other hand, believe states are often more restrained than offensive realists suggest: that they are security, rather, than power, maximizers. In this approach, survival is often best satisfied through consolidating a state's position in the international arena rather seeking to better it. This is, partly, down to the **offensive-defensive balance** where offensive behaviours are typically more costly than their defensive counterparts (see Lynne-Jones 1995). It is also, partly, because of the security dilemma, where the augmentation of military capabilities for defensive purposes is likely to trigger fear and insecurity amongst rivals, leading to counter-augmentation and, consequently, insecurity for self and other alike.

Third, whether understood by appeal to structure (international anarchy) or agency (national self-interest), realists agree that states tend to search for security via self-help behaviour. As Waltz (2001: 159) argues, within such a conflictual, anarchical environment, each 'state has to rely on its own devices, the relative efficiency of which must be its constant concern'. Two such devices, in particular, attract realist attention (see, for example, Snyder 1991; Schweller 1997). First, bandwagoning, which involves (typically smaller) states siding with a more powerful or threatening state to benefit from the security this new alliance may bring. Second, balancing, which involves offsetting (or balancing against) a more powerful or threatening state. Mechanisms for doing this include forming alliances with other states against a perceived threat (external balancing) and increasing one's own military strength, for example by growing defence spending (internal balancing). Neither strategy of bandwagoning nor balancing, however, guarantees permanent security. The former assumes that the more powerful state may be relied on into the future: a dangerous assumption given the self-interested nature of all states. In the case of the latter, external balancing via alliance construction is a difficult and time-consuming process, while internal balancing is a costly endeavour limited by the resources available to a state.

Fourth, and finally, because the root causes of conflict (whether in human nature or international anarchy) are effectively permanent and unchanging, and because of the difficulties involved in balancing and bandwagoning, national security will only ever be temporary and precarious. The emergence of revisionist powers (states seeking to alter their position in the global system), misperceptions of the security-seeking behaviours of other states, the collapse of alliances and much else besides all have the potential to spark conflict between states. This is why political realists are, 'generally pessimistic about the prospects for eliminating conflict and war' (Walt 1998: 31).

The realist scepticism toward security's durability is countered, within mainstream Security Studies, by liberal approaches. As outlined in the Introduction, there is again considerable diversity in this tradition, although three routes to the achievement of security are particularly prominent. First, and perhaps most famous, is the democratic peace thesis, described by Jack Levy as 'the closest thing we have to an empirical law in international relations' (cited in Dunn 2009: 108; see also Doyle 2005: 466; and Chapter 3). This thesis argues that democratic states very rarely enter into war with other democracies. Explanations for this vary amongst its proponents (see Maoz and Russett 1993). Structural explanations emphasize the importance of domestic public opinion, where public support for a war may prove difficult for a democratic leadership to sustain. Normative explanations, in contrast, argue that societies governed by the non-violent resolution of conflicts (such as democracies) externalize this norm in their relations with other (ostensibly similar) states. Although numerous criticisms have been levelled at the thesis (see Owen 1994: 87–9) – including over its definitional ambiguities (what, exactly, constitutes democracy and war?) and this correlation's significance (if inter-state war is itself a comparative rarity does the absence of democratic war actually mean anything significant?) – it does offer a radically different view on security's possibility from the realist assumptions with which we began.

First, this thesis implies that absolute or relative power may not be decisive in determining whether security is achieved. Inter-state relations may be affected by a whole range of factors including expectations around the interests and actions of other states (as in normative explanations), or the workings of domestic political architectures (as in structural explanations). Indeed, the importance of domestic political architectures within this approach is indicative of a broader liberal commitment to 'inside-out' analyses of global politics, where the internal organization of a state is seen as impacting upon its external, foreign policy behaviour (Burchill 1996: 61). Second, democratic peace thesis also implies the possibility of a future world order in which war – and the insecurity generated by war and its threat – is either greatly reduced or absent (Gartzke 2000: 193). Thus, while liberalism and democracy themselves offer no guarantee of pacific behaviour (democracies frequently go to war with non-democracies), a gradual expansion of liberal democracy may be an important contributor to the expansion of pacific international relations. In Doyle's phrasing, liberalism 'has strengthened the prospects for a world peace established by the steady expansion of a separate peace among liberal societies' (cited in Kinsella 2005: 453; see also Doyle 1986).

A second liberal approach to security may be termed 'commercial pacifism'. This approach puts its optimism in the benefits of economic integration (for example, via trade or transnational production arrangements) for inter-state relations (see Box 7.2).

Explanations of the consequences of commerce for peace combine a number of related arguments (see Friedman 2005: 362–3). First, is the claim that two states involved in a close economic relationship have a

---

Box 7.2 Commercial pacifism and the World Trade Organization (WTO)

The idea that economic integration aids peaceful inter-state relations arguably underpins much of the neo-liberal architecture of the current international system. One example can be found in the World Trade Organization (WTO): the International Governmental Organization (IGO) responsible for the management of transnational trade. The following demonstrates the importance of this idea to this organization's self-image:

> Peace is partly an outcome of two of the most fundamental principles of the trading system: helping trade to flow smoothly, and providing countries with a constructive and fair outlet for dealing with disputes over trade issues. It is also an outcome of the international confidence and cooperation that the system creates and reinforces.

> History is littered with examples of trade disputes turning into war. One of the most vivid is the trade war of the 1930s when countries competed to raise trade barriers in order to protect domestic producers and retaliate against each others' barriers. This worsened the Great Depression and eventually played a part in the outbreak of World War 2.

Source: World Trade Organization (2008).

---

reduced incentive to engage in military conflict because of the detrimental economic impact this might have: for example, upon demand for their exports by the other state, or in terms of harm to production facilities situated there. Second, there are also significant opportunity costs involved in going to war; an activity which is seldom as rewarding as successful commerce. And, third, regular and sustained contact via trade may foster relations of trust, even friendship, between states: relations that, again, might reduce the prospects of military conflict. This third assumption sees broadly ideational factors enter discussions of commercial pacifism to supplement rationalist arguments predicated on notions of material self-interest.

A final liberal explanation emerged within International Relations' neo-neo debate or 'synthesis' of the 1980s (see Wæver 1996; Chapter 1), and may be termed neo-liberal institutionalism. Neo-liberal institutionalism argues that cooperation, and the stability it brings, is possible even within an anarchical world dominated by self-interested states.

Crucial within this, as the name suggests, is the role of international institutions which 'can provide information, reduce transaction costs, make commitments more credible, establish focal points for coordination, and in general facilitate the operation of reciprocity' (Keohane and Martin 1995: 42). Put more simply, international institutions: first, make it more difficult for states to 'cheat' on the agreements they make; second, help to prevent disputes escalating to conflict when they do occur; and, third, assist in the solution of collective action problems where rational individual behaviour generates sub-optimal outcomes for all (see Grieco 1988: 495). Underpinning all of this is the assumption that states are interested in absolute rather than relative gains. Whether State B might benefit (and perhaps disproportionately) from cooperation through institutional arrangements, is of less concern to State A than the gains that State A itself will make via participation. Institutions, therefore, offer an opportunity for mitigating anarchy's conflictual logic assumed within realist approaches.

To recap, briefly, we have thus far explored a number of ways in which the two most prominent traditions within Security Studies have dealt with the provision of security. Each of the mechanisms we have looked at already – balancing, bandwagoning, military strengthening, democracy, trade, and international institutions – share at least three things in common. First, a prioritization of national security, wherein the security of the state as referent dominates the attention of these analyses (see Chapter 4). Second, an emphasis on mitigating the security threat posed by *other* states in the international system. And, third, a prioritization of military threats as the most significant – if not sole – security challenges (see Chapter 5). Yet, as we have argued throughout this book, a number of contemporary approaches take issue with these assumptions. As such, we should not be surprised to encounter a diversity of views on this question of security's provision from beyond the realist/liberal mainstream. To explore these differences, and their significance, further, let us return first to the Critical Security Studies (CSS) literature.

The CSS framework views security as a condition that is inseparable from emancipation (Booth 1991). In the words of Ken Booth (2007: 115):

> to practise security (freeing people from the life-determining conditions of insecurity) is to promote emancipatory space (freedom from oppression, and so some opportunity to explore being human), and to realise emancipation (becoming more fully human) is to practise security (not against others, but with them).

This reconceptualization of security poses two important implications for thinking about how this experience might be achieved. First, it cautions against the pursuit of security via instrumentalist or exclusivist means. This means that one's own security cannot be pursued either through unethical practices, or at the expense of the security of others. In this sense, there is some similarity with human security approaches to security's indivisibility (Thomas 2001: 161). Second, this framework also approaches security and emancipation as *processes*, rather than endpoints or goals. It will always be possible to free people further from constraints (material and ideational) that prohibit their living as they would choose to do. In concrete terms, these commitments lead Booth (2007: 428–41) to advocate a series of mechanisms for the advancement of security, including: (i) delegitimizing violence, including war, as a political tool; (ii) promoting democracy on the domestic and international stage; (iii) respecting national and international law; and (iv) enhancing human rights consistency.

The CSS approach obviously has some parallels with liberal views on the achievement of security, not least in its concern with: (i) the significance and value of transnational laws and norms, and (ii) the consequences of domestic political structures for security. At the same time, a rejection of the state as security's guarantor is grounded in a view of the self-interested state with greater resemblance to traditional realist thought. The CSS emphasis on security as a process rather than an achievable condition, moreover, also has parallels with the impermanence or impossibility of security within political realism. Where CSS differs from each of these traditional approaches, however, is, first, in its view of the human as the ultimate referent of security (Chapter 4). And, second, in its emphasis on **immanent critique**. This critical strategy involves seeking the potential for change – or 'concrete utopias' (Wyn Jones 1999: 76–8) – within the world as it currently exists, blighted though it may be by 'a contagion of morbid symptoms' such as child poverty, preventable diseases and environmental devastation (Booth 2007: 12; compare Burke 2007). Thus, while the international human rights regime is far from perfect, for advocates of CSS it still offers some hope for the future security of peoples across the globe. As Booth (2007: 250) puts it:

> situations have within them possibilities of a better life ... Immanent critique involves identifying those features within concrete situations (such as positive dynamics, agents, key struggles) that have emancipatory possibilities, and then working through the politics (tactics and strategies) to strengthen them.

The effort of CSS to centre individuals within the study and provision of security resonates with much contemporary debate around the related concept of human security. Each of these approaches takes concrete sources of human insecurity as the starting point for their analysis; each, too, adopts an explicitly normative stance toward security as a desirable (if never fully achievable) condition (see Chapter 8). Most important of all, however, for this chapter's purposes is a shared prioritization of people over states as security's referent.

At a minimum, advocates of human security agree that a vast range of harms afflict people across the world (see Chapter 6). These harms – including poverty, diseases, malnourishment and crime, as well as inter-state war – tend also to be viewed as addressable, albeit via considerable effort from the international community. Beyond this shared commitment, however, different interpretations of the concept lead to very different recommendations for security's provision. As Newman (2001) notes, these include: (i) support for humanitarian or peace operations where states fail to provide for their citizenry's security; (ii) basic human needs approaches which emphasize poverty reduction programmes; and (iii) support for endogenous and local development initiatives. As with CSS, discussions of human security tend to imply that further work toward the realization of security is always possible. As the 1994 UNDP Report from which much of this literature derives argued: 'In the final analysis, human security is a child who did not die, a disease that did not spread, a job that was not cut, an ethnic tension that did not explode in violence, a dissident who was not silenced. Human security is not a concern with weapons – it is a concern with human life and dignity' (UNDP 1994).

Because of considerable disagreements (ontological, epistemological and normative) within feminist scholarship on international security (and the role of gender therein) it is not possible to identify one common route toward security's provision within this literature. Liberal feminists tend to advocate an opening up of national and international political structures to the participation of women. Radical feminists emphasize the distinctiveness of men and women, associating the conflictual, aggressive, competitive character of global politics with masculinity. The assumption of radical feminists that women's insights and experiences might hold potential for a more cooperative international arena has been criticized, by some, for reinforcing essentialist arguments about the two sexes (compare Fukuyama 1998 and Tickner 1999). Post-structuralist feminists are far more sceptical about claims that women (and men) have a distinctive essence. Instead, they are interested in the ways in which representations or performances of sex and gender constitute these identities and the global political dynamics in which they are implicated. As Sjoberg (2009: 188) explains, this involves exploring how 'gendered linguistic manifestations of meaning, particularly strong/weak, rational/emotional, and public/private dichotomies, serve to empower the masculine, marginalize the feminine, and constitute global politics'. And, in so doing, working toward the deconstruction of these meanings and their manifestations, because: 'The dominant voice of militarized masculinity and decontextualised rationality speaks so loudly in our culture, it will remain difficult for any other voices to be heard until that voice loses some of its power to define what we hear and how we name the world – until that voice is delegitimated' (Cohn 1987: 717–18).

Feminist efforts to deconstruct security discourses and the policies they make possible have been particularly important in demonstrating how efforts to create security are always constituted by broader ideas about gender. Carol Cohn's (1987) work on US nuclear strategy in the late Cold War period, in which she charted the saturation of these debates with heavily gendered assumptions and constructs, is illuminating: 'white men in ties discussing missile size' (Cohn 1987: 692), as she neatly puts it. In her analysis (see also Chapter 3), she highlights the way euphemisms ('clean bombs'; 'surgical strikes'), sexualized imagery ('penetration aids'; 'missile hardening') and the like combined to make the aggressive and expensive nuclear policies of this era a possible and legitimate enterprise amongst policy communities. More recently, Laura Shepherd's (2008, 2010) research into **UN Security Council Resolution 1325** (adopted in the year 2000) has demonstrated that even well-intentioned efforts to address gendered violences risk reproducing dominant constructions of gender. This resolution – on Women, Peace and Security – called for an enhanced sensitivity to gendered violence and inequalities in all future efforts at peace-building and post-conflict reconstruction (Shepherd 2008: 383). In so doing, however, it contributed to the longstanding positioning of women as victims of violence within global politics: as passive and vulnerable to (agential) men.

Post-structuralist feminist writings echo a broader post-structuralist concern to deconstruct dominant frameworks of violence and (in)security. Binary oppositions and the work that they do in stabilizing social and political meaning attract particular interest. Binary oppositions are pairs of seemingly antithetical terms that are paradoxically dependent upon each other for their meaning, for instance: reason/emotion; mind/body; man/woman; tolerance/intolerance, universal/particular. In each case, the meaning of one term is constructed by its opposition to the other. For post-structuralists, such pairings and their dominance in Western thought are problematic for three reasons (see Borradori

2003: 138–9). First, they are rigid: each opposition marginalizes and excludes that which does not conform neatly to either term. Where, for instance, do transgendered or intersex people fit into a man/woman schema? Second, each pairing also enacts a hierarchy in which one term is privileged over its opposite: the former, in each of the above examples. And, third, the stability of each pairing in philosophical and political discourse works to mask its contingency: there is nothing inevitable about any of these labels or their perceived oppositions, they are human constructs.

This post-structuralist perspective is important because it pulls attention to the reliance of security upon its own opposition: insecurity. Within dominant discursive frameworks it makes no sense – it is impossible – to think of a territory (such as a state) or an identity (such as a nation) as secure, without contrasting this with the insecurity of other places (beyond the state's borders), or other identities (external security threats). The domestic/international dualism upon which much International Relations theory relies offers a very powerful example of this (see Walker 1993). Here, appeals to the 'inside' of the state as a space of security, order and progress depend on constructions of the 'external' international realm as a site of insecurity, anarchy, and time-lessness. National security discourses, policies and technologies, similarly, rely on the identification, or construction, of threatening others: the construction of insecurities that both threaten, and therefore mark the limit of, the self. The historical reproduction of the United States' self-identity, for instance, has relied on the articulation of a whole series of dangers and risks, including witchcraft, communism, terrorism and illegal drugs (Campbell 1998b). The point here is that security practices not only rely upon constructions of insecurity. They also frequently create or (re)produce insecurities of their own. Security initiatives – CCTV cameras, 'peace walls', armed police, humanitarian operations, anti-terrorist legislation, drug control policies, curfews – generate insecurity and fear at the same time as they seek to enhance security (see Box 7.3). As Burke (2007: 13) argues, it is therefore impossible to think, experience or enact security without also thinking, experiencing or enacting insecurity:

> dreams of security, prosperity and freedom hinge, from their earliest conceptualisations to the contemporary politics of the national security state, on the insecurity and dying of others. Our societies run, prosper and survive – however dangerously and dysfunctionally – on the back of a political economy of death and suffering that is embedded and legitimised in our most basic ethical and political ideals.

Box 7.3 The (im)possibility of (in)security

Recent discussions of (in)securitization associated with the Paris School of Security Studies emphasize the extent to which security technologies and practices generate insecurity as well as security. As an example, consider the following discussion from a focus group on anti-terrorism policy in the UK that centred on the recent installation in Birmingham of CCTV cameras using anti-terrorism monies. In debating the purpose and meaning of these cameras, the participants demonstrate security's ambiguous relation to insecurity:

> Participant 1: But you guys, don't you think it's more safe and secure, they're doing that. I mean, it's our housing, isn't it?

> Participant 2: No, it's an invasion of privacy.

> Participant 1: It's an invasion of privacy, but there is some sense of security, because there are some loonies out there. Not the cameras, but just generally, you know, if there is tight security.

> Participant 2: It's not for our security though, it's for others.

Source: *Anti-Terrorism, Citizenship and Security in the UK* research project. Available at http://www.esrc.ac.uk/my-esrc/grants/RES-000-22-3765/read.

These explorations of security's imbrication with insecurity take us some distance from the liberal optimism explored above. Indeed, we are closer, here, to our realist starting point of security's temporary and precarious character, where the quest for national (self-)security results, ultimately, in insecurity for the other and the self (see also Peoples and Vaughan-Williams 2010: 70). *Either* security *or* insecurity has been replaced with *both* security *and* insecurity. In this sense, in relation to this chapter's overarching question of security's possibility, liberalism exists as something of an outlier within IR Theory and Security Studies. While versions of human security, Critical Security Studies and feminist security studies posit opportunities for (and routes to) enhanced security, each of these approaches tend to fall short of the promise of (potential) absolute security within liberal thinking on democracy, institutions and trade. The question, then, is how are we to explain these differences? What is it that pulls realists, post-structuralists and others back from envisioning full, complete, security in the present and future?

| **Key Points** |

- For realists, security is possible only as a temporary and precarious condition. Mechanisms for achieving it include balancing, bandwagoning and military power.
- Liberal approaches to security are diverse. Major emphases, however, include democracy, trade, and international institutions. Liberal approaches tend to be more optimistic over the prospects of security's longevity.
- Advocates of CSS emphasize the need to work within but transform the current (imperfect) world to enhance security. They also appeal for a congruity of means and ends in pursuing security.
- Human security approaches agree that a range of harms afflict the security of individuals. Responses advocated include humanitarian interventions and endogenous, local, development initiatives.
- Feminist security studies emphasize the gendered nature of insecurities. Different strands of feminism, however, suggest different routes toward security, depending, in part, on different conceptions of gender and its role within global politics.
- Post-structuralist and Paris School approaches point to the interdependence of security and insecurity. Here, security as an ontologically complete condition becomes impossible.

Security Studies, continuity and change

The approaches considered above differ markedly in their view of security's possibility. Most obviously, their prioritization of different referents leads to an emphasis on quite different security challenges. This, in turn, has implications for the policy mechanisms advocated for security's satisfaction, and, indeed, for perceptions of the prospects for resolving posited threats. Thus, a framework that views poverty as the most significant contemporary challenge to (human) security will support a quite different take on the route to, and likelihood of, security than one emphasizing the threat of inter-state war to (national) security.

In this section, however, we argue that the varying degrees of optimism explored above are also connected to another key issue within the Philosophy of Social Science. That issue – the nature and rhythm of social and political change over time – is one, we suggest, on which all approaches to security take a stance. Indeed, it is an issue with which all efforts at social and political analysis must grapple in fashioning coherent explanations of the world around us. For, as Hayden White

(1980: 27) notes, it is only through ordering the world's events into recognizable forms (stories or narratives) that those events can be given meaning and hence rendered amenable to explanation, understanding or prediction:

> The notion that sequences of real events possess the formal attributes of the stories we tell about imaginary events could only have its origins in wishes, daydreams, reveries. Does the world really present itself to perception in the form of well-made stories, with central subjects, proper beginnings, middles and ends, and a coherence that permits us to see 'the end' in every beginning? Or does it present itself more in the forms that the annals and chronicles suggest, either as mere sequence without beginning or end, or as sequences of beginnings that only terminate and never conclude?

White's argument draws on a very particular understanding of time in which events and their connections only become meaningful once inserted into coherent stories. His suggestion, however, has significance beyond this, for it encourages us to ask what type of narrative – what type of story – our above approaches to security employ in their efforts to make sense of the world. How, for instance, are events in the past, present and future imagined, represented and linked in the stories they tell us? And, how do particular understandings of time's 'shape' or movement emerge from, and help sustain, these distinct stories?

In realist security studies, as we have seen, security is viewed typically as a temporary and precarious accomplishment, at best. Although defensive realists tend to be slightly more optimistic than their offensive counterparts, perpetual security remains an elusive ambition. A toxic combination of competition, uncertainty and self-interest means armed conflict is an ever-present possibility as the power and fortunes of particular states wax and wane. As such, international politics follows a similar logic today as it did decades, even centuries ago. The lessons of long-dead scholars – Thucydides, Machiavelli, Hobbes, Rousseau and the like – remain just as relevant for understanding contemporary events as they do for our analyses of the Peloponnesian wars and other past conflicts. As Robert Cox (1996: 92) summarizes nicely in relation to contemporary versions of realism: 'history becomes for neorealists a quarry providing materials with which to illustrate variations on always-recurrent themes'.

This realist approach to security relies on a very particular understanding of time as a static horizon. Although changes do occur in the international system – a particular state may see its power rise or fall, for example – the really significant aspects of global life endure relatively unchanged. History, therefore, is timeless. Security – present and future – cannot be imagined much less achieved because the dynamics and logics of international politics do not change. This is particularly true for structural variants of realism, which have difficulty in accounting for qualitative, systemic change by their very nature (see Hay 2002). Yet, as Buzan (1996: 60) notes, this emphasis on historical repetition is shared by advocates of political realism of various persuasions:

> power politics, the logic of survival, and the dynamics of (in)security do seem to be universally relevant to international relations. At any period of history it is very hard to escape from the fact that the major powers do play the central role in defining international political and economic order...Thus while the particular circumstances and conditions of history change from era to era, there does seem to be a certain continuity to some aspects of political life.

This relatively static understanding of international politics contrasts with the faith in institutions, commerce, and democracy as potential game changers within liberal thought. As we saw, liberals view each of these as having the capacity not only to alter the prospects of national and international security, but to improve them, and perhaps permanently so. Realism's timelessness, then, is substituted here for a very different understanding of time as a broadly evolutionary process. Gradual, and incremental, historical change is a genuine and real possibility, particularly given the importance of absolute security gains, and the presence of human rationality. Improvements in security may not be uninterrupted. Events – unforeseen and unpredicted – will still puncture this process of progress. Still, extending across these is the possibility of a perceptible linear trend toward human improvement, and a mitigation of humanity's and/or anarchy's worst excesses. As one of the most famous advocates of contemporary liberal thought argued about criticisms of his 'end of history' thesis: 'what I suggested had come to an end was not the occurrence of events, even large and grave events, but History: that is, history understood as a single, coherent, evolutionary process, when taking into account the experience of all peoples in all times' (Fukuyama 1992: xii).

Assumptions about timelessness and historical progress that underpin realist and liberal stories of security respectively have been questioned on a number of grounds. In the case of the former, critiques have included the following. First, an insufficient attention to moments of profound historical transformation in the history of global politics, not least the emergence of the modern state system itself. This is why political realism is so frequently criticized for having failed to predict the end of the Cold War in 1989. Second, is an inadequate recognition of the importance of the specific historical location from which claims about timelessness are written. Here, as Rengger and Thirkell-White (2007: 6) put it: 'the theorist is situated as much as a creature of the historical circumstances of the time as that which is being investigated'. And, third, the possibility that this understanding of history itself fore-closes the potential for radical change in the future of international politics (Bell 2003: 807). Here, realism has been criticized by construc-tivist theorists, amongst others, as a self-fulfilling prophecy. If state leaders believe the international realm to be inherently and inescapably competitive they will act as if that is the case. This, in turn, is likely to (re)produce the world in that image (see, for example, Wendt 1992, 1995).

In the case of liberal thinking on security's future(s), again, a number of important critiques may be made. First, the linear notion of time underpinning notions of historical progress might also be accused of insufficient self-reflection on its origins. From a post-colonial posi-tion, this view of historical change may appear profoundly Eurocentric in its emphasis on Western histories, institutions and powers; and, more importantly, in its approach to these institutions and interests as ethical and progressive (Barkawi and Laffey 2006: 340). Alternative histories of international relations – emphasizing voices and experiences from the global South, for example – would address the former, and cast considerable doubt on the latter. Second, from a radical feminist standpoint, liberal notions of linear time may also be critiqued as implicitly gendered. Here, understandings of time as a directional, progressive dynamic draw (even if unconsciously) on men's experience and expectations of time, and, as such, they might be insufficiently attuned to the cultural and corporeal experiences of women (see Kristeva 1981; O'Brien 1989: 14–16; Leccardi 1996: 173–5). Third, although much liberal thought is appropriately nuanced, there is also a danger of teleology here where contingent and unexpected events are simply incorporated into pre-existing visions of the future.

As a result of such criticisms, some of the more contemporary approaches to security attempt to steer clear of these very particular understandings of time, often by drawing on a more sophisticated approach to historical change. In CSS literatures, for instance, a belief that security can genuinely be enhanced (if not, ever, fully completed) avoids the stasis of realist thought on history at the same time as it credits human agency with the capability of enacting change in the security arena. The importance of immanent critique and the search for 'realizable utopias' (Wyn Jones 2005: 230) within this approach also signals reflection on the extent to which human futures (national and international) are borne out of the concrete, lived circumstances of the present. This is why emancipation (as the means *and* end of security) acts, for Booth (2005a: 182) and others, as a guide for tactical goal setting as well as a normative anchorage. Future security – and future insecurity – then, is not, here, determined or inevitable. The goal of (critical) scholars (and citizens) is a constant working toward improvements in the life conditions of people, especially those who are most marginalized by existing, and pernicious, structures of political, economic and social life. As Booth (2005a: 182) puts it:

> As a result of engaging in immanent critique emancipatory ideas can develop that in turn can be translated into tactical action. Praxis is the coming together of one's theoretical commitment to critique and political orientation to emancipation in projects of reconstruction.

The point of this section is not to argue for the merits of any of these understandings of change. Indeed, each understanding should be viewed as a construction in which different points in time are connected, and their relationships plotted. What is important, however, is to understand the extent to which all perspectives on security's (im)possibility depend on underlying ontological assumptions about the nature, drivers and extent of political change. These assumptions both inform, and emerge from, the discussions of democracy, bandwagoning and so on considered above. In the chapter's final section we now illustrate this by turning to recent discussions of 'the new' in the study of security, building in the process on the discussion of Chapter 6.

Key Points

- All perspectives on security draw upon ontological assumptions about the character, drivers and possibility of change.
- The impermanence of security within realist thought reflects and reinforces a particular understanding of time as a static, unchanging dynamic.
- Liberal optimism about security's possibility is rooted in an evolutionary conception of time.
- Critical Security Studies tends to view the future as open, and changeable. From this perspective it is the task of critics to shape the present and future through pursuing emancipatory projects.

Security Studies and 'the new'

The extent to which debates around international security are satu-
rated by temporal claims and imaginaries can be demonstrated further
by looking at the emphasis on novelty and newness in this field. In this
section, we explore two very prominent examples of this, focusing in
turn on 'new terrorism' and 'new wars' (see Table 7.2). As argued
below, one of the most interesting aspects of these categorizations is
the different discursive functions they perform. As we will show, 'the
new' is rarely invoked simply to describe external events or dynamics.

Debates around new terrorism came to the fore in the late 1990s
(Jackson *et al.* 2011: 165–7). For advocates of this categorization (for
example, Laqueur 1999; Simon and Benjamin 2000; Hoffman 2006), the
last decade of the twentieth century witnessed the emergence of a qualita-
tively new type of terrorism bearing strikingly limited resemblance to its
historical forebears. First, where earlier organizations, such as the
Provisional IRA, modelled themselves on national militaries with their
formal leadership structures, new groups, such as al Qaeda, were far
more diffuse in their organization, perhaps better understood as a
network, a movement, or even an ideology (see Neumann 2009; Jarvis
2012). Second, where 'old terrorism' had been motivated, primarily, by
political ambitions – whether revolutionary, nationalist-separatist, or
right-wing – new terrorism was deemed to be driven by fanatical religious
ideologies. Third, where old terrorism organized, drew support from, and
targeted its violence locally (for example, ETA in the Basque region), new
terrorism's ambitions and activities were less constrained by geographical
boundaries: their funding, recruits and targets all being international.
And, finally, where old terrorist organizations were selective in their
targets, new terrorism has been marked by a movement toward indis-
criminate, and sometimes mass casualty, attacks. New terrorism, thus,
may be seen less as a form of political communication, and more as an
acting out of irrational hatreds. As R. James Woolsey (cited in Morgan
2004: 30–1) provocatively put it: 'Today's terrorists don't want a seat at
the table, they want to destroy the table and everyone sitting at it.'

The old/new terrorism distinction is, of course, typically presented
with more nuance than the above summary allows. For Neumann
(2009), for instance, the labels are most usefully viewed as ideal types,
in that certain groups ('old' and 'new') will be more closely identifiable
with these characteristics than others. In spite of this circumspection, a
number of critics have challenged this thesis on empirical and political
grounds (compare Spencer 2006 and Kurtulus 2011). Empirically,
many have suggested that the distinctions between old and new terrorism are less profound than this binary construction implies. Tucker

(2001: 3), for instance, argues that old terrorist groups differed little in their organization from newer networks: the Red Army Faction (RAF) and Palestine Liberation Organization (PLO), for example, both lacked the hierarchical structure the distinction assumes. Others question the neatness of the thesis' separation of politics and religion, arguing that old terrorist groups were not irreligious, and that new terrorist groups interweave religious and political motivations (see Duyvesteyn 2004: 445; also, Gunning and Jackson 2011). Beyond these empirical concerns, a number of authors have also conducted performative analyses of the new terrorism thesis (see Guzzini 2007): looking at its implication in political decision-making and foreign policy behaviour. Thus, constructions of novel threats are viewed, by some, as justifications of novel counter-measures, in that 'we are being told by many of the policy makers and leading terrorism experts that the "new terrorism" we are facing today requires totally new counter-terrorism measures to deal with it effectively' (Spencer 2008: 1; also Jarvis 2008, 2009b). For Burnett and Whyte, the thesis' assumption of new incorrigibility, in particular, works both to decontextualize and homogenize a range of distinct political movements. In so doing, it performs a simplifying move that contributes scholarly support 'for the ratcheting up of punitive and military responses to terrorism' (Burnett and Whyte 2005: 6).

A related, but frequently separate, discussion to the new terrorism debate has centred around one set of prominent arguments concerning contemporary changes in the nature of warfare. As outlined in Chapter 5, numerous themes have been pursued in this context. These include debates over: the extent to which major war has become obsolete (Mueller 1990; Mandelbaum 1998); the West's contemporary reliance on air power in military confrontation (McInnes 2001); and discussions over the perceived (and latest) Revolution in Military Affairs (RMA). More relevant to us here, however, is the 'new wars' debate associated, in particular, with the work of Mary Kaldor (2007). This debate distinguishes between the conflicts of modernity fought between states for territorial or geopolitical gain, on the one hand. And, on the other, today's localized conflicts (shaped by the forces of globalization) wherein identity politics dominate, and a spread of actors participates. New wars, in this understanding, are characterized by a higher ratio of civilian to military casualties, and by far greater degrees of brutality.

The 'new wars' thesis has been hotly contested on a number of grounds; several unsurprisingly similar to responses to the 'new terrorism' debate. Henderson and Singer (2002), for instance, point to its over-simplification, describing the categorization as a 'typological hodgepodge' used to bracket a diversity of conflicts that differ as much from each other as they do from 'old wars'. Others (Newman 2004;

Melander *et al.* 2009) question the increase in brutality associated with this perceived transformation in organized violence. Kaldor's reply to criticisms such as these, interestingly, was to highlight the normative as well as descriptive aims of her thesis. Thus, in the second edition of her book, Kaldor acknowledges the starkness of the old/new war distinction. Yet, while maintaining that the 'new war argument does reflect a new reality' (Kaldor 2007: 3), Kaldor points also to the performative power of this label. In her words:

> The main point of the distinction between new and old wars was to change the prevailing perceptions of war, especially among policymakers. In particular, I wanted to emphasise the growing illegitimacy of these wars and the need for a cosmopolitan political response – one that put individual rights and the rule of law as the centrepiece of any international intervention (political, military, civil or economic). (Kaldor 2007: 3)

Although debated in largely separate literatures, there are clear connections between discussions of new terrorism and new wars. In the first instance, both locate transformations in political violence within a changing socio-political landscape. The form that contemporary violence takes, in each debate, is a product of broader developments in the world of things (for example, new technologies), and in the world of ideas. Hence, the explanatory significance afforded to identity politics and globalization within both. Second, each debate points to a contemporary shift in the agents and victims of violence. On the former, in both cases, a rising amateurism is posited: hierarchical militaries fight alongside gangs, guerrillas, and the like in new wars, while new terrorist groups no longer seek to imitate national militaries. In terms of the latter, both literatures also point to a rise in civilian casualties; a rise relative to military casualties in the new wars debate, and an absolute rise in discussions of new terrorism. Each debate also, moreover, points to a growth of violent atrocities, for example in the widespread contemporary employment of rape as a weapon of war or in hostage beheadings. Finally, both theses rest upon a claim that there has occurred a significant, and qualitative, change in political violence toward the end of the twentieth century. Returning to the argument in the section above, this claim not only relies on a particular reading of global time; a reading marked by a highlighting of discontinuity. It also, importantly, works to normatively condemn that which is described as 'new'. If old wars and terrorism were brutal and deplorable; new wars and terrorism are even more so. This condemnation, moreover, also supports a powerful appeal for restructuring

Table 7.2 *Security, old and new*

	OLD	NEW
Wars	**Motivation**: Geopolitical or ideological. **Mode**: Conventional (e.g. capture of territory). **Units**: Regular armies (hierarchical and state-organized). **Economics**: State-centric. **Examples**: Crimean War (1853–1856); World War II (1939–1945).	**Motivation**: Identity claims and politics. **Mode**: Mobilization of extremism, terror, limited direct engagement. **Units**: Diverse (e.g. paramilitaries, criminal gangs, mobs, mercenaries, regular armies). **Economics**: Globalized and deterritorialized. **Examples**: Bosnia-Herzegovina (1992–1995).
Terrorism	**Organization**: Hierarchical. **Aims**: Political (e.g. nationalism). **Violence**: Comparatively moderate (e.g. discrimination between legitimate and illegitimate targets). **Examples**: Euskadie ta Askatasuna (ETA); Fuerzas Armadas Revolucionarias de Colombia (FARC); Irish Republican Army (IRA).	**Organization**: Dispersed/fluid. **Aims**: Religious and millenarian. **Violence**: Comparatively indiscriminate (e.g. mass casualty attacks). **Examples**: al Qaeda; Aum Shinrikyo; the Earth Liberation Front (ELF).

Sources: Jackson *et al.* (2011); Kaldor (2007); Neumann (2009).

policy responses to these 'new' forms of violence. Temporal claims, therefore, not only saturate contemporary discussions of international security. They also possess significant performative power in calling for the attention of scholars, students, policymakers and citizens to specific security issues, and the characteristics they are deemed to possess.

Key Points

- Claims to novelty and newness are prominent within contemporary Security Studies. Their functions, however, extend beyond the description of empirical realities.
- Discussions of new terrorism and new wars both contain policy implications: calling for a rethinking, in each case, of how to deal with these issues.
- Opponents of these theses have criticized their conceptual frameworks and empirical claims.

Conclusion

This chapter explored the question of how and whether security might be achieved. It began by exploring a range of potential routes to security posited within realist, liberal and contemporary approaches. These spanned military expenditure, balancing, bandwagoning, democratization, local development initiatives, human rights regimes, the contestation of hegemonic masculinities, and much else besides. The chapter's first section concluded by introducing arguments from the post-structuralist and Paris School around security's impossibility. Here we explored security's conceptual and empirical interdependence on its apparent other: insecurity. In the chapter's second section, we argued that these differences derive not only from obvious conceptual disagreements over security's meaning and referent, but, in addition, from underpinning ontological assumptions about the nature and drivers of change over time. All approaches to international security, we noted, take a position on this core meta-theoretical question, even where that position remains implicit or taken for granted.

The chapter concluded by pointing to the significance of constructions of time to the study of security more broadly. Using debates around new terrorism and new wars as an example, we argued that claims to, or identifications of, novelty and change in the realm of international security perform both descriptive and performative functions. That is, they do something beyond simply describing (ostensible) empirical dynamics. These functions, as we saw, may be normative, as in Kaldor's condemnation of the barbarity and illegitimacy of new wars. They may also be prescriptive, as in debates over how to respond to new terrorism. In Chapter 8 we now take a closer look at the importance of normative claims, arguments and assumption by focusing on whether security is, indeed, a 'good' or desirable condition or experience.

Further Reading

Burke (2007) explores the imbrication of security and insecurity, particularly in the context of the War on Terror. Walker (1993) offers a deconstructive reading of International Relations, and the binary oppositions upon which dominant knowledge thereof rests. Doyle (1998) traces the guiding assumptions and antecedents of realist, liberal and socialist approaches to international political life, while Waltz (2001) provides an overview of competing explanations of the causes of war that rely upon assumptions of human nature or psychology, political life within the state, and the international order.

Internet Resources

The United Nations Millennium Campaign (2014) contains an overview of the campaign, details on each of the Millennium Development Goals, and a range of additional resources including programme reports. The United Nations Department of Economic and Social Affairs (2010) is a report on *The World's Women* which analyses key differences between the status of men and women in a range of areas of global political life.

Chapter 8

Is Security Desirable?

Chapter Overview

This chapter introduces readers to ethical questions that surround the practice and study of international security. The chapter makes two overarching arguments. The first is that all approaches to security involve ethical judgements, even if these are largely implicit. The second is that security researchers should try to remain as open as possible about their own normative commitments. The chapter begins by exploring perspectives on the 'good' that security can do. These include arguments for harnessing security's power to amplify an issue's importance, and claims about security's connection to emancipation and human well-being. A second section then picks up the discussion with which the Introduction chapter opened, exploring security's negatives or downsides. As demonstrated below, these include its capacity to foreclose democratic decision-making, and its connections to insecurity. The chapter concludes by arguing that it is vital that researchers remain as open as possible to a diversity of ways of speaking, practising, studying and experiencing security.

Chapter Contents

Introduction

Contemporary – or 'critical' – approaches to the study of security share three things in common (Browning and McDonald 2013). The first is a fundamental critique of political realism as a way of thinking about and practising security. The reasons behind this critique are multiple – and varied – but prominent amongst these are the militaristic emphasis on strategy and warfare within realist approaches, its statist vision of global politics and thereby security's referent, and a pessimism about the possibility of genuine, qualitative change in world affairs. As we saw in Chapter 7, realist approaches tend to be sceptical about the possibility of achieving anything other than temporary, precarious security. This shared rejection of realism's conservatism – rather than any common positive commitments – was identified as the thread linking different critical approaches to security in the first major discussion thereof (Krause and Williams 1996, 1997b).

The second commonality identified by Browning and McDonald (2013) is a shared concern with what they term the politics of security. This refers to a common interest in the performative issue of what security *does* (Guzzini 2007). What, in other words, happens when security discourses, practices and technologies are invoked, enacted, used or otherwise present in particular situations, be that the border control checkpoint, the prison, or the street corner. The third shared commitment – and that pursued in this chapter – is an attention to the ethics of security, or a common, 'concern with definitions of the "good" or progress regarding security' (Browning and Macdonald 2011: 243). Some approaches manifest this concern by outlining positive ethical commitments toward which we as scholars and humans should strive. This is most obvious in discussions of emancipation associated with the 'Welsh School' of Critical Security Studies (CSS). As Hynek and Chandler (2013: 47) put it: 'CSS set out "to create an alternative world" and it was this normative drive which led theorists to resist accepting the world as it was and the problems of security as they were traditionally posed – at the level of securing the national interests of states'. Others, in contrast, concentrate on deconstructing, resisting and tracing the potentially harmful consequences of security practices: whether intended or otherwise. This emphasis is particularly prominent within 'Paris School' and post-structuralist approaches. Yet, however it is framed, there exists a common concern to think through whether security is, indeed, a desirable phenomenon, and it is this concern on which this chapter focuses.

This chapter argues that all perspectives on security – 'traditional' and 'critical' alike – take an interest of one sort or another in ethical issues. Although most pronounced in the universalist and cosmopolitan impulses that inspire liberal and Critical Theory approaches, such approaches have no monopoly on these issues. Indeed, even the most seemingly 'factual' or 'scientific' discussions of statecraft and military strategy are inspired by ethical commitments, even if these remain often hidden. Beyond exploring different ethics of security, the discussion that follows seeks also to tie together the different questions on which previous chapters have focused. As demonstrated below, we need a sense of what security is (Chapter 1) to make up our minds on whether security is a good thing. We also, however, need to know who or what is being secured (Chapter 4) from whom or what (Chapters 5 and 6) and how (Chapter 7) in order to determine whether we should support particular security practices and projects.

Key Points

- An interest in the ethics of security is shared across very different positions within 'critical' security studies.
- Security can be – and, indeed, is – both embraced and rejected on ethical grounds.
- The most traditional approaches to security, however, also make ethical claims, even if these are largely implicit.

The 'good' of security

A useful place to begin reflecting on the capacity of security to do good is by thinking about the political and rhetorical force of the term. For many authors, 'security' is a 'power word' (Barnett 2001a: 25) that makes things happen when it is invoked. Specifically, when issues become widely thought of or accepted as security threats, the profile and importance of those issues tends to increase dramatically. This realization leads some to argue that there is real merit in seeking to harness this ability that 'security' has – to take an issue and prioritize it above others – and to encourage others to see non-military or non-direct forms of violence in these terms (see Chapter 6). In other words, a moral commitment to reducing harm and insecurity, coupled with a recognition of 'security's' rhetorical and political clout, should encourage us to frame non-traditional or 'new' challenges as security threats.

The important point to take from this discussion is that the decision of whether or not to frame issues as security challenges is not – or, not solely – an objective or descriptive one. Whether to use the language of security – with everything this entails – is a political and ethical decision as much as a matter of meeting empirical criteria. Although there might be dangers in trying to push disease, poverty, environmental degradation and the like on to the security agenda (discussed in the following section) there are also real potential benefits to be had. As Stefan Elbe (2006: 132) has argued, the securitization of HIV/AIDS has significant potential benefits for sufferers of this disease living in parts of the world with inadequate state infrastructure:

> The securitization of HIV/AIDS through the United Nations Security Council, because of its high public profile and unique status in international law, is one way of working toward this goal; it tries to increase the political pressure on governments to begin addressing the issue in a way that would help to ensure the survival of millions of persons living with HIV/AIDS, and it tries to encourage them to do so through early and prompt responses to the pandemic.

Discussions about environmental security offer another useful example. Although some authors are sceptical of the need for any 'rhetorical' (Levy 1995: 60) linkage between these two phenomena, there is again potential value in seeking to commandeer the importance connoted by the term 'security'. As Barnett (2001b: 12) puts it, having acknowledged the problems of securitization: 'Security communicates a certain gravitas that is arguably necessary in climate change policy. In that climate change is a security problem for certain groups, identifying it as such suggests that it is an issue that warrants a policy response commensurate in effort if not in kind with war.' To be really clear, the debate here is not – or, at least, not only – about whether the environment and HIV/AIDS *are* security issues. The debate is over whether the environment and HIV/AIDS *should be thought of* as security issues.

A second powerful argument for security's desirability is found within classical realist literature on the nature of the state. As we saw in Chapter 1, Thomas Hobbes' (1985) *Leviathan* imagines the state as a response to the anarchical 'state of nature' in which life is 'nasty, brutish and short' and all need beware the actions of others. Here, the establishment of a sovereign power provides some measure of relief from the insecurity associated with its absence. Thus, because individuals enter into a social contract with the sovereign to abide by the laws of the land, they and others experience some degree of security. Importantly, however, this realist approach is one in which these commitments to the security of others end at the state's borders (although, see Ashley 1981). Outsiders, such as those living in other countries, may not expect the same protections as insiders for two reasons. First, because they have not entered into this contract with the sovereign power; and, second, because no such agreement exists at the level of the international system which is characterized by anarchy.

Box 8.1 Securing the individual in international politics and law

An ethical commitment to the security of every individual is contained within numerous important documents pertaining to international politics and law. The following are excerpts from some of the most prominent of these.

The Universal Declaration of Human Rights – adopted by the United Nations General Assembly on 10 December 1948:

recognition of the inherent dignity and of the equal and inalienable rights of all members of the human family is the foundation of freedom, justice and peace in the world. (Preamble)

All human beings are born free and equal in dignity and rights. They are endowed with reason and conscience and should act towards one another in a spirit of brotherhood. (Article 1)

Everyone has the right to life, liberty and security of person. (Article 3)

No one shall be subjected to torture or to cruel, inhuman or degrading treatment or punishment. (Article 5)

Everyone has the right to a standard of living adequate for the health and well-being of himself and of his family, including food, clothing, housing and medical care and necessary social services, and the right to security in the event of unemployment, sickness, disability, widowhood, old age or other lack of livelihood in circumstances beyond his control. (Article 25)

United Nations Charter, Preamble, signed on 26 June 1945 in San Fransisco:

WE THE PEOPLES OF THE UNITED NATIONS DETERMINED to save succeeding generations from the scourge of war, which twice in our lifetime has brought untold sorrow to mankind, and to reaffirm faith in fundamental human rights, in the dignity and worth of the human person, in the equal rights of men and women and of nations large and small, and to establish conditions under which justice and respect for

→

Interestingly, given their ontological differences, approaches to security focusing on the individual human often make similar ethical claims to those advocated by state-centric approaches such as political realism. Although thrust into International Relations scholarship relatively recently, it is important to remember that a political concern with the worth of – and the need to secure – individual human beings goes back at least several decades (see Box 8.1). As Axworthy (2001: 19) argues:

→

the obligations arising from treaties and other sources of international law can be maintained, and to promote social progress and better standards of life in larger freedom

United Nations General Assembly Resolution 60(1), adopted on 16 September 2005:

> We stress the right of people to live in freedom and dignity, free from poverty and despair. We recognize that all individuals, in particular vulnerable people, are entitled to freedom from fear and freedom from want, with an equal opportunity to enjoy all their rights and fully develop their human potential. To this end, we commit ourselves to discussing and defining the notion of human security in the General Assembly.

Convention (IV) relative to the Protection of Civilian Persons in Time of War. Geneva, 12 August 1949.

> (1) Persons taking no active part in the hostilities, including members of armed forces who have laid down their arms and those placed 'hors de combat ' by sickness, wounds, detention, or any other cause, shall in all circumstances be treated humanely, without any adverse distinction founded on race, colour, religion or faith, sex, birth or wealth, or any other similar criteria.
> To this end, the following acts are and shall remain prohibited at any time and in any place whatsoever with respect to the above-mentioned persons:
> (a) violence to life and person, in particular murder of all kinds, mutilation, cruel treatment and torture;
> (b) taking of hostages;
> (c) outrages upon personal dignity, in particular humiliating and degrading treatment;
> (d) the passing of sentences and the carrying out of executions without previous judgment pronounced by a regularly constituted court, affording all the judicial guarantees which are recognized as indispensable by civilized peoples.
> (2) The wounded and sick shall be collected and cared for.

A recognition that people's rights are at least as important as those of states has been gaining momentum since the end of World War II. The Holocaust forced a serious examination of the place of international moral standards and codes in the conduct of world affairs. It also caused us to rethink the principles of national sovereignty. The Nuremburg Trials acknowledged that grotesque violations of people's rights could not go unpunished. The United

Nations Charter, the Universal Declaration of Human Rights, and the Genocide and Geneva Conventions all recognised the inherent right of people to personal security.

People-centric approaches to security tend to value security for at least two reasons. The first is that security either implies, or increases the chances of, survival. Beginning with the premise that human life merits preserving – or perhaps better, that people have a right to life – we should value and work toward security out of a respect, here, for the lives of others. In this sense, we should work toward and advocate for the meeting of basic human welfare needs upon which life depends. As seen in Chapter 7, these needs include access to food, water, shelter, and so forth. Restricting our focus to the militaristic threats of Chapter 5, given that preventable diseases, poverty and pollution cause far more harm to individuals across the globe is, in other words, ethically inadequate (Newman 2010: 80).

A second people-centric way of thinking about security's moral worth arises in 'Welsh School' debates around security's relation to emancipation. For authors such as Ken Booth (2007: 115), these two phenomena are inseparable such that:

> to practise security (freeing people from the life-determining conditions of insecurity) is to promote emancipatory space (freedom from oppression, and so some opportunity to explore being human), and to realise emancipation (becoming more fully human) is to practise security (not against others, but with them).

Seen in this way, security is a desirable condition for two reasons. As we saw in Chapter 7, the first – and most familiar one – is that enhancing security means working toward the reduction or removal of 'those physical and human constraints which stop them carrying out what they would freely choose to do' (Booth 1991: 31). These constraints relate to all those drivers of insecurity – or all forms of direct and structural violence – that have a negative impact upon the everyday life of individuals and communities across the world. As Booth continues, 'War and the threat of war is one of those constraints, together with poverty, poor education, political oppression and so on' (Booth 1991: 319). Underpinning this support for security's progressive potential is a conviction that our current world of entrenched and enormous inequalities and (dis)advantages is not 'the best of all possible worlds' (Booth 2007: 250–1). Qualitative improvements in the lives of people in different parts of the world are possible. Indeed, not only possible, but our responsibility – as scholars of security as well as citizens – to work toward their achievement. As Booth (2005a: 268) argued in contrast to Krause and Williams' (1997b) initial – deliberately open – attempt to formulate a 'critical' security studies:

> Critical security theory is both a theoretical commitment and a political orientation...As a political orientation it is informed by the aim of enhancing security through emancipatory politics and networks of community at all levels, including the potential community of communities – common humanity.

Security should be pursued, then, in the first instance because it signifies the absence of a host of military and non-military harms that afflict peoples' everyday lives. It is importantly also desirable, for Booth, as a *means* as well as an *end* in itself because being secure gives people the opportunity to explore different ways of authoring their own lives: to explore different ways of pursuing, 'what it might be to be a human being' (Booth 2007: 257). A life that is preoccupied with surviving current or potential threats is some way from realizing the fullness of its potential. Working toward true security – 'survival-plus' in Booth's terms – therefore means working toward providing space – for all humans – to do more than simply stay alive (see Box 8.2).

Box 8.2 Poverty and human becoming

The impact of different types of insecurity on the pursuit of exploring different ways of being human – or different ways of living one's life – is suggested in a recent study on the impact of poverty upon cognitive ability. This study found that a constant preoccupation with money concerns had an impact on a person's mental energy equivalent to a reduction of 13 IQ points, the loss of a whole night's sleep, or being chronically alcoholic. People experiencing acute financial problems of this sort spend, 'so much mental energy on the immediate problems of paying bills and cutting costs that they are left with less capacity to deal with other complex but important tasks, including education, training or managing their time' (Jha 2013). It is dynamics such as these that Booth and others have in mind in discussing security as 'survival-plus'. Security is more than simply staying alive, and more than an end worthy of protecting for its own sake.

Source: Jha (2013).

Communitarian and cosmopolitan approaches

State-centred approaches toward security's desirability tend to draw upon broadly **communitarian** moral frameworks. Communitarian thinking proceeds from the view that our moral responsibilities end at the boundaries of the community in which we live. Human beings, as Adler (2005: 4) puts it, 'are members of multiple and sometimes over-lapping communities, whose lowest common denominator consists of a shared identity or "we-feeling", shared values and norms, and face-to-face interactions – or, at least, a discourse, practice, moral conviction, or some combination thereof that is shared with other people and dif-ferentiates the group from other groups'. These communities might be territorially bounded – for example with fellow nationals; anchored, yet dispersed – for example with diasporas; or genuinely global – for example with religions. Because moral principles, commitments and norms emerge within human communities such as these, and because these are the context for human associations, it is these communities – rather than the individual humans privileged by people-centric approaches – which form the basis for communitarians' normative commitments. For political realists such as Hans Morgenthau, then, ethical commitments within global politics are built up from the foun-dation of the 'national interest' (Molloy 2009: 95) that supports and follows his state-centric visions of global politics. Thus, while an emphasis on statecraft, guns, bombs and *Realpolitik* is often submitted as evidence of realism's amoral or immoral leanings, a powerful con-ception of ethics actually underpins this broad family of ideas.

People-centric approaches affirming security's desirability tend to draw upon cosmopolitan rather than communitarian ethics. This is the view that our moral commitments are not, and should not be, con-tained by the existence of spatial or other borders: such as the bound-aries of the state in which we happen to live. There is no legitimate moral or legal foundation for prioritizing particular individuals over others when thinking about the obligations I owe to whom. Rather, our responsibilities cut across any national, religious, ethnic, gender or other differences we might identify. As David Held puts it: 'Cosmopolitanism elaborates a concern with the equal moral status of each and every human being and creates a bedrock of interest in what it is that human beings have in common, independently of their partic-ular familial, ethical, national and religious affiliations' (2010: x). This emphasis upon human equality is central, too, for Mary Kaldor (2003: 19) who argues that, 'the cosmopolitan ideal combines a commitment to humanist principles and norms, an assumption of human equality, with a recognition of difference, and indeed a celebration of diversity'.

Approaches of this sort might be grounded in claims about the commonalities between people living different lives in different parts of the world: commonalities that might include universal needs such as food, water and shelter (see also Walker 2010: 13). They might also be rooted in concerns about the emergence of collective risks and the indivisibility of human security wherein dangers and threats such as SARS or ozone depletion are no respecters of the integrity of sovereignty and its territorial claims. Moreover, in a world in which commitments to national identities are – for some – becoming more fragile due to migration patterns, the rise of diaspora politics, global social movements, and transformations within particularistic identity politics, 'many individuals now seem to be, more than ever, prone to articulate complex affiliations, meaningful attachments and multiple allegiances to issues, people, places and traditions that lie beyond the boundaries of their resident nation-state' (Vertovec and Cohen 2002: 2).

Cosmopolitanism, in this sense, offers a route out of the moral 'iron cage' that realism provides us (Booth 2005b). A recent explicit, and interesting, articulation of a cosmopolitan ethics can be found in the work of Anthony Burke (2013) who seeks to address the lack of explicit engagement with cosmopolitan themes within contemporary Security Studies. Burke's (2013: 20) approach to cosmopolitanism is set out as a project of reducing insecurity for all human beings, and involves working toward a major transformation of three key drivers of global political outcomes: state behaviour, global governance frameworks, and the actions of non-state actors such as corporations. This project of 'security cosmopolitanism' (in his terms) is underpinned by three ethical principles which vividly spell out the scale of commitment implied within this type of approach. Burke's first principle is that, 'the responsibility of all states and security actors is to create deep and enduring security for all human beings in a form that harmonises human social, economic, cultural and political activity with the integrity of global ecosystems'. Burke's (2013: 22) second principle is a temporal one which focuses on the *future* consequences of decisions and actions that take place in the here and now: 'all states and security actors have fundamental responsibilities to future generations and the long-term survival of global ecosystems: to consider the impact of their decisions, choices and commitments through time'. This principle is complemented by a third which is a command upon individuals, states, corporations, NGOs and any other individual or collective actor whose actions will impact upon the security of others to: 'act as if both the principles and consequences of your action will become global, across space and through time, and act only in ways that will bring a more secure life for all human beings closer' (Burke 2013: 23). Taken together, Burke's principles offer a code of conduct by which the actions of all actors within the global system can be assessed. These actors, Burke argues, should follow these principles in working toward the end of improving the security of all humans and ecosystems across the world: taking responsibility for an open and distant future where the outcomes of our actions can never be fully known.

Burke's cosmopolitan framework is not the only such approach to the ethical questions raised by international politics. David Held, for example, identifies four fundamental principles that establish the core of the cosmopolitan 'moral and political universe' (2003: 471). These principles (see Table 8.1), Held argues, form a political project thoroughly suited to the challenges globalization poses to international security, social justice and beyond. To implement them, however, would require the establishment of cosmopolitan institutions, norms and polities based around multilayered governance, democratic fora, and enhanced transparency within International Governmental Organizations (Held 2003: 478). Mary Kaldor's work on 'new wars' (see Chapter 7) offers another prominent example in which the assertion of cosmopolitan norms and principles is presented as an alternative to the exclusivist identity claims underpinning contemporary conflicts such as in post-2003 Iraq which blur war, crime and human rights transgressions. In a recent clarification of her thesis, Kaldor (2013: 14) argues that, 'policing, the rule of law, justice mechanisms and institution-building depend on the spread of norms at local, national and global levels'. This spread, however, is the responsibility of both researchers and citizens, given that 'norms are constructed both through scholarship and public debate' (Kaldor 2013: 14).

Table 8.1 *David Held's principles of cosmopolitanism*

Principle	Meaning
Egalitarian individualism	Individual people are the ultimate units of moral concern. Each person is equally worthy of respect and consideration.
Reciprocal recognition	Each person's status of equal moral worth should be recognized by everyone.
Consent	A commitment to everyone's equal moral worth requires non-coercive political processes for negotiation and dispute settlement.
Inclusiveness and subsidiarity	Those significantly affected by public processes or issues should have an equal opportunity to influence them.

Source: Held (2003).

Box 8.3 Eurocentrism

The term **Eurocentrism** is commonly employed to critique taken-for-granted assumptions about Europe's especial role in the world. As we saw in Chapter 2, it is central to post-colonial challenges toward many of the standard epistemological positions within Security Studies. Matin (2013: 354) argues that Eurocentrism has four interconnected assumptions at its centre. First, the *historical* argument that modernity emerged in Europe independent to developments in the rest of the world: that modernity was a distinctive European experience, in other words. Second, the *normative* belief that this experience is indicative of European superiority. Third, a *prognostic* assumption that this experience of modernity and the political institutions and norms (democracy, freedom, etc.) of its expression will become universal. And, fourth, a *stadial* assumption that this development will happen in stages in different parts of the world.

Perhaps the most common charge against cosmopolitan approaches is that they rely upon a set of moral standards that have a very specific foundation in Western thought and (more specifically) the European enlightenment. That is, although claims to equal moral worth and demands for representative political institutions might be presented as universal, these are actually rooted in very particular – Eurocentric – experiences attached to specific times and places (see Box 8.3). Thus, universal arguments about what security is, how it should be pursued, and whether we are to desire it run the risk of homogenizing different ways of thinking, doing and desiring security.

Second, cosmopolitan arguments are also criticized for paying insufficient attention to the nature of 'the political' itself. For some, such as Chantal Mouffe (2005), the faith of their advocates in democratic institutions, global governance, human rights regimes and the like, are no doubt noble. At the same time, this faith serves to ignore or neglect the importance of power relations and the drawing of self/other boundaries that are fundamental to political life and the very essence of democratic politics. Dialogue, reconciliation and the building of consensus between individuals of equal moral worth might seem desirable. Yet, it is, in fact, dissent and 'agonism' based around competition and differences of interest that are vital to the working of democracy and therefore worth preserving.

Third, and related to the above, cosmopolitan claims are also often subject to the charge of utopianism (Held 2003: 478–80). The argument that we should set aside our real or apparent differences (of nationality, of religion, and so on) when acting – and the idea that our global elites should do the same – is, potentially, a far cry from our current world order. Antagonisms and hostility based on perceived 'clashes' of cultures, races or civilizations are as prominent in the early twenty-first century as in early epochs. Rather than hospitality and recognition, those seeking refuge or security in a state other than that of their birth are as likely to encounter resentment, ill-treatment, imprisonment or worse. 477 deaths were recorded by the US Border Patrol along the American south-western border with Mexico in 2012 alone (Gomez 2013). In the UK, a man – Jimmy Mubenga – was unlawfully killed by border control guards aboard the flight deporting him to Angola (Barling 2013). And, at Australia's borders, between January 2000 and October 2013 alone, there have been over 1,480 recorded deaths, many of them of people unknown. This continuing propensity of states to wage or permit violence against outsiders demonstrates the challenges that cosmopolitan visions confront.

A fourth set of criticisms focuses upon the political practices that cosmopolitan claims enable. One obvious example is the use of such claims to legitimize military interventions and other forms of security endeavour around the world with the considerable human and other costs that tend to follow. Recent conflicts in Afghanistan, Iraq, Libya and beyond have been justified – in part – by claims to the moral worth of suffering humans or demographics (Kurds, women, ordinary Afghans and so on) therein. And claims to human security also frequently underpin the construction of international political architectures such as the United Nations with their legal and moral frameworks. For advocates of the state and sovereign power, these political incarnations of cosmopolitanism are problematic because of their violation of non-intervention norms, and their imposition of limits upon the internal and external behaviours of states (Jabri 2012: 631). For advocates of cosmopolitanism (e.g. Burke 2013), on the other hand, criticisms such as this miss the mark. States' use of cosmopolitan rhetoric around the suffering of others and our 'responsibility to protect' strangers in order to legitimize military and other endeavours is really an exercise in aggressive liberalism or instrumentalist *Realpolitik*, rather than one of cosmopolitan politics *per se*.

The cosmopolitan/communitarian debate is, of course, a stylized one. There have been numerous efforts to bridge or disturb this binary, and to nuance these competing conceptions of moral duties. Within the field of International Relations, its most famous expression is perhaps found in the distinction that is frequently drawn between **pluralism** and solidarism. This distinction is associated, in particular, with the writings of Hedley Bull (2002): the key theorist within the so-called

'English School' approach to this field (see Bellamy 2003: 323–5). Pluralists approach the international system as one that contains a plurality of actors with their own ways of life and minimal agreement about substantive issues across the international system. Universal ethical norms and principles, here, are unlikely to be reached as they will always be rooted in particular cultures and hence expressions of particular interests. Solidarists, in contrast, argue that shared moral standards do exist between states and therefore agreement about the rights and wrongs of particular decisions – such as whether or not to intervene in the affairs of another state – is far from impossible.

Reus-Smit's (2002: 496–7) summary of Hedley Bull's writing demonstrates the connection between pluralism and communitarianism, on the one hand; and, solidarism and cosmopolitanism on the other. As he puts it, Bull discerned a fundamental distinction between, 'those who see international society as bound together in solidarity by common values and purposes, and those who hold that states have a plurality of different purposes and that international society rests solely on the observation of common rules of coexistence' (Reus-Smit 2002: 496–7). Thus, while a lack of shared ethical commitments (pluralism) might not lead to conflict (because rules of coexistence – such as sovereignty – might be observed), those that understand the international system as a society characterized by solidarism are likely to be more optimistic about the constraining force of moral concerns upon statecraft.

Key Points

- Security's advocates point to its power to amplify an issue's importance and urgency.
- Security is also deemed desirable by some for the protection and possibilities it offers people and states.
- State-centric approaches to security's desirability tend to draw upon communitarian moral claims.
- People-centric approaches tend to draw upon cosmopolitan moral claims.
- The cosmopolitan/communitarian distinction has found expression in the debate between solidarists and pluralists within International Relations.

The 'negatives' of security

It is difficult, in some senses, to see how and why one might wish to oppose security on ethical grounds. In a similar way to human rights or freedom, we might see security as an unqualified 'good'. This good might be because security is seen as a desirable end in itself: who, given a choice, would opt for less security? Or, because we might see security as an important means toward other ends, perhaps liberty (for Hobbes) or choosing how to live (for Booth). Yet, as with human rights and freedom, however, things are not quite so straightforward. There are a number of potential ethical concerns with the drive for security that merit reflection to which we now turn.

A first normative dilemma emerges when the quest for security leads to unintended, but deleterious consequences for the self or for others (human and otherwise). An important example is the environmental harm frequently brought about by military technologies, operations and other activities (see Box 8.4). As Deudney (1990: 463) argues, 'war and the preparation for war are clearly environmental threats and consume resources that could be used to ameliorate environmental degradation'. In the first instance, war itself often directly causes environmental damage. The bombing of the Jiyeh power station during the Israeli–Lebanese conflict in 2006, for instance, led to the release of an estimated 12,000 to 15,000 tons of fuel oil into the Mediterranean Sea (United Nations Environment Programme 2009: 8). Perhaps better known is the deliberate destruction of oil wells by the Iraqi army during the Persian Gulf War of 1990 (ibid). The Vietnam War which ended in 1975 saw the dropping of 72 million litres of chemicals upon Vietnam, two-thirds of which was Agent Orange, according to (contested) official figures (Scott-Clark and Levy 2003). Beyond the long-

---

Box 8.4 Scorched earth

Scorched earth tactics are a form of military activity that attempts to destroy everything of potential use to one's enemy in a conflict (Hulme 1997: 49). The strategy has considerable environmental costs, and has been historically widespread as Hulme (1997: 58) summarizes:

> scorched earth is a policy whereby a retreating belligerent directly causes damage or destruction to anything in his tracks, in order to impede, prevent or frustrate a pursuing army. Such tactics have been popular throughout history... In 1918 whilst retreating from Belgium and France, the German army drenched the ground with Mustard Gas destroying everything in its wake. Similar action occurred during the Second World War as German troops fled from the Soviet army in the Danish province of Finmark.

Source: Hulme (1997).

term harm these chemicals caused to generations of human lives in Vietnam, they also rendered large parts of the land infertile.

Second, preparations for war undertaken by the national security state are also a potential source of harm, including (again) to the environment (Deudney 1990: 463). These include the production of emissions in the manufacturing of weapons and other defence technologies, or the production and storage of hazardous waste materials used in non-traditional weapons. Many of the world's militaries and defence departments are, however, attempting to address these costs. The UK's Ministry of Defence (MoD), for example, is committed to meeting a series of targets associated with the coalition government's 'Greening Government Commitments'. These include reducing water consumption and emissions from energy usage on MoD estates, through to commitments to sustainable procurement (Ministry of Defence 2013). The Australian Department of Defence, similarly, has its own Defence Environmental Strategic Plan with six sets of policy objectives. These translate into commitments to do such things as monitor noise levels at major Air Force bases and to identify strategies to minimize the disposal of waste at sea by the Navy (Australian Government Department of Defence 2010). However, although plans and frameworks such as these indicate some level of commitment to 'greening' defence, their adequacy has been questioned given the scale of environmental harm caused by military preparations and activities.

A third issue is with the opportunity costs of the resources that are ploughed into security (Deudney 1990: 463; Barnett 2001b: 10). Resources that are dedicated to improving national security, in terms of military procurement, salaries for armed forces, border control technologies, internal policing and so forth, are major aspects of national expenditure. Global military expenditure in 2012, for instance, was $1,753 billion – a fall on the previous year! – or 2.5% of global gross domestic product (Perlo-Freeman *et al.* 2013). The US alone spent $682 billion, China $166 billion, Russia $90.7 billion and the UK $60.8 billion. These are obviously resources that could have been dedicated to other areas of public policy – poverty reduction, education and literacy programmes, healthcare, welfare and so on – that may or may not be related security depending on how the term is understood (see Chapter 1). The then US President Dwight Eisenhower made this argument very explicitly in his discussion of the opportunity costs of military expenditure in a speech he delivered in April 1953 (see Box 8.5).

An alternative, and potentially more developed, set of ethical concerns is raised by the securitization literature associated with the Copenhagen School approach. As outlined in earlier chapters (see Introduction) this approach views security as a social practice whereby

---

Box 8.5 Opportunity costs of military expenditure

Former US President Dwight Eisenhower gave a speech to the American Society of Newspaper Editors in April 1953. Delivered in the context of the Cold War and shortly before Eisenhower's death, the speech highlighted the opportunity costs of military expenditure. As it makes clear, this is an ethical as much as a political or economic decision: a question about the type of life we wish to pursue. The section of the speech reproduced below has reverberated with progressive political movements and campaigns since its delivery:

> Every gun that is made, every warship launched, every rocket fired signifies, in the final sense, a theft from those who hunger and are not fed, those who are cold and are not clothed. This world in arms is not spending money alone. It is spending the sweat of its laborers, the genius of its scientists, the hopes of its children. The cost of one modern heavy bomber is this: a modern brick school in more than 30 cities. It is two electric power plants, each serving a town of 60,000 population. It is two fine, fully equipped hospitals. It is some 50 miles of concrete highway. We pay for a single fighter plane with a half million bushels of wheat. We pay for a single destroyer with new homes that could have housed more than 8,000 people. This, I repeat, is the best way of life to be found on the road the world has been taking. This is not a way of life at all, in any true sense. Under the cloud of threatening war, it is humanity hanging from a cross of iron.

---

an authoritative figure designates something as a security threat, and a relevant audience accepts this designation. Security, in other words, is the process of constructing a particular issue (e.g. climate change or poverty) or actor (e.g. Osama bin Laden or the USA) as a threat to the very existence of some referent (e.g. Iran, the West, Christianity, etc.). This constructivist approach therefore offers an analytical framework for exploring how issues become securitized by particular actors within particular contexts. Its value, in that sense, is its applicability to a potentially infinite range of constructed threats. The securitization approach also, however, offered one of the earliest ethical critiques of the dangers of speaking and doing 'security'.

According to securitization theory, when an issue is successfully securitized its importance is dramatically increased. If the very existence of something – our nation, our way of life, our biosphere, etc. – is at stake, then dealing with that threat becomes an urgent priority. As a consequence, normal political processes are suspended, and emergency powers are legitimized to deal with the threat. Numerous examples of this can be identified. During World War II, the securitization of Japan as a threat to American security led to the imprisonment of over 110,000 people within the US because of their Japanese origins (Cole 2002, 2003). Early attempts to deal with HIV/AIDS instituted enormous levels of security measures in misguided efforts to prevent the spread of this virus (see Box 8.6). Emergency powers such as these may, moreover, become institutionalized over time and simply accepted as the proper way to deal with a particular issue, or seemingly similar issues. Related to this is the danger that the securitization of threats will lead to their militarization. Barnett (2001b: 11), for example, argues that this was the consequence of the earliest debates around environmental security. Rather than ushering in newer and more progressive ways of dealing with environmental damage, the environment has often been inserted into existing statist and militaristic frameworks that may be inappropriate and even counter-productive for its address:

> Environmental security was originally written with the intention of exposing the inadequacy of militarised practices of security, the porous nature of sovereignty in the face of environmental change, and to elevate environmental problems from the level of 'low politics' to 'high politics' so that states would commit as much energy and resources to address environmental problems as they do to other security problems (this is what meant by 'securitisation'). However, the result has not been trade-offs in military security for environmental security, or increased resources and energy devoted to enhancing environmental security. Instead, environmental change problems have been militarised; the emphasis has been placed on environmental change as cause of violent conflict rather than human insecurity; and on exogenous environmental threats to the state for which unspecified Others were seen to be responsible, as opposed to attending to domestic causes of environmental change.

Paul Roe (2012), drawing on the work of Claudia Aradau (2004), argues there are two broad types of normative criticism that are levied against securitization. The first focuses on the ways in which security politics interrupt or suspend the democratic process. Once something is accepted as a security issue, deliberation, debate and review come to an end and the openness of routine, normal politics is replaced with hasty and secretive decision-making. Political, military or other elites acting on undisclosed information are substituted for an accountable government and a well-informed citizenry. The second set of criticisms identified by

Box 8.6 Securitizations of HIV/AIDS

When awareness of HIV/AIDS began to emerge in the late 1970s and early 1980s, the virus was quickly securitized with often horrific consequences for sufferers, and their families. Public health posters (see 'web resources') employed instantly recognizable and often graphic imagery associated with death such as skeletons and tombstones. The bodies of those killed by the virus were treated as contaminated, and a threat to the health and security of others. The following is taken from a report from the UK daily newspaper, *The Independent*, in a story from 1988:

> A young man dies in hospital. His parents are not allowed to see his body. He is put into two sealed bags, one inside the other. He is taken away to be buried in a special steel coffin. Over the place where he is buried, heavy flagstones are laid. The young man died, of course, of AIDS.

Roe (2012) concentrates on the outcomes of securitization. These not only include questions around the efficacy of treating issues such as the environment or poverty as security concerns, but also the tendency of security politics to institute boundaries between 'us' and 'them'. Beyond the obvious human rights concerns associated with emergency politics in cases such as internment and the like, then, securitization is also integral to the creation of antagonistic, exclusionary politics.

Although securitization's inherent negativity is questioned by Roe (2012) and others (for example, Floyd 2007; see also Browning and McDonald 2013), one response to these concerns is to attempt to desecuritize issues that have been socially constructed as security threats. In contrast to those who appeal to the harnessing of security's rhetorical and political power in order to highlight and then address social harms, this approach argues for the opposite: that we should work to take issues *out of* the realm of security. The concept and dynamics of **desecuritization** – understood as, 'the shifting of issues out of emergency mode and into the normal bargaining processes of the political sphere' (Buzan *et al.* 1998: 4) – remain far less well understand than those of securitization. Identified strategies (see Huysmans 1995; Roe 2004) include the following. First, an objectivist approach which involves discrediting constructions of security with empirical facts or arguments to demonstrate that the apparent threat does not exist. Climate change sceptics, for example, seek to do this by providing data that purports to challenge received scientific wisdom. Imams and others similarly work hard to contest the widespread (and pernicious) securitization of Islam (see Croft 2012) by challenging depictions of this faith and its followers as a threat to British identity, values and ways of life. Second, constructivist strategies toward desecuritization involve demonstrating *how* a particular threat has been constructed as a security issue and attempt to reveal the discursive claims and logics upon which this construction depends. Hansen and Nissenbaum's (2009: 1157) exploration of the securitization of cyberspace, for instance, argues that there are three distinctive 'modalities' at work in this area:

> *hypersecuritization*, which identifies large-scale instantaneous cas-cading disaster scenarios; *everyday security practices*, that draws upon and securitizes the lived experiences a citizenry may have; and *technifications*, that captures the constitution of an issue as reliant upon expert, technical knowledge for its resolution and hence as politically neutral or unquestionably normatively desirable.

Myriam Dunn Cavelty (2013) attempts something similar, demon-strating how three different types of threat are securitized in cyber-space: digital accidents, professional hackers, and systemic vulnerabilities within critical and interconnected infrastructures. Importantly, she demonstrates that a range of actors are involved in these securitizations: governmental and non-governmental, elite and non-elite. By providing a fuller understanding of the securitization process in this area, these analyses therefore offer potential for desecu-ritizing such threats: treating them as less exceptional than they may at times seem.

A third strategy toward desecuritization discussed by Huysmans and Roe is a deconstructivist strategy. This involves re-telling the security 'drama' differently from the 'inside' out, such that the seeming stability of security threats and referents are brought into question. Matt McDonald (2005), for example, argues that one response to the securi-tization of asylum seekers and undocumented migrants as a threat to Australia in the early twentieth century would be to re-cast this secu-rity drama in such a way that the security of asylum seekers was placed at its centre. This would have the effect of pulling into question the antagonistic relationship between Australia and asylum seekers. A fuller deconstruction still would be to work to deconstruct the very sta-bility of these identities (as well as their relationship) and to problema-tize categories such as 'Australia' and 'asylum seeker'. As with the objectivist and constructivist strategies for desecuritization, this approach – at least implicitly – begins with an ethical concern around the 'panic politics' of security and its tendency to harden political identities, disrupt political processes, and legitimize emergency powers and frameworks. Rather than seeking to make use of security's discursive and political power – by moving public policy concerns into security frameworks – the solution here is the opposite: to seek to challenge the 'security' of security issues.

Other very significant criticisms of security are found within writings associated with the Paris School approach to international political sociology and post-structuralism. Authors in these traditions share a scepticism toward the view that security can be separated from insecurity. In the case of the former, this scepticism is often a product of sociological analyses of the impacts of security technologies, professionals and practices on those that are subject to them. The building and arming of gated communities, for instance, might make their residents both more and less secure at the same time: rendering external threats more distant from the 'inside', yet heightening – and constructing – fear of those threats through the constant reminder offered by walls, guns and dogs. The same is true, of course, in the building of peace walls or border fences such as the Israeli West Bank Barrier, or those that continue to populate the city of Belfast in Northern Ireland over fifteen years after the signing of the Good Friday Agreement.

Post-structuralists, too, point to the inseparability of security and insecurity, exploring, amongst other things, how constructions of threat and 'otherness' are central to the drawing of the boundaries of the 'self'. Given the common concern in demonstrating the contingency of – and deconstructing – oppositions such as self/other, security/insecurity (Chapter 3), when post-structuralist authors write explicitly about ethics they tend to view cosmopolitan and communitarian approaches with equal suspicion. This is because both cosmopolitan and communitarian approaches fall back on some notion of prior, autonomous subjects that exist before and beyond their relations to one another (see also Campbell and Shapiro 1999). For cosmopolitans – such as advocates of human security – this subject is the individual human. For communitarians – such as realists – this subject is a collective community, such as the nation or the state. Many post-structuralists, in contrast, conceptualize ethics in terms of an openness to difference – drawing, often, on the writings of Emmanuel Levinas in particular. This involves a refusal to accept the status quo and a fight to confront simplified, exclusionist discourses and practices of security such as, for example, in right-wing accounts of migration. As David Campbell (1998a: 513) argues, this is an ethos in which:

> the overriding concern is the struggle for – or on behalf of – alterity rather than a struggle to efface, erase, or eradicate alterity... It

would declare that we should actively nourish and nurture antagonism, conflict, plurality, and multiplicity, not at the expense of security or identity – for this is not an either/or option – but in terms of security's and identity's contamination by and indebtedness to otherness.

From this perspective, once we accept that self/other, security/insecurity, power/resistance and so forth are fluid and inseparable, our task becomes neither securing the self from the other, nor seeking to build institutions and provide security for already-existing humans. Instead, it is about an ethos based on the affirmation of difference and even antagonism: of opening the self up to the other rather than seeking to close it off.

Key Points

- The quest for security is responsible for considerable harm to a range of actors and other phenomena, including the natural environment.
- The quest for security also has major opportunity costs.
- Securitizing issues may have deleterious consequences for democratic processes and outcomes.
- Security may also create, and be inseparable from, its apparent antithesis: insecurity.

Conclusion

This chapter has explored a range of perspectives on the ethics of security. In particular, it has concentrated on two questions that are vitally important for any serious discussion of this term. The first of these questions is whether security is, or should be thought of, as a 'good' or desirable thing: something that is to be pursued or sought after. The second question, which naturally follows, relates to what we as scholars and students – as well as people or citizens – should be doing in relation to security. Should we, for instance, seek to give voice to the marginalized and oppressed, and allow them to speak, in their own terms, on their own insecurities? Or, should we concentrate our efforts on deconstructing discourses of national security for the harms that they cause? Alternatively, still, perhaps we should seek to harness security's perlocutionary power and apply the word to as many sources of suffering as we can such that they might be taken more seriously within the global political system.

It is vital, we argue, to remember that all discussions of security involve some form of answer to questions such as these: even if that answer is only implicit and hidden. As we have tried to demonstrate, even the two approaches most often accused of lacking any normative concern – political realism and post-structuralism – rely upon identifiable ethical commitments, even if these commitments do not translate into a concrete programme for (moral) action. Indeed, as we have tried to demonstrate throughout this book, it is simply not possible to research, write about, or make claims to security from a value-less and neutral vantage point stripped of ideas, values and interests. Such a point simply does not exist, and we are always already embedded in historical, social, political, professional and a host of other contexts and relations as soon as we move to think or speak of security. These relations cannot be escaped, and we may not even be able to fully articulate them and their impacts. What we can, however, attempt to do is be as explicit as possible about our commitments, vantage points and positionalities from which we are writing. This involves refusing to hide (or to hide behind) dynamics of authorship and authority in the security knowledge we create.

A second thing we can do is to try to make use of a pluralizing impulse and work to allow as many perspectives, experiences and conceptions of (in)security as possible to come forward in debates around what security is, how it might be achieved, and whether it is desirable. In so doing, we could do far worse than follow Matt McDonald (2009: 121) in seeking, 'the freeing up of space to think, speak, and write differently about what [security] means, how it might be studied, and how to make sense of effective responses to it'. Viewed in this way, studying (in)security is part of the practising and doing (in)security. Although the outcomes of particular security projects or claims cannot be known in advance, neither can the outcomes of doing nothing. Better, then, to accept that security is riddled with ethical considerations, and to work as hard as we can to articulate, defend, and where necessary adjust those which we hold. Given that security 'saturates the language of modern politics [such that] our political vocabularies reek of it and our political imagination is confined by it' (Dillon 2002: 12), refusing to do otherwise would be as unrealistic as it would be ethically dubious. For, as Mark Neocleous (2008: 3) puts it in a heavily referenced paragraph worth citing at length:

> This saturation of the political and social landscape with the logic of security has been accompanied by the emergence of an academic industry churning out ideas about how to defend and

improve it. Security has been defined and redefined. It has been re-visioned, re-mapped, gendered, refused. Some have asked whether there is perhaps too much security, some have sought its civilisation, and thousands of others have asked how to 'balance' it with liberty. Much of this redefining, re-visioning, remapping, and so on, has come about through a more widespread attempt at widening the security agenda so as to include societal, economic and a broad range of other issues such as development or the environment. These moves have sought to forge alternative notions of 'democratic' and 'human' security as part of a debate about whose security is being studied, the ontological status of insecurities and questions of identity, and through these moves security has come to be treated less as an objective condition and much more as the product of social processes.

Key Points

- No value-less or neutral vantage point for the analysis or experience of security exists.
- In our view, it is desirable that security researchers remain as open as possible about their own normative commitments.
- It is also, we suggest, desirable to be open to as many perspectives, experiences and conceptions of (in)security as possible.

Further Reading

Barnett (2001a) provides a critical discussion of the concept of environmental security, while Burke (2013) details his understanding of 'security cosmopolitanism' and the contribution such an approach might make. Campbell (1998a) explores normative issues around security from a post-structuralist perspective, and Roe (2012) investigates normative debates in relation to securitization. Browning and McDonald (2013), finally, provide an excellent overview of the stakes involved in, and differences between competing visions of, critical security studies. As they argue, whatever 'critical security studies' is, it has something to do with the politics and ethics of security.

Internet Resources

United Nations (2014) contains a series of web pages relating to the Universal Declaration of Human Rights. The pages contain the Declaration's full text as well as an account of its history and further resources. Wellcome Collection (2014) is host to a collection of images of public health posters from across the world on HIV/AIDS. While some securitize the virus, others appeal for destigmatization and an end to prejudice. Oxford Research Group (2014) contains publications and other resources on sustainable security while Australia Border Deaths Database (2014) keeps a record of all known deaths associated with Australia's borders.

Conclusion

Chapter Overview

In this conclusion we do three things. First, we recap and summarize the book's content and arguments. Second, we highlight the diversity and importance of Security Studies in the contemporary world. Third, we sketch some of the future directions available to contributors and newcomers to this discipline; pointing to its porous and shifting boundaries, and to linkages with other fields of study including, amongst others, Geography, Sociology and Neuroscience. We argue that it is unnecessary, and indeed counter-productive, to isolate the field of Security Studies from the insights, approaches and methods of related disciplines.

Chapter Contents

Introduction

Conclusions can take many forms, attempting to summarize, synthesize and, perhaps, speculate on the preceding arguments, their significance, and future directions. In this conclusion, we attempt each in turn. First, we recap the central arguments the book has put forward in attempting to map a critical introduction to the subdiscipline of Security Studies. Here, drawing on Hay (2002), we revisit questions of ontology, epistemology and methodology in studying security, as well as noting what is at stake in their possible answers. This is achieved, in part, by drawing out the ways in which competing answers to underlying questions concerning the philosophy of social science lead researchers to divergent understandings of issues and dynamics within Security Studies. Second,

223

building on divergent approaches to common (empirical) issues, as well as questions of the politics, policy and possibility of security, we turn to the inherent interdisciplinarity of a subdiscipline which might be more fruitfully understood as a subfield, crossing porous and constructed (sub)disciplinary boundaries. Fortunately, the concerns and approaches of the subdiscipline/subfield of security are fluid and in motion, evolving, as we have suggested, in line with, and in response to, both the 'fierce urgency of now' and more parochial paradigmatic preoccupations. We suggest that the twin dynamics of widening and deepening – as well as new realities inspiring new depths and modes of analysis – encourage and, perhaps, demand a renewed devotion to interdisciplinary enquiry. Third, we briefly conclude with an attempt at the hardest of all tasks, and one which has proven particularly difficult for International Relations and its subdisciplines: we speculate as to what the future might hold for security and its study.

Landscapes of international security

We began this book by asking a fundamental question: what is security? It is a question which inspires further reflection and enquiry, rather than offering up immediate or obvious answers: is security objective or subjective; is security measurable; is security absolute or relative; is security a sense, a process, or a condition? Identifying what security is, therefore, is certainly not a straightforward task. Moreover, its answer shapes how it is that students and scholars in Security Studies will go about conducting their work and formulating knowledge of security and insecurity (the topics of Chapters 3 and 2, respectively). After exploring what this means for the study of various potential threats and referents, we complicated matters further still (in Chapters 7 and 8), by questioning security's very possibility and desirability.

To begin with, we simply rejected one extreme, parsimonious and limiting answer to the question, what is security? Theorizations of security as survival, it seems to us, are simply too narrow. They fail to adequately conceptualize the range of insecurities a person, group, or thing might face. In contrast, more expansive accounts of security, such as those found in debates over human security and the Critical Security Studies (CSS) literature, acknowledge that insecurity is possible despite continued survival (as we saw with the experience of the 33 miners trapped underground in Chile, for example). This realization enables a more specific question to be asked: what conditions – or basic needs – must therefore be met for the achievement of security? Here, again, we rejected one extreme position within the debates that emanate from this question. Security is not reducible to brute material realities at any level of analysis (state, human, community, or beyond). To make this argument, we sketched recent challenges to ontological materialism within the IR and Security Studies literature, pointing to the contemporary prominence of constructivist thought, as well as Foucauldian approaches. Such approaches enable a more complex understanding of security, in which identities, interests and threats exist and interact as social productions, rather than as pre-given entities. Of course, these arguments have developed in line with the changing contexts in which security has been studied, shifting in accordance with history and politics. Security Studies, as outlined in Chapter 1, has had two principal opening moments; following the fall of the Berlin Wall in 1989 and the Twin Towers of the World Trade Center in 2001. The emergence and consolidation of human security, feminist security studies, constructivist and critical approaches to security were but some of the impacts of these transformatory events.

In Chapters 2 and 3, we developed these arguments, considering their implications for how we might 'know' and 'do' security. Chapter 2 focused on the question: what can be known about security and insecurity? Here, again, we rejected one particularly extreme (if dominant) and limiting approach, which views Security Studies as a scientific enterprise. Much more difficult to answer, given the implications of taking a stance, is whether security is universal, or a particular and localized experience (e.g. Burke *et al.* 2014). Either way, we showed that what one thinks is knowable shapes the types of knowledge one tries to generate; you are unlikely to seek universal laws if your focus is on case studies (and vice versa). These founding assumptions are also vital for the way in which researchers are likely to attempt to produce such knowledge. Turning to methodology and methods, in Chapter 3, we explored a range of approaches for doing just this, including mathematical methods such as regression analysis and formal modelling, as well as 'qualitative' techniques such as ethnography, discourse analysis and focus group research. While there are, unsurprisingly, strengths and limitations to each, this growing diversity and the interest fuelling it is to be welcomed, not least because thinking carefully about knowledge production processes generates higher quality research.

In the middle section of the book, in Chapters 4, 5 and 6, we turned to some of the more substantive issues facing researchers of security, namely: security *for* whom and *from* what? Since its inception, Security Studies has traditionally answered the question 'what is security?' in a blunt and troubling way: security is national security, i.e. that of the state. But it is far from clear that the nation-state should be privileged as security's referent, for analytical and normative reasons. Rather, security's traditionally favoured referent has been privileged for reasons of politics, power and treasure: Security Studies, like International Relations more broadly, was a US-centric discipline, partly funded and directed by the US government during the early stages of the Cold War. As a result, the guiding assumptions of this subfield were set according to the questions, interests, and concerns of powerful actors therein.

Our argument, in Chapter 4 was that there are a lot of reasons to question this imbrication of an academic field – Security Studies – and the more prosaic, parochial concerns of national politics. These reasons included ontological concerns over the diversity rather than homogeneity of states; normative concerns surrounding the role of the state as security's guarantor within or outwith (illustrated by recent violences against protestors in Libya and Syria); arguments that agency should not be included as a criterion for decisions about referents; and challenges to the conflation of state and nation implicit in many discussions of national security. Its principal challenger, though, has an equally contentious claim to be security's referent. Human security, some feminist approaches, and Critical Security Studies (CSS) all present different justifications for focusing on people rather than states. Whilst a seemingly attractive proposition for critics of *Realpolitik*, these approaches confront challenges of their own, including: the ease with which states can co-opt 'human security' discourses; the heterogeneity of humans and their needs, wants and fears; and, the challenges of knowing and speaking about the security of other people we have not met and may never meet. In response, we introduced a range of alternative suggestions that have also been made, such as taking the biosphere as security's referent in discussions of ecological security, or Copenhagen School explorations of societal security with their emphasis on collective identities. What this debate revealed, however, is that claims to security and insecurity are integral to the (re-)production of referent objects at all levels of analysis, while claims to identity are complicit in the identification and management of security issues. In other words, constructions of threat are part of constructions of the thing that is threatened: representations of the Soviet Union in the Cold War were part of the process by which American national identity was forged (and vice versa).

In answering the second part of the above question – security from what? – it is no exaggeration to state that no security threat has achieved anything like the attention afforded to the military threat posed by other states. Such exercises of 'hard power' have been the preoccupation of academics and practitioners of Security Studies since the subdiscipline's inception. Indeed, much of its history has been a story of the study of the consequences of war at different levels of analysis and an identification of its principal determinants and forms. The changing nature of warfare was discussed in Chapter 5, considering transformations in the likelihood of military conflict, the geographies and practices of war, as well as the privatization of contemporary warfare. Evolutions in weapons technologies, we showed, have helped to drive these changes, as they have the relatively recent developments in contemporary terrorism. Chapter 6 built on and extended this discussion of security threats, emphasizing the importance of Peace Studies debates for moving scholars and activists away from a restrictive focus on direct, observable, and somatic forms of harm. We introduced here a range of contemporary non-military security threats and their consequences, including climate change, famine, poverty, organized crime and gendered violences. These forms of harm, we argued, are responsible for far more human suffering than more 'traditional' security issues. At the same time, they have largely – and unproductively – been discussed within Security Studies for the impact they can have on national security.

In Chapters 7 and 8, we posed our final questions: is security possible and desirable, and how might it be achieved? Here, we discussed the normative decisions that scholars of international security make in their studies, focusing on what ethical commitments actually consist of, from where they derive, and how far they extend in the context of a Westphalian state system. How, for example, can we understand the ethical commitments of former US President George W. Bush's election statement in 1999 that the United States should not use force to end genocide. This argument was put forward only half a decade after the massacre of nearly one million 'innocent' Rwandans, but was seen to be a populist rallying cry in the context of Bill Clinton's America. In contrast to communitarian commitments such as these, we also discussed the more cosmopolitan ethical commitments embodied in the UN Millennium Development Goals, which function as an effort to further human security around the world. And, again, we contrasted the liberal conceptualization of historical progress that these goals embody with less optimistic readings of insecurity's potential permanence. Attempts to achieve security through balancing and hegemonic stability are surely only ever temporary and precarious. In part because security can only ever be achieved fleetingly, partially, and in isolated spaces and places. Conceptualizing continuity and change, we suggest(ed), is an important and too-often implicit backdrop to considerations of ethical and empirical debates. Ultimately, we argue that the toleration of some degree of risk or insecurity is necessary in contemporary life. This is the case for two reasons. First, to avoid the erosion of other similarly significant political values. And, second, to counter the over-zealous and often counter-productive responses to perceived insecurities that have characterized recent security paradigms such as the 'global war on terror'. It is these sorts of concerns that have motivated our own research within Security Studies.

Shifting landscapes of international security

Our critical analysis of security and Security Studies has revealed a constructed, fluid subdiscipline which is constantly in motion (see also Croft 2008). It is important to note two further points on this. First, security and its study is as wide and diverse as it has been at any point since World War II. This is a good thing, since it helps 'us' (understood as a global 'us') to address a greater variety of the harms that befall people all over the planet, in the hope of improving the conditions of a our global existence. It also increases the likelihood that these issues will be faced creatively and critically, with novel solutions to emerging problems, which are nonetheless reflexively arrived at and validated. Second, the boundaries of the 'subdiscipline' of Security Studies are constantly shifting to incorporate new and exciting theoretical and academic developments (that often parallel 'real-world' issues). In fact, as Croft (2008) notes, Security Studies is perhaps better conceptualized as a subfield rather than a subdiscipline. While it is certainly true that novel insights within International Relations have permeated an increasingly critical and heterogeneous Security Studies subdiscipline, the subfield of Security Studies straddles multiple cognate disciplines, finding different concerns and insights across the social sciences. Geography, Sociology, and Psychology, to name only three, all have important insights on security issues.

Three useful examples can highlight the impact that Security Studies is having as an interdisciplinary subfield, as well as the benefits of engaging with disciplines beyond International Relations. First, consider the recent impact of work on affect, emotion and memory, inspired by developments in neuroscience. Memory studies and the 'affective turn' are producing a burgeoning literature in Security Studies, as scholars turn to consider the role that emotions play in foreign policy and international relations more generally (e.g. Crawford 2000; Bleiker and Hutchison 2008; Mercer 2010; Ross 2006). This body of work has been influenced by social theorist Brian Massumi, political theorist William Connolly (2002) and neuroscientist

Antonio Damasio, amongst many others. For example, in Geography, Nigel Thrift has become synonymous with non-representational theory. For Thrift (2008: 25), 'understanding affect requires some sense of the role of biology' because humans do 'not stand outside nature'; we are, in fact, 'full of all kinds of impulses which are outside its comprehension'. In this sense he insists that 'social science needs to draw on approaches that are willing to countenance a formative role for the biological' (ibid: 26). Often, these approaches are to be found outside of the discipline of International Relations. Such insights help Security Studies to acknowledge that the 'contours and contexts of what happens constantly change: for example, there is no stable "human" experience, because the human sensorium is constantly being reinvented as the body continually adds parts into itself' (ibid: 2).

Second, new theories of space and time, based on shifting global geographies, have helped to inspire work in International Relations. Work in Radical Geography, by the likes of David Harvey (2005), for example, has helped to inspire analyses of security issues, which encompass critical theoretical approaches, and the role of political economy. Likewise, David Campbell's work (e.g. 1998) has straddled Geography and International Relations, enabling a critical analysis of US foreign policy, which is sensitive to the politics of space and place, as well as language, culture and identity. This is a line of thinking that has found significant avenues of enquiry within Critical Geopolitics more broadly. Relevant examples include the work of Gerard Toal (1996) on foreign policy and the writing of global political space, as well as Simon Dalby (2009) on issues pertinent to environmental security. Perhaps, however, the usefulness of interdisciplinarity generally, and the borderlands of Geography and International Relations specifically, is best emphasized by the work of Derek Gregory (2004), which remains chronically under-read in International Relations. Gregory's project to map the spatial and temporal connections between colonial relations in the past, present and likely future is one which should certainly find greater resonance within critical approaches to security, especially in a post 9/11 security environment (see Jarvis and Holland 2014).

Third, practitioners facing demanding counter-terrorism requirements are seeking insights from across a range of sectors that manage risk effectively. From Economics, to International Political Sociology, via Environmental Science, there is growing awareness amongst policymakers and their advisers that terrorism requires insights from a range of academic specialisms, including work on neuroscience and emotion, but also less-explored alternatives such as anthropology. Living with and talking to terrorists, for example, while difficult to get past university ethics committees, is increasingly recognized as a particularly useful approach to generating new knowledge about the drivers of terrorism, and an essential basis of understanding upon which to formulate counter-terrorism policies. Likewise, following the 2008 financial crash, attempts to incorporate unavoidable risk – insecurities – within the 'system' are being adopted from financial markets, where the regulation of inexorable vulnerability is acknowledged as a necessary component of ensuring the survival of overarching structures. Interdisciplinary insights therefore are not merely the preserve of academics, but are also increasingly seen as a potential avenue for the formulation of better policy and the realization of security, or at least the minimization and incorporation of insecurity within a stable system.

Future landscapes of international security

Where then might we go from here? First, and perhaps most obviously, the relatively recent diversification of Security Studies should be applauded and will hopefully continue. The benefits of cross-disciplinary activities based on underlying research synergies are manifest in a variety of Security Studies' different schools and approaches. It is only relatively recently that excellent work in Geography, Sociology and Psychology has been read and cited in Security Studies as the subdiscipline has accelerated its transition into something more amorphous than traditional Strategic Studies, with its narrow military focus. We hope that the relationship between Geographers and Security Studies will continue to develop. To date, this relationship has, with a few prominent exceptions, been under-explored, with especially few scholars in International Relations reading work in Geography. This is a great shame, given the critical theoretical sophistication of a discipline that can help to elucidate the power relations underlying and emanating from the constructed cartography of world politics. Critical Theory, constructivist and post-structural approaches in Security Studies share very many of the same concerns as radical Geographers. Critical Geopolitics, for example, is a subdiscipline split between those of a more Marxist influence and those of a more Foucauldian background, in a manner not entirely dissimilar to the fissures characterizing critical security approaches in Europe.

As for Sociology, the work of Didier Bigo and the so-called Paris School has explicitly attempted to develop an International Political Sociology centred on the work of Social Science's second most cited author of all time: Pierre Bourdieu. This work and its terminology of field, habitus and the like has already inspired novel and insightful research on the borders of Politics, International Relations, and Sociology (e.g. Huysmans 2005; Bigo *et al.* 2010; Williams 2007). The success of the subfield of International Political Sociology has been reflected in the formation of new working groups, international networks and prominent journals. Similarly, as agendas have shifted the focus of security scholars towards terrorism, there has been a reawakened interest in social movement theory and processes of radicalization, which has raised awareness of work in cognate disciplines (Baker-Beall *et al.* forthcoming). Attempts at deeper, more sophisticated and realistic conceptualizations of processes of radicalization have already permeated policymaker and practitioner debates, as counter-terrorism and counter-radicalization strategies now acknowledge the plurality of ways in which a person might be drawn to espouse violent extremism. Interdisciplinary work in Security Studies has been able to show that, despite its heuristic usefulness, there is no single process through which terrorists are made; academia and now policy is rejecting the 'conveyor-belt' theory of radicalization, thanks in part to interdisciplinary research.

In Psychology and Neuroscience, huge strides in the possibilities of imaging the brain have only recently indicated what the potential benefits for Security Studies might be. Discussions of affect and emotion, to date, have often been principally theoretical affairs, since the technology to gather primary data has only recently been developed. These advances will give researchers the ability to study the way the brain works. Since so much of the critical turn in Security Studies has been premised upon the constructivist mantra that ideas matter, the ability to study the site of these ideas and witness the different ways in which information is processed and ideas formed is particularly exciting. These developments will surely be particularly interesting for post-structural approaches as well. Testing the Wittgensteinian notion that the limits of language are the limits of the world, neuroscience can open the possibility of the formative role of the pre-conscious, non-linguistic functions of the brain, as humans respond to everyday and non-everyday stimuli in ways in which they are not aware of.

In addition to the benefits of interdisciplinary research, the future of Security Studies is likely to be driven by the cold hard reality of research funding. The history of Security Studies suggests that the sub-discipline has long had a trajectory set by the availability of grants and awards, rather than, necessarily, the demands of knowledge or detached intellectual enquiry. The subdiscipline's centre of gravity remains skewed towards the west of the Atlantic. The hegemony of positivist approaches in the United States remains unabashed, despite critical developments and interventions in Europe, Canada and elsewhere. Today, we see a situation developing in United States academia that is not too distant from that of 1947. Once again, funding for Political Science and International Relations research is heavily biased in favour of work that will further the national security (or economic interests) of the United States. Driven by an austere economic backdrop and the partisan political climate of Congress, the National Science Foundation (NSF) announced in 2013 that Political Science funding would be limited to research that 'promotes national security or the economic interests of the United States'. There are three possible and even likely outcomes of this arrangement.

First, Security Studies as a discipline is likely to grow, since it can be expected that scholars working in areas close to the study of security will make the short hop across to the policy field, driven by imperatives to secure research funds. As several European academics joked following the NSF's announcement, securitization theorists such as Ole Wæver are likely to be very popular in the United States over the coming years, as scholars discover that anything can potentially be securitized. Second, the answer to the most fundamental question – what is security? – is likely to remain artificially weighted in favour of a particular, limiting and troubling response: security is national security. The pre-eminence of state security and traditional understandings of military threat will likely continue to dominate, given the added impetus of financial drivers. Critical approaches and a desire to study new security issues and threats will likely therefore continue to play second fiddle to the demands of state security. Third, Security Studies will remain a deeply divided discipline, with the 'critical quadrangle' (Croft 2008) of schools in Europe working towards greater harmony and sophistication as linkages and overlaps are sought (Browning and McDonald 2013), with the risk that critical partners in the United States will remain far harder to find.

Of course, as Browning and McDonald (2013) have shown, the future of Security Studies, and especially critical approaches within Security Studies, will be determined as much by internal dynamics and developments as outside influence. Critical security approaches remain very much a work in progress: as they should be. The political implications of security dynamics are still being worked out, while the ethical drivers and consequences of security and its politics continue to be contested and theorized (e.g. Burke *et al.* 2014). For Browning and McDonald (2013) the need to find overlapping spaces between schools of critical security studies is paramount. These are, after all, constructed schools and divisions (Croft 2008). Likewise, Security Studies needs to continue to work through the implications of the approaches that have been developed, refining, for example, notions of emancipation, possibilities of ethical security policy, and the politics of exceptional security measures vis-à-vis everyday insecurities and unease. We argue that scholars have already begun to tackle these challenges and, therefore, that this is an exciting time to be working within Security Studies.

Conclusion

This book has provided a critical introduction to Security Studies. While we have summarized and introduced topics for particular heuristic reasons, we have also developed a number of critical arguments, advocating the study of security in certain forms and specific ways that do not always receive sufficient attention within the subdiscipline. Throughout, we have argued that Security Studies benefits from its diversity and heterogeneity, so long as dialogue is maintained across and outside of the subdiscipline. We have also suggested that Security Studies scholars must be reflexively aware of the context-specific (and funding/government specific) manner in which Security Studies has developed as a subdiscipline. Security Studies is too important only to be a tool of those who hold power. The plight of the majority of people around the world is evidence enough that the subdiscipline must work for the voiceless as well as the strong, as much as it must encourage reflection on such categories as 'voiceless' and 'strong'. Strategic Studies and military-premised analyses of state security are a core and important component of Security Studies and they should continue to be. This preoccupation with national security, however, must not be allowed to lead to a lazy and dangerous conflation of security with state security. Security, as we have argued throughout, is far more than that, and recognizing as much is the first step to a better Security Studies.

If that is our ontological starting point, we have also made a series of related epistemological and methodological arguments. We reject the notion that empirics and knowledge do not count if they cannot be counted. Methodological pluralism should be the bedrock of the subdiscipline. Quantitative and qualitative, positivist and post-positivist approaches are richer for their dialogue, triangulation and synergy. We resist, however, the exclusion of critical alternatives on the basis of paradigmatic norms and gate-keepers in the traditional centres of Security Studies: in the US and beyond. Very many of the most important subjects in Security Studies demand non-numerical approaches to knowledge production. And all require reflective and reflexive modes of enquiry. On all sides, it is imperative that research is presented and disseminated in a manner that can lead to greater specialization and sophistication as well as wider understanding across and outside the subdiscipline. Of course, these imperative demands are already being met. New journals such as *International Political Sociology* and *Critical Studies on Security* have added to established sites of critical engagement with issues of security such as *Security Dialogue*, *Millennium Journal of International Studies* and *European Journal of International Relations*. On top of this, issue-specific journals – such as *Critical Studies on Terrorism* – have also begun to make a major critical impression even in subject areas so traditionally dominated by policy-relevant, problem-solving research.

Intellectual diversity and methodological pluralism can help Security Studies to tackle the burning issues of the day, and to consider the ways in which human experience might be improved. As we write this Conclusion, the international news media is awash with reports from the funeral service for Nelson Mandela. His life-long struggle is illustrative of the plethora of demands facing Security Studies. A colonial history and lingering colonial relations in the present day require historical and geographical analysis. As Slavoj Žižek (2013) has pointed out, engrained inequality has not ended with Mandela's rise to prominence (nor, in the terms set out in Chapter 6, has violence); instead, it demands a socio-economic frame to help us make sense of and resist these injustices. Race relations too require insights from critical approaches in Sociology, Political Science and International Relations. But let us not also forget that burning issues of identity and relations between people must be complemented by considerations of South African foreign policy, as the region's hegemon. Moreover, the country offers one of the few examples of how a nuclear weapons-free world might one day be realized. At the intersection of the Western and non-Western worlds, where leaders of the Global North and Global South have come together to honour the legacy of a man famed for fighting injustice, let us reflect on the range of issues that Security Studies can, should, and must comment on.

Glossary of Terms

AfPak Contraction of Afghanistan and Pakistan, the term reflects the US military's (post-2008) view of the region as one theatre of operations – rather than two states – requiring a coordinated strategic approach. The term is associated, in particular, with Richard Holbrooke.

Anarchy A form of political organization characterized by the absence of any central authority or power. Many International Relations (IR) scholars believe the global system to be anarchical, although the consequences of this for the interactions of states and other actors are heavily debated.

Anthropogenic Created or caused by human behaviour: often used in debates around climate change.

Arms Race Whereby two or more states compete to develop military superiority. The logic of arms races binds states into a competitive series of responses to the actions of other states. The development of nuclear warheads in the US and USSR during the Cold War is a prime example.

Autoethnography A qualitative research method that concentrates on the personal experience, reflections and narratives of a researcher embedded in a particular context.

Bipolarity A situation characterized by a relatively even distribution of power between two different actors, or poles. The Cold War rivalry between the United States and the Soviet Union is often viewed as a period of bipolarity, as it was dominated by two superpowers with nuclear weapons capabilities.

Blowback Has come to be understood as the inadvertent consequences of (often covert) foreign policy when circumstances and alliances have shifted with time. The US decision to support Mujahedeen fighters in Afghanistan in their fight against Soviet forces during the 1980s is often cited as leading to blowback, given the changed priorities of the United States after 2001.

BRICs Acronym formed out of the four major rising powers of the early twenty-first century: Brazil, Russia, India, China.

Ceteris paribus Latin phrase translating as 'all other things being equal' to describe the process of attempting to control a research environment in order to concentrate only on the variables under study.

Many post-positivist approaches argue the assumption cannot be made within social scientific research.

Clash of Civilizations Academic thesis originally developed by Samuel Huntington in a *Foreign Affairs* article in 1993 which argued that the future of global politics would be cultural and dominated by conflict between civilizations such as the West, the Eastern world, and the Muslim world. Huntington's ideas grew in popularity after 9/11, but have been subject to widespread conceptual and normative criticism.

Clausewitz, Carl von Prussian soldier and military theorist, his book, *On War*, remains one of the most famous discussions of military strategy ever published. It gave concepts to Strategic Studies such as the 'fog of war' which remain well-used today, as well as the insight that war is a continuation of politics by other means.

Coalition of the Willing A term used to describe an informal alliance of states supporting and potentially cooperating in a military intervention. Often these temporary convergences of interest mask more fundamental divisions between coalition states.

Cold War The period of global political history between the end of World War II in 1945 and the collapse of the Soviet Union and fall of the Berlin Wall in the early 1990s. The Cold War was dominated by an East/West rivalry between the Soviet Union and the United States. It was characterized by periods of heightened tension – for example around the 'Cuban Missile Crisis' of 1962 – and less antagonistic periods of 'détente' – for example in the early 1970s.

Communitarianism A conception of ethics in which moral commitments emerge within and are limited by particular communities. Communitarianism is often contrasted to cosmopolitanism which is far more optimistic about the possibility of universal moral standards.

Constructivism/Constructivist A broad theoretical approach that has become increasingly influential within International Relations and Security Studies. Constructivists tend to view political and social outcomes as the product of an interplay between material and ideational factors.

Containment A strategy or policy commonly attributed to George Kennan and used by the US to prevent the expansion of the Soviet Union during the Cold War.

Copenhagen School A constructivist approach to critical security studies that focuses on the ways in which different types of security threat are 'securitized' by well-positioned 'securitizing actors'. The approach is associated with Barry Buzan and Ole Wæver and was a major influence in the broadening of Security Studies to include non-military threats.

Correlates of War (CoW) Academic research project based in the United States aimed at accumulating scientific knowledge about war. The project hosts a number of data sets which researchers can use.

Cosmopolitanism In contrast to communitarianism, cosmopolitanism emphasizes the common humanity of all people and the political and ethical implications of this realization.

Critical constructivism Located on an IR theoretical spectrum between conventional (thin) constructivism and post-structuralism, critical constructivists emphasize the importance of ideas and identity to foreign and security policy.

Critical discourse analysis (CDA) A form of discourse analysis that pays particular attention to the relations between language and power. Influences include Karl Marx, the Frankfurt School, and Michel Foucault, and major figures within this approach include Teun van Dijk, Norman Fairclough, and Ruth Wodak.

Critical Security Studies (CSS) Where capitalized, Critical Security Studies typically refers to the 'Welsh School' approach to Security Studies and its emphasis on the relation between security and emancipation. Without capitals, the term usually refers to all approaches to security that stand outside of the liberal and realist orthodoxies, including post-colonialism, feminism, Marxism and post-structuralism.

Critical Terrorism Studies (CTS) A comparatively new and broad research agenda that emerged in the early twenty-first century in the context of the post-9/11 War on Terror. Those identifying as, or associated with, critical terrorism studies tend to share a scepticism toward dominant terrorism discourses and counter-terrorism practices. Influences include critical theory, post-structuralism, historical materialism and literature on state terrorism.

Critical Theory Where capitalized, Critical Theory usually refers to writers associated with, or influenced by, the Marxian Frankfurt School, such as Theodor Adorno and Max Horkheimer. Although diverse in their interests, the Frankfurt School were concerned with the role of knowledge as a practice of emancipatory social change. Uncapitalized, the term becomes broader and refers to social and political approaches that are critical of established approaches and their ontological, epistemological and methodological constraints.

Deduction/Deductive An approach to the generation of knowledge that works through the application of reason to initial principles and formulations.

Deepening A key aim within much critical security research, deepening seeks to uncover the political thoughts and agendas underpinning conceptions and theories of security.

Democratic peace thesis Academic thesis which argues that democracies very rarely, if ever, go to war with other democracies. Explanations for the thesis vary and include domestic political cultures, and economic interdependencies.

Democratization The process of instituting and embedding democracy in a country where it was previously absent.

Desecuritization This is a less-developed concept than securitization, but generally refers to the process by which a security issue is returned to 'normal' politics. Desecuritization is typically seen as normatively desirable, because of security's association with exceptional measures and antagonistic others.

Deterrence The effort to prevent another actor from acting in some way. Nuclear deterrence, linked to principles of Mutually Assured Destruction, was a major focus within Strategic Studies during the Cold War era.

Discourse In its broadest sense, discourse refers to a system of meaning incorporating linguistic and symbolic elements as well as material phenomena and objects. The Higher Education discourse, for example, includes ideas about the purposes of education, institutions such as universities and libraries, objects such as books, pens and tablet computers, and subjects including students and professors. In a narrower sense, the term discourse is reserved for the use of language: spoken and written.

Discourse analysis Usually associated with narrow understandings of discourse (see above), discourse analysis is a research method for studying uses of language. It can be qualitative and concentrated on a detailed analysis of a small number of texts; or quantitative aimed at statistical analysis of large corpuses of material.

Empiricism Epistemological perspective in which direct experience of the world is seen as the most reliable pathway to knowledge.

English School More optimistic than realism, the English School focuses on 'international society' – the society of states – and the rules, laws and norms that comprise it. A divided approach, Solidarists prioritize international justice, whereas Pluralists prioritize international order, which inform competing normative positions on the question of humanitarian intervention.

Environmental security Security sector that focuses on threats to, or emerging from, the environment. These may include global climate change, biodiversity loss, drought, and pollution induced by war.

Epistemology The study of knowledge, focusing on questions about what the researcher can know of the world around her and of her place within it.

Essentially contested concept Term made famous by Gallie to describe those concepts for which more than one plausible meaning exists. Security, justice, terrorism and freedom are viewed by many – although not all – as examples of essentially contested concepts.

Ethnography Anthropological research method of growing popularity within Security Studies. Ethnography involves a researcher immersing themselves in an environment, often for long periods of time, to try to develop an 'insider's' account of that which they are studying.

Eurocentric Knowledge claims or perspectives that privilege Western or European interests and experiences over those of others. Eurocentrism is almost always employed as a criticism.

Existential threat A threat to the continuing existence of something or someone. For some approaches – such as the Copenhagen School – threats have to be existential to count as 'security' issues.

Female genital mutilation (FGM) Otherwise known as female circumcision, it is the practice of removing the external female genitalia for reasons other than medical necessity.

Feminism Broad term for a diverse collection of theoretical approaches and interests that share a concern with the ways relations and practices are gendered. Feminism has had a major impact on the broadening, deepening and recasting of contemporary security studies.

Focus groups A research method that focuses on the conversations and dynamics that take place within small groups of (usually) less than ten participants. The researcher's role is to guide and moderate the discussion, but she is often less directly involved in the conversation than in the use of interviews as a research method.

Fourth generation warfare Emphasizes the complexity of de-centralized warfare, characterized by new, asymmetric, and guerrilla wars, for example.

Foreign Policy Analysis (FPA) A subdiscipline within Politics and International Relations which seeks to understand and explain foreign policymaking processes and outcomes.

Functional equivalence (of states) A way of describing that states tend to do the same types of thing, irrespective of how powerful they are. These include providing health and education for their citizens, policing their borders, and maintaining military or defence capabilities.

Game theory Studies and models decision-making. Can explain that less-than-optimal outcomes are arrived at logically and rationally.

Genealogy A method of historical analysis associated with Friedrich Nietzsche and Michel Foucault, and influential amongst post-structuralist approaches to International Relations and elsewhere. Genealogy involves attempting to demonstrate the contingency of the present and the dependence of contemporary social arrangements (including truths) upon historical power relations. In this sense, genealogical studies challenge evolutionary narratives of historical progress.

Great Power War Conflicts between states which possess the necessary power to influence international order.

Groupthink An outcome resulting from the social and psychological pressure for conformity of thinking within a group. Traditionally viewed as a potential explanation of sub-optimal decision-making.

Hard power The ability to make others do what they would otherwise choose not to, using either threats or rewards. The phrase 'hard power' was popularized within IR by Joseph Nye.

Hegemony The exercise of power by a dominant actor through the consent of subordinate actors. In the international system, this may involve providing public goods such as international institutions, from which other actors as well as the hegemon benefit.

Hegemonic transition theory Associated with Robert Gilpin, this theory attempts to explain (cyclical) transitions in international hegemony by reference to conflicts over issues of leadership, organization and order within the international system.

Historiography Refers to the (context of the) development of the discipline of International Relations. In particular, the historiography of IR flags up the development of the discipline in a particular period (the end of the World Wars and onset of the Cold War) in a particular state (the USA) that gave the discipline particular biases.

Human Rights A set of entitlements and protections deemed – by their advocates – to apply universally to all people across the world, irrespective of factors such as residence, gender, ethnic identity, sexuality, or government. A vast body of international and national law has been established to protect these rights which include freedom of expression, freedom of religion, freedom from torture, and the right to a fair trial. Human rights are often associated with, and criticized for, their liberal emphasis on the equal moral worth of each individual.

Human Security An approach to Security Studies that focuses on the individual – rather than the state – as the referent object to be secured. The United Nations Development Project's (UNDP) 1994 Human Development Report brought the concept to prominence by emphasizing the importance of non-military forms of harm or insecurity suffered by people across the world.

Humanitarian intervention Military intervention conducted with reference to human rights rationale/justification, over and above the concerns of the national interest.

Immanent critique A form of analysis which assesses policy or theory on its own terms, seeking the potential for positive change in the concrete specifics of the present. For example, it is possible to critique the policies of the War on Terror as having failed to make us safer, despite the fact we were promised by politicians that they would.

Induction/Inductive As opposed to deduction, inductive reasoning begins with empirical observations, which are located in broader patterns and used as the basis for hypothesis testing and subsequent theory generation.

International Atomic Energy Agency (IAEA) International organization seeking to promote the peaceful use of nuclear technology. The IAEA was established in 1957 as the United Nations' 'Atoms for Peace' organization, and exists as an independent organization with a special agreement regulating its relationship to the UN.

International order A way of describing the dominant mode of political organization at the global level, for example in discussions of the 'neo-liberal international order'. International order implies some measure of stability and an architecture of institutions, norms, rules and expectations upon which the status quo depends.

International Relations (IR) Capitalized, International Relations refers to the academic discipline focusing on global political dynamics and the interactions between states and other actors. Without capitals, the term refers directly to those interactions rather than their study.

International system Two or more states interacting with one another. The phrase is associated with realist and English School approaches to International Relations.

Interviews A research technique usually based on a one-to-one interaction between the researcher and their subject. Interviews were traditionally conducted face-to-face, with the researcher posing questions directly to the interviewee. Technological advancements mean this is no longer necessarily the case, and interviews can now be conducted at a distance. It is common to distinguish between structured, semi-structured and unstructured interviews to refer to a respective declining level of interviewer control over the interview's content.

Kantian Tripod Trade, democracy and institutions. Proposed by Immanuel Kant as the three features that might create the conditions for perpetual peace.

Leviathan Metaphorical term alluding to an overarching power/government of the international realm. The term is heavily associated with Thomas Hobbes, and forms the title of his famous book.

Liberalism A major theoretical approach within the discipline of International Relations, with roots in modern political theory. Liberal approaches tend to emphasize the possibility of absolute gains within the international system, the role of non-state actors, and the potential for cooperation between states and other actors. Liberal approaches emphasize the importance of trade dynamics, political institutions and democracy for understanding state behaviour.

Method The tool or technique used to collect or generate knowledge via research. An enormous range is used within Security Studies and beyond, including interviews, regression analysis, and autoethnography.

Methodology A term to describe the overarching process through which research is understood and conducted. The term methodology includes research methods as well as meta-theoretical commitments.

Millennium Development Goals Eight UN goals, formulated in 2000, aimed at eradicating extreme poverty, and ensuring sustainability while promoting development.

Mutually Assured Destruction (MAD) The guarantee of second strike capability following nuclear attack, knowledge of which, the theory suggests, will stop a state from attacking in the first place.

National identity Commonly perceived characteristics associated with a particular state. National identity refers to how a state – or components of a state, such as executive decision-makers – views itself and its role in the world.

National missile defence System of missile defence designed to shield a state from attack.

National security A term typically employed to refer to the security of the state rather than a nation, and therefore something of a misnomer. National security has tended to be prioritized within the disciplines of International Relations and Security Studies, given the state-centric ontologies of these approaches.

Neo-liberalism An economic theory prioritizing free market capitalism and minimizing state intervention.

Neo-neo synthesis A term used to describe the coming together of IR's two principal theories – liberalism and realism – around a relatively narrow range of questions and shared assumptions.

Neo-realism An attempt to render realism a more scientific theory during the 1970s. Neo-realism shifted explanations for world politics up from human nature to the rational pursuit of survival by states inhabiting an anarchical international environment. It is widely associated with Kenneth Waltz, whose 1979 book *Theory of International Politics* was pivotal in the establishment of the neo-realist theoretical framework.

New security challenges/issues Misleading term used to describe a range of security threats that were previously excluded by the narrow parameters of Security Studies. Examples of so-called new security challenges include environmental degradation, disease pandemics, poverty and malnourishment.

New terrorism A controversial term to describe the apparent transformation of terrorist organizations at the end of the twentieth century. Proponents of the 'new terrorism' thesis argue that groups such as al Qaeda are less centralized than their predecessors, more intent on mass casualty violence, and motivated by religious rather than political ambitions. Critics view the thesis as simplistic, and argue that it is potentially implicated in excessive and exceptional approaches to countering terrorism evident within aspects of the post-9/11 war on terrorism.

New wars A term developed within Mary Kaldor's work on transformations of warfare under conditions of globalization. New wars allude to decentralized and asymmetric conflicts (such as guerrilla and civil wars), often fought around exclusivist identity claims, and where the lines between civilian and combatant, war and peace can be blurred.

New world order A term first used by Gorbachev but popularized by George H.W. Bush alluding to the post-Cold War international order.

Nominal variable A variable without a natural numerical ordering, for example colours.

Non-state actors Actors other than states, which nonetheless possess sufficient agency to influence the dynamics of world politics. Non-state actors include non-governmental organizations, terrorist organizations, and transnational criminal organizations.

Normative Value claims about what 'should' or 'ought' to be the case.

Nuclear Non-Proliferation Treaty (NPT) The Treaty attempts to ensure that nuclear weapons states will help non-nuclear weapons states develop nuclear technology for peaceful means, in return for non-nuclear weapons states not developing nuclear technology for non-peaceful means.

Nuclear weapons states States possessing nuclear weapons, whether or not they are signatories to the NPT.

Ontology The philosophical study of the nature of reality or existence. Ontological claims focus on what exists in the world.

Offensive-defensive balance Associated with neo-realist thought, the term refers to the distance between offensive and defensive military capabilities in a particular circumstance. This distance is seen as having potential explanatory value for the likelihood of conflict or cooperation.

Ordinal variable A type of variable allowing for increasing and decreasing values within cases. Ranking countries by their level of economic development on a scale of one to five, for instance, would make use of ordinal variables.

Orientalism Developed by Edward Said, building on the work of Foucualt, Orientalism is the system of discourses and practices which together created or constituted the 'Orient' by 'the Occident' and structures unequal (imperial) power relations between them.

1947 US National Security Act Significant restructuring of the US military and intelligence agencies, at the end of the Second World War and start of the Cold War. The Act led to the creation of the Department of Defense and National Military Establishment.

Paradigm Associated with T.S. Kuhn, a paradigm is an agreed upon set of ideas, which might structure the way a community of (social) scientists go about doing research.

Paris School A comparatively new framework for the study of security most prominently associated with the writings of Didier Bigo. The Paris School approach draws insights from sociology, criminology and migration studies to explore the role of security professionals (such as border patrol guards) and technologies (such as CCTV cameras) in the organization and governance of security fields. A key philosophical influence in this work is the French sociologist Pierre Bourdieu.

Parsimony/Parsimonious Simplicity, often deliberate, for the purposes of elegance or explanatory power.

Patriarchy, Sexism and Misogyny Set of practices, institutions, power relations and ideas that together produce a hierarchical relationship between men and women in which the former are privileged. These may be conscious and deliberate, or embedded within cultural practices, and social, political and legal architectures such as the family, parliaments, and universities.

Peace Research/Peace Studies Academic field of research that emerged in the post-World War II era. Peace Studies has been particularly important for contemporary Security Studies, given its emphasis on structural violences and other forms of harm.

Pluralism/Pluralists The branch of the English School prioritizing international order over international justice, and therefore usually opposed to humanitarian interventions.

Positivism/Positivist An epistemological standpoint whose advocates seek to model the social sciences on the natural sciences.

Post-colonialism Academic framework that seeks to centre the voices and experiences of marginalized or majority world populations in order to destabilize and contest the implicitly Eurocentric nature of knowledge claims that are framed as universal. Post-colonialism pulls our attention to the histories and legacies of colonialism and the importance of these for the construction of contemporary world politics.

Post-modernism Variously refers to a particular period of time – that which comes after modernity; a particular aesthetic or cultural milieu associated with the mid- to late twentieth century; or, an intellectual sensibility associated with a scepticism toward truth, grand narratives, and established forms of authority. The term's imprecision is one reason for its rejection by many authors often associated with it, notably the French theorist Michel Foucault.

Post-structuralism Notoriously difficult to define, post-structuralism may be thought of as a set of theoretical commitments associated with continental philosophers including Michel Foucault and Jacques Derrida. Post-structuralists share an epistemological scepticism toward absolute meta-narratives or absolute 'Truths', and emphasize the contingent, perspectival and partial nature of truth claims. Post-structuralism has had an increasing influence within International Relations and Security Studies, as well as in other social sciences.

Power Understood in different ways by different theories of International Relations. For example, realists equate power with relative material capability, whereas constructivists look to the power of norms and narratives to shape behaviour.

Pre-emption The employment of military power to counter the imminent threat of an enemy mobilizing for war. Pre-emption differs from preventive actions (which focus on potential but imprecise future threats), although the two are often conflated in political rhetoric.

Private military corporations/Private military companies (PMCs) Private corporations – and therefore distinct from a state's military forces – that provide support for military and security operations, including logistical support, consultancy and direct engagement. PMCs have played an increasingly significant role within several contemporary wars (especially Afghanistan post-2001 and Iraq post-2003), raising considerable questions about the privatization of violence.

R2P Shorthand for 'Responsibility to Protect', R2P has become a major norm within the international system since its establishment in the UN in 2005. R2P suggests that states have a responsibility to their own citizens and to those in other countries. States are, therefore, obliged to address mass atrocities abroad which may involve military and other forms of intervention.

Rationalism Epistemological perspective in which the use of reason is seen as the most reliable pathway to knowledge.

Rationality Where a decision or action is coherent with the criterion of reason. Assumptions about the rational nature of actors – especially states – have had a major influence within International Relations and Political Science, underpinning neo-realist thought in the former, and rational choice theory in the latter.

Realism/Political realism IR's pre-eminent theory, emphasizing human nature and rationality, and presenting a relatively pessimistic view on international relations.

Realpolitik The conduct of politics based on the national interest, usually understood materially (and/or economically).

Referent (object, of security) That whose security is under consideration. For example, in discussions of French national security, France is the referent object. In discussions of gendered violence against women, women are the referent object. In discussions of human security, it is the human who takes up this position.

Regression analysis Statistical technique for measuring the impact of a change in one variable on another variable.

Relative Material Capability A material measure of power, premised on a state's military force, measured relative to that of others.

Relativism Refers to the idea that there is no external criterion by which to evaluate the validity of different truth claims, social practices, or moral standards.

Reliability A measure of the consistency of the findings of a particular research project, reliability is an important consideration within positivist research, in particular.

Replicability The capacity of an experiment or piece of research to be reproduced and engender the same outcomes. Replicability is an important consideration of research validity within positivist approaches.

Researcher effect The impact that the presence of a researcher has on the context or dynamics they are researching. Although inescapable, it is possible to be sensitive to the possible impacts of one's presence as well as to reflect upon these at the analysis stage.

Risk/Risk Management Risk refers to the likelihood and potential consequences of some future event. The category has become increasingly important within Security Studies, where it is often viewed as a social construction. Risk management is a set of techniques, technologies and professionals that together seek to reduce the probability or harm of the posited risk.

Revolution in Military Affairs (RMA) The Revolution in Military Affairs is a term used to describe changes in warfare based on technological advancement and new strategic environments.

Rogue states/Rogues A term used to designate particular states as potential security risks given their perceived indifference to international law.

Second strike capability The ability of a state to launch a retaliatory nuclear strike in response to nuclear attack.

Securitization/securitized/securitize Refers to the process by which a political issue is transformed into a security threat, usually through a powerful actor describing it as such. The concept is associated with the Copenhagen School approach to Security Studies and conceptualises security as a 'speech act' – hence a social construction – rather than an objective condition.

Security An enormously, and perhaps essentially, contested term. In common usage security typically refers to the absence of threats and the safety this produces. Within academic discussion, the meaning, referent, desirability and possibility of security are all heavily debated.

Security community/Security communities Term associated with Karl Deutsch, a security community is a situation whereby a population inhabiting a particular area expects that shared social problems will be solved via peaceful means rather than violence. The European Union may be viewed as a security community today given the unlikelihood of its members going to war with one another.

Security dilemma The risk that efforts to augment one's defensive capabilities will be interpreted as hostile or offensive actions by others. This may lead to reduced security for all actors involved.

Security spiral The logical condition that can arise from the security dilemma, as states descend into an arms race, with consistent mutual reinforcements of the others' need to build up military capability.

Security Studies An academic discipline seen by some as a sub-field of International Relations. Security Studies has expanded dramatically in recent years, largely because of the growth of explicitly critical approaches. Although very different in focus, these approaches all share an interest in unpacking what security and insecurity mean, as well as how these experiences or conditions are produced.

Self-interest That which is wanted or needed by the self. Within IR, actors – such as states – that are widely believed to behave rationally are so because they appear to be following their self-interest.

Semiotics The study of how meaning is produced and conveyed through signs and other symbolic practices.

7/7 Shorthand for four suicide bomb attacks carried out in London on 7 July 2005. The attacks were led by Mohammad Sidique Khan, and justified with reference to radical Islamist ideas. Fifty-two people were killed, as well as the perpetrators.

Small and Light Weapons (SALW) Weapons that are portable and designed for use by small numbers of people, such as handguns, rocket launchers and light machine guns. SALW result in more deaths than any other type of weapon in the international system.

Societal security A particular sector of security associated with the Copenhagen School approach to Security Studies. Societal security refers to perceived threats to collective, shared identities.

Solidarists A branch of the English School prioritizing international justice over international order and consequently more inclined to support humanitarian interventions.

State The most prominent unit of political organization within the international system today. The state is the institutional architecture through which the territory of a country is governed. For many, the continuing importance of the state within global politics is brought into question by dynamics such as globalization and the emergence of new actors and agents. These include International Governmental Organizations such as the United Nations, International Non-Governmental Organizations such as Greenpeace, and non-state actors such as terrorist groups and transnational criminal movements.

Strategic culture Refers to a body of shared beliefs and values on issues of security and defence, usually derived from the perception of mutual historical experience.

Strategic Defense Initiative (SDI) Otherwise known as 'Star Wars' this was a defence initiative launched by US President Reagan in 1983 to prevent missile attacks from hostile countries.

Strategic Studies Academic subdiscipline of International Relations and widely seen as the progenitor of Security Studies. Strategic Studies focuses on military strategy, and the use of military force.

Structural violence Term coined by Johan Galtung to describe and explain the harms suffered by people across the world as a result of impersonal structures such as global capitalism.

Subject/Object The relationship between the researcher (the subject) and the thing (object) being researched.

Superpower Term coined by William Fox to refer to the most powerful states in the international system.

Survival-plus The notion that security is about more than continued existence and should include measures of life quality.

Terrorism A term that is notoriously difficult to define, given its pejorative connotations. Terrorism tends to be associated with the instrumental use of violence conducted by non-state groups for the communication of a political message; for instance, attacks by al Qaeda or the Provisional Irish Republican Army. For many critical scholars, it is important to remember that states, too, engage in terrorism and that the label is often used to demonize rather than describe the actions of others in the international system.

Threat inflation The process of exaggerating the significance and/or scale of a security threat.

Total war The rare condition in which all the resources of the state are geared towards fighting and winning war.

Transnational criminal organizations Organized and relatively coherent criminal networks that exist or operate across national boundaries.

Treaty of Westphalia A series of Peace Treaties signed in 1648 between major European powers. These, and the peace they engendered, are often seen as the birth of the modern state system, codifying the principle of non-intervention which is frequently viewed as integral to sovereignty.

United Nations (1994) Human Development Report Published by the UNDP in 1994 this report thrust the concept of 'human security' on to the global stage.

Unmanned aerial vehicles (UAVs) Aircrafts controlled and guided in the absence of a human pilot aboard the vehicle. UAVs are widely referred to as 'drones' and have become increasingly important in contemporary conflict: most famously in the AfPak region under President Obama.

UNSC Resolution 1325 Resolution of the United Nations Security Council on women, peace and security. The resolution has been lauded by some for recognizing the distinctiveness and importance of gendered violences, and critiqued by others for its essentialist assumptions about women (and men).

Uppsala Conflict Data Programme A database containing information on armed conflicts taking place across the world.

Washington Consensus This has broadened in its usage and meaning to encompass a general market-based and neoliberal economic approach.

Welsh School Sometimes known as the 'Aberystwyth School' or 'Critical Security Studies', the Welsh School is an explicitly critical approach to Security Studies. It aims at promoting security via emancipatory politics, seeing security and emancipation as integral to one another. Major thinkers include Ken Booth and Richard Wyn Jones.

Widening An important move within Security Studies in the late 1990s that saw the incorporation of a far broader range of issues and challenges within this field's remit. Critics argue that the widening of Security Studies has led to a blurring of its focus and coherence.

Bibliography

Achen, C. and Snidal, D. (1989) 'Rational Deterrence Theory and Comparative Case Studies', *World Politics*, 41(2): 143–69.

Adams, R. (2011) 'Palestinian UN bid for statehood: as it happened', *Guardian Online*. Available via: http://www.theguardian.com/world/blog/2011/sep/23/alestinian-statehood-un-general-assembly-live, accessed 9 October 2013.

Adler, E. (1997) 'Seizing the Middle Ground: Constructivism in World Politics', *European Journal of International Relations*, 3(3): 319–63.

Adler, E. (2005) *Communitarian International Relations: The Epistemic Foundations of International Relations*, Abingdon: Routledge.

Adler, E. and Barnett, M. (1998) 'Security Communities in Theoretical Perspective', in E. Adler and M. Barnett (eds), *Security Communities*, Cambridge: Cambridge University Press, pp. 3–28.

Åhäll, L. and S. Borg (2013) 'Predication, Presupposition and Subject-positioning', in Shepherd, L. (ed.), *Critical Approaches to Security: An Introduction to Theories and Methods*, Abingdon: Routledge, pp. 196–207.

Alexander, R. (2013) 'Reinhart, Rogoff... and Herndon: The student who caught out the profs', *BBC News Online*. Available via: http://www.bbc.co.uk/news/magazine-22223190, accessed 9 October 2013.

Alford, R. (1998) *The Craft of Inquiry: Theories, Methods, Evidence*, Oxford: Oxford University Press.

Allison, G. (2012) 'How it Went Down', *Time*, 7 May 2012.

Amoore, L. (2013) *The Politics of Possibility: Risk and Security Beyond Probability*, Durham, NC: Duke University Press.

Anderson, B. (1991) *Imagined Communities: Reflections on the Origin and Spread of Nationalism*, London: Verso.

Aradau, C. (2004) 'Security and the Democratic Scene', *Journal of International Relations and Development*, 7(4): 388–413.

Ashley, R. (1981) 'Political Realism and Human Interests', *International Studies Quarterly*, 25(2): 204–36.

Ashley, R. (1984) 'The poverty of neorealism', *International Organization*, 38(2): 225–86.

Ashley, R. (1988) 'Untying the Sovereign State: a double reading of the anarchy problematique', *Millennium-Journal of International Studies*, 17(2): 227–62.

Atkins, J. (2013) 'A Renewed Social Democracy for an "Age of Internationalism": An Interpretivist Account of New Labour's Foreign Policy', *British Journal of Politics and International Relations*, 15(2): 175–91.

Australia Border Deaths Database (2014) Available online via: http://arts

online.monash.edu.au/thebordercrossingobservatory/publications/australian-border-deaths-database/, accessed 1 July 2014.

Australian Government Department of Defence (2010) *Defence Environmental Strategic Plan, 2010–2014*. Available via: http://www.defence.gov.au/environment/strat_plan.pdf, accessed 27 November 2013.

Axworthy, L. (2001) 'Human Security and Global Governance: Putting People First', *Global Governance*, 7(1): 19–23.

Badie, D. (2010) 'Groupthink, Iraq, and the War on Terror: Explaining US Policy Shift toward Iraq', *Foreign Policy Analysis*, 6(4): 277–96.

Baker-Beall, C. (2009) 'The Discursive Construction of EU Counter-Terrorism Policy: Writing the Migrant "Other", Securitisation and Control', *Journal of Contemporary European Research*, 5(2): 188–206.

Baker-Beall, C., Heath-Kelly, C. and Jarvis, L.. (eds) (forthcoming) *Counter-radicalisation: Critical Perspectives*, Abingdon: Routledge.

Baldwin, D. (1995) 'Security Studies and the End of the Cold War', *World Politics*, 48(1): 117–41.

Balzacq, T. (2011) 'Enquiries into Methods: a new framework for securitization analysis', in Balzacq, T. (ed.), *Securitization Theory: How Security Problems Emerge and Dissolve*, Abingdon: Routledge, pp. 31–54.

Barkawi, T. and Laffey, M. (2006) 'The postcolonial moment in security studies', *Review of International Studies*, 32(2): 329–52.

Barling, K. (2013) 'Deportee Jimmy Mubenga's last moments of struggle', *BBC News Online*. Available via: http://www.bbc.co.uk/news/uk-england-london-23180872, accessed 21 November 2013.

Barnett, J. (2001a) *The Meaning of Environmental Security: Ecological Politics and Policy in the New Security Era*, London: Zed.

Barnett, J. (2001b) 'Security and Climate Change', *Tyndall Centre for Climate Change Research Working Paper No. 7 (October 2001)*. Available online via: http://www.tyndall.ac.uk/sites/default/files/wp7.pdf, accessed 12 November 2013.

Barnett, M. (1999) 'Culture, Strategy and Foreign Policy Change: Israel's Road to Oslo', *European Journal of International Relations*, 5(1): 5–36.

Baudrillard, J. (1995) *The Gulf War Did Not Take Place*, Bloomington: Indiana University Press.

Baylis, J., Smith, S. and Owens, P. (eds) (2014) *The Globalization of World Politics: An Introduction to International Relations*, 6th edn, Oxford: Oxford University Press.

Beck, U. (1992) *Risk Society, Towards a New Modernity*, London: Sage Publications.

Beier, J. (2008) 'Thinking and Rethinking the Causes of War', in Craig A. Snyder (ed.), *Contemporary Security and Strategy*, 2nd edn, Basingstoke: Palgrave Macmillan.

Belasco, A. (2011) 'The Cost of Iraq, Afghanistan, and Other Global War on Terror Operations Since 9/11', Congressional Research Service, http://www.fas.org/sgp/crs/natsec/RL33110.pdf

Bell, D. (2003) 'Review Article. History and Globalization: Reflections on Temporality', *International Affairs*, 79(4): 801–14.

Bell, D. (2009) 'Introduction: Under an Empty Sky – Realism and Political Theory', in D. Bell (ed.), *Political Thought and International Relations: Variations on a Realist Theme*, Oxford: Oxford University Press, pp. 1–25.

Bellamy, A. and McDonald, M. (2002) '"The Utility of Human Security": Which Humans? What Security? A Reply to Thomas & Tow', *Security Dialogue*, 33(3): 373–77.

Bellamy, A. (2003) 'Humanitarian Responsibilities and Interventionist Claims in International Society', *Review of International Studies*, 29(3): 321–40.

Berenskoetter, F. (2007) 'Thinking about Power', in Berenskoetter, F. and Williams, M.J. (eds), *Power in World Politics*, Abingdon: Routledge, pp. 1–22.

Betts, K. (2005) 'Maybe I'll Stop Driving', *Terrorism and Political Violence*, 17(4): 507–10.

Bevir, M., Daddow, O. and Hall, I. (eds) (2014) *Interpreting Global Security*, Abingdon: Routledge.

Biddle, S., Friedman, J. and Shapiro, J. (2012) 'Testing the Surge: Why did Violence Decline in Iraq in 2007?', *International Security*, 37(1): 7–40.

Bigo, D., Carrera, S., Guild, E. and Walker, R.B.J. (2010) *Europe's 21st Century Challenge: Delivering Liberty and Security*, London: Ashgate.

Bilgin, P. (2002) 'Beyond Statism in Security Studies? Human Agency and Security in the Middle East', *The Review of International Affairs*, 2(1): 100–18.

Bilgin, P. (2003) 'Individual and Societal Dimensions of Security', *International Studies Review*, 5(2): 203–22.

Bilgin, P. (2010) 'The Western-Centrism of Security Studies', *Security Dialogue*, 41(6): 615–22.

Bilgin, P. and A. Morton (2004) 'From "Rogue" to "Failed" States? The Fallacy of Short-termism', *Politics*, 24(3): 169–80.

Bilgin, P. and Morton, A. (2002) 'Historicising Representations of "Failed Atates": beyond the cold-war annexation of the social sciences?', *Third World Quarterly*, 23(1): 55–80.

Blaikie, N. (1993) *Approaches to Social Enquiry*, Cambridge: Polity.

Blair, A. (1999) 'Doctrine of International Community', Chicago, 24 April 1999.

Blair, B. (2011) 'Revisiting the "Third Debate" (part I)', *Review of International Studies* 37(2): 825–54.

Blakeley, R. (2013) 'Elite Interviews', in Shepherd, L. (ed.), *Critical Approaches to Security: An Introduction to Theories and Methods*, Abingdon: Routledge, pp. 158–68.

Bleiker, R. and Hutchison, E. (2008) 'Fear No More: emotions in world politics', *Review of International Studies*, 34(1): 115–35.

Bleiker, R. (2003) 'A Rogue is a Rogue is a Rogue: US foreign policy and the Korean nuclear crisis', *International Affairs*, 79(4): 719–37.

Booth, K. (1991) 'Security and Emancipation', *Review of International Studies*, 17: 313–26.

Booth, K. (1994) 'Security and Self: Reflections of a Fallen Realist', *YCISS Occasional Paper*, No. 26. Available online via: http://yorkspace.

library.yorku.ca/xmlui/bitstream/handle/10315/1414/YCI0073.pdf?sequence
=1. Accessed: 8 May 2014.

Booth, K. (2005a) 'Emancipation: Introduction to Part 3', in Booth, K. (ed.). *Critical Security Studies and World Politics*, London: Lynne Rienner, pp. 181–7.

Booth, K. (2005b) *Critical Security Studies and World Politics*, London: Lynne Rienner.

Booth, K. (2007) *Theory of World Security*, Cambridge: Cambridge University Press.

Booth, K. (2011) 'Realism Redux: contexts, concepts, contests', in K. Booth (ed.), *Realism and World Politics*, London: Routledge, pp. 1–14.

Borradori, G. (2003) 'Deconstructing Terrorism: Derrida', in G. Borradori (ed.), *Philosophy in a Time of Terror: Dialogues with Jürgen Habermas and Jacques Derrida*, Chicago, IL: Chicago University Press: 137–72.

Bormann, N. (2008) *National Missile Defence and the Politics of US Identity: A Poststructural Critique*, Manchester: Manchester University Press.

Brenner, W. (2006) 'In Search of Monsters: Realism and Progress in International Relations Theory after September 11', *Security Studies*, 15(3): 496–528.

Brown, C. (2013) 'Interview – Chris Brown', *E-International Relations*. Available online via : http://www.e-ir.info/2013/05/28/interview-chris-brown/, accessed 1 July 2014.

Browning, C. and McDonald, M. (2013) 'The Future of Critical Security Studies: ethics and the politics of security', *European Journal of International Relations*, 19(2): 235–55.

Bull, H. (2002) *The Anarchical Society: A Study of Order in World Politics*, New York: Columbia University Press.

Bulley, D. (forthcoming) 'Foreign Policy as Ethics: Towards a Re-evaluation of Values', *Foreign Policy Analysis*.

Burchill, S. (1996) 'Liberal Internationalism', in Burchill, S. and Linklater, A. with Devetak, R., Paterson, M. and True, J. (eds), *Theories of International Relations*, Basingstoke: Macmillan, pp. 28–66.

Burchill, S. and Linklater, A. (eds) (2013) *Theories of International Relations*, 5th edn, Basingstoke: Palgrave Macmillan.

Burke, A. (2001) *In Fear of Security: Australia's Invasion Anxiety*, Annandale: Pluto Press Australia.

Burke, A. (2007) *Beyond Security, Ethics and Violence: War against the Other*, London: Routledge.

Burke, A. (2013) 'Security Cosmopolitanism', *Critical Studies on Security*, 1(1): 13–28.

Burke, A. McDonald, M. and Koo, K. (2014) *Ethics and Global Security*. Abingdon: Routledge.

Burke, J. (2011) *The 9/11 Wars*, London: Allen Lane.

Burnett, J. and Whyte, D. (2005) 'Embedded Expertise and the New Terrorism', *Journal for Crime, Conflict and the Media*, 1(4): 1–18.

Bush, G.W. (2001) 'Address to the Nation', 7 October 2001.

Buus, S. (2009) 'Hell on Earth: Threats, Citizens and the State from Buffy to Beck', *Cooperation and Conflict*, 44(4): 400–19.

Buzan, B. (1991) *People, States and Fear: An Agenda for International Security in the Post Cold War Era*, New York: Harvester Wheatsheaf.

Buzan, B. (1996) 'The timeless of wisdom of realism?', in S. Smith, K. Booth and M. Zalewski (eds), *International Theory: Positivism and Beyond*, Cambridge: Cambridge University Press, pp. 47–65.

Buzan, B. (1997) 'Rethinking Security after the Cold War', *Cooperation and Conflict*, 32(1): 5–28.

Buzan, B. (2014) (2013) 'Security – Concept'. Available online via: http://www.youtube.com/watch?v=dqdzRjSlz34&list=PLA6D0C1EA78DEA 1A9, accessed 1 July 2014.

Buzan, B. and Hansen, L. (2009) *The Evolution of International Security Studies*, Cambridge: Cambridge University Press.

Buzan, B., Waever, O. and de Wilde, J. (1998) *Security: A Framework for Analysis*, London: Lynne Rienner.

Byman, D. (2005) 'A Corrective That Goes Too Far?', *Terrorism and Political Violence*, 17(4): 511–16.

Campbell, D. and Shapiro, M. (1999) 'Introduction from Ethical Theory to the Ethical Relation', in Campbell, D. and Shapiro, M. (eds), *Moral Spaces: Rethinking Ethics and World Politics*, Minneapolis: University of Minnesota Press, pp. vii–xx.

Campbell, D. (1998a) 'Why Fight? Humanitarianism, Principles, and Post-structuralism', *Millennium: Journal of International Studies*, 27(3): 497–521.

Campbell, D. (1998b) *Writing Security: United States Foreign Policy and the Politics of Identity* (Revised Edition), Manchester: Manchester University Press.

Campbell, D. (2001) 'Time Is Broken: The Return of the Past in the Response to September 11', *Theory and Event*, 5(4): 1–11.

Campbell, D. (2012) 'Visual Storytelling', personal website. Available at: http://www.david-campbell.org/.

Caplan, B. (2006) 'Terrorism: The Relevance of the Rational Choice Model', *Public Choice*, 128(1–2): 91–107.

Caprioli, Mary and Trumbore, F. (2003) 'Identifying "Rogue" States and Testing their Interstate Conflict Behaviour', *European Journal of International Relations*, 9(3): 377–406.

Card, C. (1996) 'Rape as a Weapon of War', *Hypatia*, 11(4): 5–18.

Carr, E. (2001) *The Twenty Years' Crisis 1919–1939: An Introduction to the Study of International Relations* (reissued), Basingstoke: Palgrave Macmillan.

Choi (2012) 'Fighting to the Finish: Democracy and Commitment in Coalition War', *Security Studies*, 21(4): 624–53.

Clausewitz, C. (1968) *On War*, London: Penguin Books.

Clay, E.J. (2012) http://www.odi.org.uk/opinion/details.asp?id=6656&title= food-assistance-convention-hunger-food-price.

Cohen, A. (1996) 'Personal Nationalism: A Scottish View of Some Rites, Rights, and Wrongs', *American Ethnologist*, 23:4: 802–15.

Cohn, C. (1987) 'Sex and Death in the Rational World of Defense

Intellectuals', *Signs: Journal of Women in Culture and Society*, 12(4): 687–718.

Coker, C. (2001) *Humane Warfare*, London: Routledge.

Cole, D. (2002) 'Enemy aliens', *Stanford Law Review*: 953–1004.

Cole, D. (2003) 'Judging the Next Emergency: judicial review and individual rights in times of crisis', *Michigan Law Review*, 101(8): 2565–95.

Collins, A. (ed.) (2013) *Contemporary Security Studies*, Oxford: Oxford University Press.

Connolly, W. (2002) *Neuropolitics: Thinking, Culture, Speed*, Minnesota: University of Minnesota Press.

Correlates of War (2014) Available online at: http://www.correlatesofwar. org/, accessed 1 July 2014.

Cox, R. (1981) 'Social Forces, States and World Orders: Beyond International Relations Theory', *Millennium*, 10(2): 126–55.

Cox, Robert W. (1996) *Approaches to World Order*, Cambridge: Cambridge University Press.

Crawford, N. (2000) 'The Passion of World Politics: Propositions on Emotions and Emotional Relationships', *International Security*, 24(4): 116–56.

Crelinsten, R. (2009) *Counterterrorism*, Cambridge: Polity.

Crick, E. (2012) 'Drugs as an Existential Threat: an analysis of the international securitization of drugs', *International Journal of Drug Policy*, 23(5): 407–14.

Croft, S. (2007) 'British Jihadis and the British War on Terror', *Defence Studies*, 7(3): 317–37.

Croft, S. (2008) 'What Future for Security Studies', in Williams, P. (ed.), *Security Studies: An Introduction*, London: Routledge.

Croft, S. (2012) *Securitizing Islam: Identity and the Search for Security*, Cambridge: Cambridge University Press.

D'Aoust, A. (2013) 'Do you have what it takes? Accounting for emotional and material capacities', in Salter, M. and Mutlu, C. (eds), *Research Methods in Critical Security Studies: An Introduction*, Abingdon: Routledge, pp. 33–6.

Daddow, O. and Gaskarth, J. (2014) 'From Value Protection to Value Promotion: interpreting British security policy', in Bevir, M., Daddow, O. and Hall, I. (eds) (2014) *Interpreting Global Security*, Abingdon: Routledge, pp. 73–91.

Daddow, O. (2013) *International Relations Theory: The Essentials*, 2nd edn, London: Sage.

Dalby, S. (2002) *Environmental Security*, Minneapolis: University of Minnesota Press.

Dalby, S. (2009) *Security and Environmental Change*, Cambridge: Polity.

Dannreuther, R. (2013) *International Security: The Contemporary Agenda*, 2nd edn, Cambridge: Polity.

Debrix. F. (2002) 'Language as Criticism: Assessing the Merits of Speech Acts and Discursive Formations in International Relations', *New Political Science*, 24(2): 201–9.

Der Derian, J. (2001) *Virtuous War: Mapping The Military- Industrial-media-entertainment Network*, Basic Books.

Der Derian, J. and Shapiro, M. (1989) (eds) *International/Intertextual Relations: Postmodern Readings of World Politics*, Lexington, Mass.: Lexington Books.

Derrida, J. (1997) 'The Villanova Roundtable: A Conversation with Jacques Derrida', in Caputo, J. (ed.), *Deconstruction in a Nutshell: A Conversation with Jacques Derrida*(New York: Fordham Press): 3–28.

Deudney, D. (1990) 'The Case Against Linking Environmental Degradation and National Security', *Millennium: Journal of International Studies*, 19(3): 461–76.

Deudney, D. (1999) 'Environmental Security: A Critique', in Deudney, D. and Matthew, M. (eds), *Contested Grounds: Security and Conflict in the New Environmental Politics* (Albany: State University of New York Press).

Devetak, R. (2009) 'After the Event: Don DeLillo's White Noise and September 11 narratives', *Review of International Studies*, 35(4): 795–815.

Dillon, M. (2002) *Politics of Security: Towards a Political Philosophy of Continental Thought*, Abingdon: Routledge .

Dixit, P. (2012) 'Relating to Difference: Aliens and Alienness in *Doctor Who* and International Relations', *International Studies Perspectives*, 13(3): 289–306.

Doty, R. (1993) 'Foreign Policy as Social Construction: A Post-Positivist Analysis of US Counterinsurgency Policy in the Philippines', *International Studies Quarterly*, 37(3): 297–320.

Doyle, M. (1986) 'Liberalism and World Peace', *The American Political Science Review*, 80(4): 1151–69.

Doyle, M. (1998) *Ways of War and Peace: Realism, Liberalism and Socialism*, New York, NY: W.W. Norton & Company.

Doyle, M. (2005) 'Three Pillars of the Liberal Peace', *The American Political Science Review*, 99(3): 463–6.

Dumbrell, J. (2002) 'Unilateralism and "America First"? President George W. Bush's Foreign Policy', *The Political Quarterly*, 73(3): 279–87.

Dunn Cavelty, M. (2013) 'From Cyber-bombs to Political Fallout: Threat Representations with an Impact in the Cyber-Security Discourse', *International Studies Review*, 15(1): 105–22.

Dunn, T. (2009) 'Liberalism, International Terrorism and Democratic Wars', *International Relations*, 23(1): 107–14.

Duyvesteyn, I. (2004) 'How New is the New Terrorism?', *Studies in Conflict and Terrorism*, 27(5): 439–54.

Dyenrenfurth, N. (2007) 'John Howard's Hegemony of Values: The Politics of Mateship in the Howard Decade', *Australian Journal of Political Science*, 42(2): 211–30.

Edkins, J. (2003) *Trauma and the Memory of Politics*, Cambridge: Cambridge University Press.

Elbe, S. (2006) 'Should HIV/AIDS be Securitized? The Ethical Dilemmas of Linking HIV/AIDS and Security', *International Studies Quarterly*, 50(1): 119–44.

Enloe, C. (2008) 'Women and Men in the Iraq war: what can feminist curiosity reveal?', Lecture delivered on 24 March 2008 at the Clarke Forum on Contemporary Issues, Dickinson College'. Available online at: http://www.youtube.com/watch?v=XXUCLahznqs, accessed 1 July 2014.

Epstein, C. (2008) *The Power of Words in International Relations: Birth of an Anti-Whaling Discourse*, Cambridge: CUP.

Fairclough, N. (2003) *Analysing Discourse: Textual Analysis for Social Research*, Abingdon: Routledge.

Faludi, S. (2007) *The Terror Dream: What 9–11 Revealed About America*, Cornwall: MPG Books.

Faludi, S. (2008) *The Terror Dream: Fear and Fantasy in Post-9/11 America*, New York: Metropolitan Books.

FAO, WFP and IFAD (2012) *The State of Food Insecurity in the World 2012: Economic Growth is Necessary but not Sufficient to Accelerate Reduction of Hunger and Malnutrition*. Rome, Food and Agriculture Organization of the United Nations.

Fierke, K. (1996) 'Multiple Identities, Interfacing Games: The Social Construction of Western Action in Bosnia', *European Journal of International Relations*, 2(4): 467–97.

Fierke, K. (2007) *Critical Approaches to International Security*, Cambridge: Polity.

Floyd, R. (2007) 'Towards a Consequentialist Evaluation of Security: bringing together the Copenhagen and the Welsh Schools of security studies', *Review of International Studies*, 33(2): 327–50.

Floyd, R. (2010) *Security and the Environment: Securitisation Theory and US Environmental Security PPolicy*, Cambridge: Cambridge University Press.

Foucault, M. (1980) *Power/Knowledge: Selected Interviews and Other Writings, 1972–1977*, London: Longman.

Freedman, L. (1994) *War*, Oxford: Oxford Paperbacks.

Friedman, G. (2005) 'Commercial Pacifism and Protracted Conflict: Models from the Palestinian–Israeli Case', *Journal of Conflict Resolution*, 49(3): 360–82.

Fukuyama, F. (1992) *The End of History and the Last Man*, London: Penguin.

Fukuyama, F. (1998) 'Women and the Evolution of World Politics', *Foreign Affairs*, 77(5): 24–40.

Gaddis, J. (2005) 'Grand Strategy in the Second Term', *Foreign Affairs*, 84(1): 2–15.

Galtung, J. (1971) 'A Structural Theory of Imperialism', *Journal of Peace Research*, 8(2): 81–117.

Galtung, J (1985) 'Twenty-five Years of Peace Research: Ten Challenges and Some Responses' , *Journal of Peace Research*, 22(2): 141–58.

Garfinkel, M. (2004) 'Stable Alliance Formation in Distributional Conflict', *European Journal of Political Economy*, 20(4): 829–52.

Garnett, J. (2007) 'The Causes of War and the Conditions of Peace', in Baylis, J., Wirtz, J., Gray, C.S. and Cohen, E. (eds), *Strategy in the Contemporary World*, Oxford: Oxford University Press.

Garrett, S. (2004) 'Terror Bombing of German Cities in World War II', in Primoratz, I. (ed.), *Terrorism: The Philosophical Issues*, Basingstoke: Palgrave Macmillan, pp. 141–60.

Gartzke, E. (1998) 'Kant we all just get along? Opportunity, willingness and the origins of the democratic peace', *American Journal of Political Science*, 42(1): 1–27.

Gartzke, E. (2000) 'Preferences and the Democratic Peace', *International Studies Quarterly*, 44(2): 191–212.

Gee, J. (2005) *An Introduction to Discourse Analysis: Theory and Method*, Abingdon: Routledge.

Geertz, C. (2003) 'Thick Description: Toward an Interpretive Theory of Culture', in Lincoln, Y. and Denzin, N. (eds), *Turning Points in Qualitative Research: Tying Knots in a Handkerchief*, Walnut Creek, CA: Altamira Press, pp. 143–68.

George, L. (2005) 'Pharmacotic War and the Ethical Dilemmas of Engagement', *International Relations*, 19(1): 115–25.

Gharib, A. (2011) 'Poll: Iraqis say they're worse off after war', *Think Progress*, 20 December 2011. Available online at: http://thinkprogress.org/security/2011/12/20/393290/poll-iraq-war-iran/

Giacomello, G. (2004) 'Bangs for the Buck: A Cost–Benefit Analysis of Cyberterrorism', *Studies in Conflict & Terrorism*, 27(5): 387–408.

Giddens, A. (1999) 'Risk and Responsibility', *Modern Law Review*, 62(1): 1–10.

Gilpin, R. (1984) 'The Richness of the Tradition of Political Realism', *International Organization*, 38(2): 287–304.

Giraldo, J. and Trinkunas, H. (2007) 'Transnational Crime', in Collins, A. (ed.), *Contemporary Security Studies*, Oxford: Oxford University Press.

Glaser, C. (2003) 'Structural Realism in a more complex world', *Review of International Studies*, 29(3): 403–14.

Glasius (2008) 'Human Security from Paradigm Shift to Operationalization: Job Description for a Human Security Worker', *Security Dialogue*, 39(1): 31–54.

Goldstein, A. (2013) 'First Things First: The Pressing Danger of Crisis Instability in U.S.–China Relations', *International Security*, 37(4): 49–89.

Gomez, A. (2013) 'Big Surge in Border Crossing Deaths Reported', *USA Today*, 18 March 2013. Available via: http://www.usatoday.com/story/news/nation/2013/03/18/immigrant-border-deaths/1997379/, accessed 21 November 2013.

Gordon, P. (2001) 'Bush, Missile Defense and the Atlantic Alliance', *Survival*, 43(1): 17–36.

Gray, C. (1996) *Postmodern War: The New Politics of Conflict*, New York, NY: The Guildford Press.

Gregory, D. (2004) *The Colonial Present: Afghanistan, Palestine, and Iraq*, Malden: Blackwell Publishing.

Grieco, J. (1988) 'Anarchy and the Limits of Cooperation: A Realist Critique of the Newest Liberal Institutionalism', *International Organization*, 42(3): 485–507.

Guardian Online (2013) 'World's Deadliest Migration Routes'. Available via: http://www.theguardian.com/news/datablog/2013/oct/03/migration-routes-migrants-boat-italian-lampedusa. Accessed 1 July 2014.

Guerrina, R. (2012) 'Birthing on the Front Line: A Tale of Military Feminity', *E-International Relations*, 26 September. Available at: http://www.e-ir.info/2012/09/26/birthing-on-the-front-line-a-tale-of-military-femininity/

Gunning, J. and Jackson, R. (2011) 'What's so "Religious" about "Religious Terrorism"?', *Critical Studies on Terrorism*, 4(3): 369–88.

Gunning, J. (2007) 'A Case for Critical Terrorism Studies', *Government and Opposition*, 42(3).

Guzzini, S. (2007) 'The Concept of Power: A Constructivist Analysis', in Berenskoetter, F. and Williams, M.J. (eds), *Power in World Politics*, London: Routledge, pp. 23–42.

Halperin, S. (2007) 'Iraq and the Political Economy of Anglo-American Foreign Policy', presented at the British International Studies Association annual conference, Cambridge University, 17–19 December.

Halperin, S. and Heath, O. (2012) *Political Research: Methods and Practical Skills*, Oxford: Oxford University Press.

Hampson, F. (2008) 'Human Security', in Williams, P. (ed.), *Security Studies: An Introduction*, London: Routledge.

Hansen, L. and Nissenbaum, H. (2009) 'Digital Disaster, Cyber Security, and the Copenhagen School', *International Studies Quarterly*, 53(4): 1155–75.

Hansen, L. (2000) 'The Little Mermaid's Silent Security Dilemma and the Absence of Gender in the Copenhagen School', *Millennium*, 29: 285–306.

Hansen, L. (2001) 'Gender, Nation, Rape: Bosnia and the Construction of Security', *International Feminist Journal of Politics*, 3(1): 55–75.

Hansen, L. (2006) *Security as Practice: Discourse Analysis and the Bosnian War*, Abingdon: Routledge.

Hansen, L. (2011) 'Theorizing the Image for Security Studies: visual securitization and the Mohammed Cartoon Crisis', *European Journal of International Relations*, 17(1): 51–74.

Hartung, W. (2008) 'The International Arms Trade', in Williams, P. (ed.), *Security Studies: An Introduction*, London: Routledge.

Harvey, D. (2005) *The New Imperialism*, Oxford: Oxford University Press.

Hassan, O. (2012) *Constructing America's Freedom Agenda for the Middle East: Democracy or Domination*, Abingdon: Routledge.

Hassan, O. (2013) 'Computer-Assisted Qualitative Data Analysis Software', in Shepherd, L. (ed.), *Critical Approaches to Security: An Introduction to Theories and Methods*, Abingdon: Routledge: 169–80 pp. x–y.

Hay (2002) *Political Analysis: A Critical Introduction*, Basingstoke: Palgrave Macmillan.

Hay, C. (2004) 'Theory, Stylized Heuristic, or Self-Fulfilling Prophecy? The Status of Rational Choice Theory in Public Administration', *Public Administration*, 82(1): 39–62.

Heath-Kelly, C. (2010) 'Critical Terrorism Studies, Critical Theory and the "Naturalistic Fallacy"', *Security Dialogue*, 41(3): 235–54.

Held, D. (2003) 'Cosmopolitanism: Globalisation Tamed?', *Review of International Studies*, 29(4): 465–80.

Held, D. (2010) *Cosmopolitanism: Ideals and Realities*, Cambridge: Polity.

Heller, F. (1983) 'The Dangers of Groupthink', *The Guardian*, 21 January 1983.

Henderson, E. and Singer, D. (2002) '"New Wars" and Rumours of "New Wars"', *International Interactions*, 28(2): 165–90.

Herring, E. and Stokes, D. (2011) 'Critical Realism and Historical Materialism as Resources for Critical Terrorism Studies', *Critical Studies on Terrorism*, 4(1): 5–21.

Herz, J. (1951) *Political Realism and Political Idealism*, Chicago: University of Chicago Press.

Hillyard, P. (1993) *Suspect Community: people's experiences of the prevention of terrorism acts in Britain*, London: Pluto.

Histories of Violence (2014) Available online at: http://historiesofviolence. com/, accessed 1 July 2014.

Hobbes, T. (1985) *Leviathan*, London: Penguin.

Hoffman, B. (2006) *Inside Terrorism* (revised edition), New York, NY: Columbia University Press.

Holland, J. (2009) 'From September 11th 2001 to 9–11: From Void to Crisis', *International Political Sociology*, 3(3): 275–92.

Holland, J. (2013a) 'Foreign Policy and Political Possibility', *European Journal of International Relations*, 19(1): 48–67.

Holland, J. (2013b) *Selling the War on Terror: Foreign Policy Discourses after 9/11*, London: Routledge.

Holland, J. and Jarvis, L. (2014) 'Night Fell on a Different World: Experiencing, Constructing and Remembering 9/11', *Critical Studies on Terrorism*, 7(2): 187–204.

Hollis, M. and Smith, S. (1991) *Explaining and Understanding International Relations*, Oxford: Clarendon Press.

Hollis, M. and Smith, S. (1996) 'A Response: why epistemology matters in international theory', *Review of International Studies*, 22(1): 111–16.

Hopf, T. (1998) 'The Promise of Constructivism in International Relations Theory', *International Security*, 23(1): 171–200.

Howard, J. (2002) 'Address to Joint Meeting of the US Congress', 12 June 2002.

Howard, P. (2004) 'Why not Invade North Korea? Threats, language games, and US foreign policy', *International Studies Quarterly*, 48(4): 805–28.

Howarth, D. (2004) 'Hegemony, Political Subjectivity, and Radical Democracy', in Critchley, S. and Marchart, O. (eds), *Laclau: A Critical Reader*, Abingdon: Routledge, pp. 256–76.

Howarth, D. (2005) 'Applying Discourse Theory: The Method of Articulation', in Howarth, D. and Torfing, J. (eds), *Discourse Theory in European Politics: Identity, Policy and Governance*, Basingstoke: Palgrave Macmillan, pp. 316–49.

Hoyt, P. (2000) 'The "Rogue State" Image in American Foreign Policy', *Global Society* 14(2): 297–310.

Hudson, H. (2005) '"Doing" Security as Though Humans Matter: A Feminist Perspective on Gender and the Politics of Human Security', *Security Dialogue*, 36(2): 155–74.

Hughes, C. and Meng, L. (2011) (eds), *Security Studies: A Reader*, Abingdon: Routledge.

Hulme, K. (1997) 'Armed Conflict, Wanton Ecological Destruction and Scorched Earth Policies: How the 1990–91 Gulf Conflict Revealed the Inadequacies of the Current Laws to Ensure Effective Protection and Preservation of the Natural Environment', *Journal of Armed Conflict Law*, 2(1): 45–82.

Humanitarian Policy Group (2011) 'Counter-Terrorism and Humanitarian Action', Overseas Development Institute. Available online via: http://www. odi.org.uk/sites/odi.org.uk/files/odi-assets/publications-opinion-files/7347.pdf, accessed 1 July 2014.

Hunt, K. (2006) '"Embedded Feminism" and the War on Terror', in K. Hunt and K. Rygiel (eds), *(En)Gendering the War on Terror: War Stories and Camouflaged Politics*, Aldgate: Ashgate, pp. 51–72.

Huysmans, J. (1995) 'Migrants as a Security Problem: Dangers of "Securitizing" Societal Issues', in Miles, R. and Thranhardt, D. (eds), *Migration and European Integration: The Dynamics of Inclusion and Exclusion*, London: Pinter, pp. 53–72.

Huysmans, J. (2005) *The Politics of Insecurity: Fear, Migration and Asylum in the EU*, Abingdon: Routledge.

Hyde-Price, A. (2007) *European Security in the Twenty-First Century: The Challenge of Multipolarity*, Abingdon: Routledge.

Hynek, N. and Chandler, D. (2013) 'No Emancipatory Alternative, No Critical Security Studies', *Critical Studies on Security*, 1(1): 46–63.

Iraq Body Count (2014) Available online at: http://www.iraqbodycount.org/, accessed 3 June 2012.

ICCM (2014) International Collaboratory on Critical Methods in Security Studies. Available online via: http://www.open.ac.uk/researchprojects/iccm/, accessed 1 July 2014.

Isenberg, D. (2012) 'Showing the Private Contracting Military Sector the Money', *Huffington Post*, http://www.huffingtonpost.com/david-isenberg/showing-the-pmsc-sector-t_b_864372.html, accessed 18 November 2013.

Jabri, V. (2012) 'Cosmopolitan Politics, Security, Political Subjectivity', *European Journal of International Relations*, 18(4): 625–44.

Jackson, R. and G. Hall (2012) 'Knowing Terrorism: A Study on Lay Knowledge of Terrorism and Counter-terrorism', Paper prepared for the 5th biennial Oceanic Conference on International Studies (OCIS), 18–20 July, University of Sydney, Australia.

Jackson, R. (2005a) 'A Reply to Jonathon Rodwell', *49th Parallel*, 15.

Jackson, R. (2005b) *Writing the War on Terrorism*, Manchester: Manchester University Press.

Jackson, R. (2007) 'Language, Policy and the Construction of a Torture Culture in the War on Terror', *Review of International Studies*, 33(3): 353–71.

Jackson, R., Breen Smyth, M. and Gunning, J. (eds) (2009) *Critical Terrorism Studies: A New Research Agenda*, (London: Routledge).

Jackson, R., Jarvis, L., Gunning, J. and Breen Smyth, M. (2011) *Terrorism: A Critical Introduction*, Basingstoke: Palgrave Macmillan.

Janis, I. (1982) *Groupthink: psychological studies of policy decisions and fiascoes*, New York: Houghton Mifflin.

Jarvis, L. and Holland, J. (2014) 'We [For]got him: Remembering and Forgetting in the Narration of bin Laden's Death', *Millennium: Journal of International Studies*, 42(2): 425–47.

Jarvis, L. and Lister, M. (2013a) 'Disconnected Citizenship? The Impacts of Anti-terrorism Policy on Citizenship in the UK', *Political Studies*, 61(3): 656–75.

Jarvis, L. and Lister, M. (2013b) 'Disconnection and Resistance: Anti-terrorism and Citizenship in the UK', *Citizenship Studies*, 17(6–7): 756–69.

Jarvis, L. and Lister, M. (2013c) 'Vernacular Securities and their Study: A Qualitative Analysis and Research Agenda', *International Relations*, 27(2): 158–79.

Jarvis, L. (2008) 'Times of Terror: Writing Temporality into the War on Terror', *Critical Studies on Terrorism*, 1(2): 245–62.

Jarvis, L. (2009a) 'The Spaces and Faces of Critical Terrorism Studies', *Security Dialogue*, 40(1).

Jarvis, L. (2009b) *Times of Terror: Discourse, Temporality and the War on Terror*, Basingstoke: Palgrave Macmillan.

Jarvis, L. (2010) 'Remember, Remember, 22 September: Memorializing 9/11 on the Internet', *Journal of War and Culture Studies*, 3(1): 69–82.

Jarvis, L. (2011) '9/11 Digitally Remastered?: Internet Archives, Vernacular Memories and WhereWereYou.Org', *Journal of American Studies*, 45(4): 793–814.

Jarvis, L. (2012) 'No: al Qaeda a diminishing threat', in Jackson, R. and Sinclair, S. (eds), *Contemporary Debates on Terrorism*, London: Routledge, pp. 97–103.

Jarvis, L. (2013) 'Conclusion: The Process, Practice and Ethics of Research', in Shepherd, L. (ed.), *Critical Approaches to Security: An Introduction to Theories and Methods*, Abingdon: Routledge, pp.236–47.

Jervis, R. (1978) 'Cooperation Under the Security Dilemma', *World Politics*, 30(2): 186–214.

Jervis, R. (1999) 'Realism, Neoliberalism, and Cooperation: Understanding the Debate', *International Security*, 24(1): 42–63.

Jha, A. (2013) 'Poverty Saps Mental Capacity to Deal with Complex Tasks, say Scientists', *Guardian Online* 29 August 2013. Available via: http://www.theguardian.com/science/2013/aug/29/poverty-mental-capacity-complex-tasks, accessed 12 November 2013.

Johnson, A. (2007) 'New Wars and Human Security: An Interview with Mary Kaldor', *Democratiya*, 11. Available at: http://dissentmagazine.org/democratiya/article_pdfs/d11Kaldor.pdf, last accessed 16 April 2014.

Johnson, H. (2013) 'Listening to Migrant Stories', in Salter, M. and Mutlu, C. (eds), *Research Methods in Critical Security Studies: An Introduction*, Abingdon: Routledge, pp. 67–71.

Kagan, R. (2003) *Paradise and Power: America and Europe in the New World Order*, London: Atlantic.

Kaldor, M. (1999 or 2007) *New Wars and Old Wars: Organized violence in a global era*, Stanford: Stanford UP.

Kaldor, M. (2003) 'American Power: From "Compellance" to Cosmopolitanism', *International Affairs*, 79(1): 1–22.

Kaldor, M. (2013) 'In Defence of New Wars', *Stability*, 2(1): 1–16.

Kaplan, R. (1994) 'The Coming Anarchy', *The Atlantic*, 20 October. Available at: http://www.theatlantic.com/magazine/archive/1994/02/the-coming-anarchy/304670/

Katzenstein, P. (2003a) 'Same War, Different Views: Germany, Japan, and the War on Terrorism', *Current History*, 101: 731–60.

Katzenstein, P. (2003b) 'September 11 in Comparative Perspective: The Antiterrorism Campaigns of Germany and Japan', *Dialogue IO*, 1, (2003): 45–56.

Kennedy-Pipe, C (2007) 'Gender and Security', in Collins, A. (ed.), *Contemporary Security Studies*, Oxford: Oxford University Press: 75–90.

Keohane, R. and Martin, L. (1995) 'The Promise of Institutionalist Theory', *International Security*, 20(1): 39–51.

Kerr, P. (2007) 'Human Security', in Collins, A. (ed.), *Contemporary Security Studies*, Oxford: OUP.

Kettell, S. (2009) 'The Curious Incident of the Dog that Didn't Bark in the Night-Time: Structure and Agency in Britain's War with Iraq', *Politics and Policy*, 37(2): 415–39.

Kettell, S. (2013) 'Dilemmas of Discourse: Legitimising Britain's War on Terror', *British Journal of Politics and International Relations*, 15(2): 263–79.

King, G. and Murray, C. (2001) 'Rethinking Human Security', *Political Science Quarterly*, 116(4): 585–610.

Kinsella, D. (2005) 'No Rest for the Democratic Peace', *American Political Science Review*, 99(3): 453–7.

Kitzinger, J. and Barbour, R. (1999) 'Introduction: The Challenge and Promise of Focus Groups', in Barbour, R. and Kitzinger, J. (eds), *Developing Focus Group Research*, London: Sage, pp. 1–20.

Klein, B. (1990) 'How the West was One: Representational Politics of NATO', *International Studies Quarterly*, 34(3): 311–25.

Krasner, S. (1999) *Sovereignty: Organized Hypocrisy*, Princeton: PUP.

Krause, K. and Williams, M. (1996) 'Broadening the Agenda of Security Studies: Politics and Methods', *Mershon International Studies Review*, 40(2): 229–54.

Krause, K. and Williams, M. (1997a) 'Preface: Toward Critical Security Studies', in Krause, K. and Williams, M. (eds) (1997) *Critical Security Studies: Concepts and Cases*, London: UCL Press, pp. vii–xxii.

Krause, K. and Williams, M. (eds) (1997b) *Critical Security Studies: Concepts and Cases*, London: UCL Press.

Krebs, R. and Jackson, P. (2007) 'Twisting Tongues and Twisting Arms: The Power of Political Rhetoric', *European Journal of International Relations*, 13(1): 35–66.

Krebs, R., and Lobasz, J. (2007) 'Fixing the Meaning of 9/11: Hegemony, Coercion, and the Road to War in Iraq ', *Security Studies*, 16(3): 409–51.

Kristeva, J. (1981) 'Women's Time', *Signs*, 7(2): 13–35.

Kurtulus, E. (2011) 'The "New Terrorism" and its Critics', *Studies in Conflict & Terrorism*, 34(6): 476–500.

Lacina, B., Gleditsch, N. and Russett, B. (2006) 'The Declining Risk of Death in Battle', *International Studies Quarterly*, 50(3): 673–80.

Laclau, E. (2004) 'Glimpsing the Future', in Critchley, S. and Marchart, O. (eds), *Laclau: A Critical Reader*, Abingdon: Routledge, pp. 279–328.

Laclau, E. and Mouffe, C. (1985) *Hegemony and Socialist Strategy: Towards a Radical Democratic Politics*, London: Verso.

Langlois, J. (1989) 'Modelling Deterrence and International Crises', *The Journal of Conflict Resolution*, 33(1): 67–83.

Laqueur, W. (1999) *The New Terrorism: Fanaticism and The Arms of Mass Destruction*, New York, NY: Oxford University Press.

Lawler, P. (2008) 'Peace Studies', in Williams, P. (ed.), *Security Studies: An Introduction*, London: Routledge.

Layne, C. (1994) 'Kant or Cant: The Myth of the Democratic Peace', *International Security*, 19(2): 5–49.

Leander, A. (2005) 'The Power to Construct International Security: On the Significance of Private Military Companies', *Millennium*, 33(3): 803–25.

Leccardi, C. (1996) 'Rethinking Social Time: Feminist Perspectives', *Time & Society*, 5(2): 169–86.

Legro, J. and Moravcsik, A. (1999) 'Is Anybody Still a Realist?', *International Security*, 24(2): 5–55.

Levy, M. (1995) 'Is the Environment a National Security Issue?', *International Security*, 20(2): 35–62.

Lisle, D. (2008) 'Humanitarian Travels: ethical communication in Lonely Planet Guidebooks', *Review of International Studies*, 34(S1): 155–72.

Lisle, D. (2013) 'Frontline Leisure: securitizing tourism in the War on Terror', *Security Dialogue*, 44(2): 127–46.

Löwenheim, O. (2010) 'The "I" in IR: an autoethnographic account', *Review of International Studies*, 36(4): 1023–45.

Lynne-Jones, S. (1995) 'Offense–Defense Theory and its Critics', *Security Studies*, 4(4): 660–91.

Lyotard, J.F. (1984) *The Postmodern Condition: A Report on Knowledge*, Minneapolis: University of Minnesota Press.

Macdonald, S. (2009) 'Why We Should Abandon the Balance Metaphor: A New Approach to Counterterrorism Policy', *ILSA Journal of International and Comparative Law*, 15(1): 95–146.

Mack, A. (2005) 'Human Security Report: War and Peace in the 21st Century', New York: Oxford UP.

Mäksoo, M. (2006) 'From Existential Politics to Normal Politics? The Baltic States in the Enlarged Europe', *Security Dialogue*, 37(3): 275–97.

Mandelbaum, M. (1998) 'Is Major War Obsolete?', *Survival* 40(4): 20–38.

Mann, M. (1988) *States, War and Capitalism: Studies in Political Sociology*, Oxford: Blackwell.

Maoz, Z. and Russett, B. (1993) 'Normative and Structural Causes of Democratic Peace, 1946–1986', *American Political Science Review*, 87(3): 624–38.

Martin, L. (1999) 'The Contributions of Rational Choice: A Defense of Pluralism', *International Security*, 24(2): 74–83.

Massumi, B. (2005) 'The Future Birth of the Affective Fact', conference pro-
ceedings: Genealogies of Biopolitics. Available at: http://browse.reticular.
info/text/collected/massumi.pdf

Massumi, B. (2007) 'Potential Politics and the Primacy of Preemption', *Theory
and Event*, 10(2).

Matin, K. (2011) 'Redeeming the Universal: postcolonialism and the inner life
of Eurocentrism', *European Journal of International Relations*, 19(2):
353–77.

May, T. (2012) 'The Dignity of Non-Violence'. Available at http://histo-
riesofviolence.com/reflections/todd-may-the-dignity-of-non-violence/

Mazaar, M. (2003) 'George W. Bush, Idealist?', *International Affairs*, 79(3):
503–22.

McCourt, D. (2013) 'Embracing Humanitarian Intervention: Atlanticism and
the UK Interventions in Bosnia and Kosovo', *British Journal of Politics and
International Relations*, 15(2): 242–62.

McDonald, M. (2002) 'Human Security and the Construction of Security',
Global Society, 16(3): 277–95.

McDonald, M. (2005) 'Constructing Insecurity: Australian security discourse
and policy post-2001', *International Relations*, 19(3): 297–320.

McDonald, M. (2009) 'Emancipation and Critical Terrorism Studies', in
Jackson, R., Breen Smyth, M. and Gunning, J. (eds), *Critical Terrorism
Studies: A New Research Agenda*, Abingdon: Routledge, pp. 109–23.

McDonald, M. (2011a) 'Deliberation and Resecuritization: Australia, Asylum-
Seekers and the Normative Limits of the Copenhagen School', *Australian
Journal of Political Science*, 46(2): 281–95.

McDonald, M. (2011b) *Security, the Environment and Emancipation:
Contestation over Environmental Change*, Abingdon: Routledge.

McDonald, M. and Merefield, M. (2010) 'How was Howard's War Possible?
Winning the War of Position over Iraq', *Australian Journal of International
Affairs*, 64(2): 186–204.

McDonald, M. and Jackson, R. (2008) 'Selling War: The Coalition of the
Willing and the "War on Terror"'. Presented at the International Studies
Association annual conference, San Francisco, April 2008.

McInnes, C. (2001) 'Fatal Attraction? Air Power and the West', *Contemporary
Security Policy*, 22(3): 28–51.

McInnes, C. (2002) *Spectator Sport War: The West and Contemporary
Conflict*, London: Lynne Rienner.

McMillan, S.M. (1997) 'Interdependence and Conflict', *Mershon International
Studies Review*, 41(1): 33–58.

Mearsheimer, J. (2001) *The Tragedy of Great Power Politics*, New York, NY:
W.W. Norton & Company.

Mearsheimer, J. (2009) 'Reckless States and Realism', *International Relations*,
23(2): 241–56.

Mearsheimer, J. and Walt, S. (2013) 'Leaving Theory Behind: Why Simplistic
Hypothesis Testing is Bad for International Relations', *European Journal of
International Relations*, 19(3): 427–57.

Meernik, J. (2004) *The Political Use of Military Force in US Foreign Policy*,
Burlington, VT: Ashgate.

Megoran, N. (2005) 'The Critical Geopolitics of Danger in Uzbekistan and Kyrgyzstan', *Environment and Planning D*, 23(4): 555–80.

Meikle, J. (2012), 'Iranian Nuclear Scientist Killed in Tehran Bomb Explosion', 11 January. Available at http://www.guardian.co.uk/world/2012/jan/11/bomb-kills-iranian-nuclear-scientist.

Melander, E., Öberg, M., and Hall, J. (2009) 'Are "New Wars" More Atrocious? Battle Severity, Civilians Killed and Forced Migration Before and After the End of the Cold War', *European Journal of International Relations*, 15(3): 505–36.

Mercer, J. (2010) 'Emotional Beliefs', *International Organization*, 64(1): 1–31.

Millennium (2013) Special issue on 'Materialism in World Politics', 41(3).

Milliken, J. (1999) 'The Study of Discourse in International Relations: A Critique of Research and Methods', *European Journal of International Relations*, 5(2): 225–54.

Ministry of Defence (2013) 'Ministry of Defence Greening Government Commitments Annual Report 2012/2013'. Available via: https://www.gov.uk/government/uploads/system/uploads/attachment_data/file/236895/MOD_GGC_Report_2012_13.pdf, accessed 25 November 2013.

Molloy, S. (2009) 'Hans J. Morgenthau Versus E. H. Carr: Conflicting Conceptions of Ethics in Realism', in Bell, D. (ed.), *Political Thought and International Relations: Variations on a Realist Theme*, Oxford: Oxford University Press, pp. 83–104.

Morgan Centre (20142014) Morgan Centre for Research into Everyday Lives. Available online at: http://www.socialsciences.manchester.ac.uk/morgan-centre/, accessed 1 July 2014.

Morgan, D. (1996) 'Focus Groups', *Annual Review of Sociology*, 22(1): 129–52.

Morgan, D. (1997) *Focus Groups as Qualitative Research*, 2nd edn, London: Sage.

Morgan, M. (2004) 'The Origins of the New Terrorism', *Parameters*. xxxiv(1): 29–43.

Morgenthau, H. (1978) *Politics Among Nations: The Struggle for Power and Peace*, 5th edn, New York: Alfred Knopf.

Morgenthau, H. (1993) *Politics Among Nations: The Struggle for Power and Peace* (Brief Edition), New York, NY: McGraw-Hill.

Mouffe, C. (2005) *Politics and The Political*, Abingdon: Routledge.

Mueller, J. (1990) 'The Obsolescence of Major War', *Security Dialogue*, 21(3): 321–28.

Mueller, J. (2005) 'Six Rather Unusual Propositions About Terrorism', *Terrorism and Political Violence*, 17(4): 487–505.

Mueller, J. (2006) *Overblown: How politicians and the terrorism industry inflate national security threats, and why we believe them*, New York: Simon and Schuster.

Mueller, J. and Stewart, M. (2011) *Terror, Security and Money: Balancing the Risks, Benefits, and Costs of Homeland Security*, Oxford: Oxford University Press.

Mustapha, J. (2013) 'Ontological Theorisations in Critical Security Studies:

Making the Case for a (Modified) Post-Structuralist Approach', *Critical Studies on Security*, 1(1): 64–82.

Mutimer, D. (2007) 'Critical Security Studies: A Schismatic History', in Collins, A. (ed.), *Contemporary Security Studies*, Oxford: OUP.

Nasseri, L. and Gaoueette, N. (2012) 'Iran says Nuclear Scientists Murder Shows Evidence of Foreign Backed Terror', 12 January. Available at http://www.bloomberg.com/news/2012-01-11/iran-nuclear-scientist-killed-by-magnetic-bomb-under-his-car-fars-reports.html.

Navon, E. (2001) 'The "Third Debate" Revisited', *Review of International Studies*, 27(4): 611–25.

Nayak, M. and Selbin, E. (2010) *Decentring International Relations*, London: Zed.

Neal, A. (2013) 'Empiricism without Positivism: King Lear and critical security studies', in M. Salter and C. Mutlu (eds), *Research Methods in Critical Security Studies: An Introduction*, Abingdon: Routledge.

Neocleous, M. (2008) *Critique of Security*, Edinburgh: Edinburgh University Press.

Neumann, P. (2009) *Old and New Terrorism: Late Modernity, Globalization and the Transformation of Political Violence*, Cambridge: Polity.

Newman, E. (2001) 'Human Security and Constructivism', *International Studies Perspectives*, 2(3): 239–51.

Newman, E. (2004) 'The New Wars Debate: A Historical Perspective is Needed', *Security Dialogue*, 35(2): 173–89.

Newman, E. (2010) 'Critical Human Security Studies', *Review of International Studies*, 36(1): 77–94.

Nossel, S. (2004) 'Smart Power', *Foreign Affairs*, 83(2): 131–42.

Nye, J. (2005) *Soft Power: the means to success in world politics*, New York: Public Affairs.

O'Brien, M. (1989) 'Periods', in Forman, F. (ed.), *Taking Our Time: Feminist Perspectives on Temporality*, Oxford: Pergamon Press, pp. 11–18.

Oneal, J.R. Oneal, F. H., Maoz, Z., and Russett, B. (1996) 'The Liberal Peace: interdependence, democracy, and international conflict, 1950–85', *Journal of Peace Research*, 33(1): 11–28.

Onuf, N. (1989) *World of Our Making: Rules and Rule in Social Theory and International Relations*, University of South Carolina Press.

Østerud, O. (1996) 'Antinomies of Postmodernism in International Studies', *Journal of Peace Research*, 33(4): 385–90.

Owen, J. (1994) 'How Liberalism Produces Peace', *International Security*, 19(2): 87–125.

Owen, T. (2004) 'Human Security – Conflict, Critique and Consensus: Colloquium Remarks and a Proposal for a Threshold-Based Definition', *Security Dialogue*, 35(3): 373–87.

Oxford Research Group (2014) 'Sustainable Security'. Available online via: http://www.oxfordresearchgroup.org.uk/ssp#publications, accessed 1 July 2014.

Paris, R. (2001) 'Human Security: Paradigm Shift or Hot Air?', *International Security*, 26(2): 87–102.

Parmar, I. (2006) '"I'm Proud of the British Empire": Why Tony Blair Backs George W. Bush', *Political Quarterly*, 72(2): 218–31.

Patomäki and Wight (2000) 'After Postpositivism? The Promises of Critical Realism', *International Studies Quarterly*, 44(2): 213–37.

Peoples, C. andVaughan-Williams, N. (2010) *Critical Security Studies: An Introduction*, London: Routledge.

Perlo-Freeman, S., Skons, E., Solmirano, C. and Wilandh, H. (2013) *Trends in World Military Expenditure, 2012*, SIPRI Fact Sheet April 2013. Available via: http://books.sipri.org/files/FS/SIPRIFS1304.pdf, accessed 27 November 2013.

Peters, K. and Richards, P. (1998) '"Why We Fight": Voices of Youth Combatants in Child Soldiers', *Africa: Journal of the International African Institute*, 68(2): 183–10.

Pettmann, J. (2005) 'Questions of Identity: Australia and Asia', in Booth, K. (ed.), *Critical Security Studies and World Politics*, London: Lynne Rienner.

Picarelli, J. (2008) 'Crime', in Williams, P. (ed.), *Security Studies: An Introduction*, London: Routledge.

Powell, R. (1999) 'The Modelling Enterprise and Security Studies', *International Security*, 24(2): 97–106.

Price, R. (1995) 'A Genealogy of the Chemical Weapons Taboo', *International Organization*, 49(1): 73–103.

Rabinow, P. and Sullivan, W. (1987) 'The Interpretive Turn: A Second Look', in Rabinow, P. and Sullivan, W. (eds), *Interpretive Social Science: A Second Look*, Berkeley, LA: University of California Press, pp.1–30.

Rapoport, A. (1968) 'Editor's Introduction', in Clausewitz, C., *On War*, Penguin Books.

Reagan, R. (1983) 'Address to the Nation on Defense and National Security'. Available online at: http://www.atomicarchive.com/Docs/Missile/Starwars.shtml, accessed 3 June 2012.

Rengger, N. and Thirkell-White, B. (2007) 'Still Critical After All These Years? The past, present and future of Critical Theory in International Relations', *Review of International Studies*, 33(S1): 3–24.

Reus-Smit, C. (2002) 'Imagining Society: Constructivism and the English School', *British Journal of Politics and International Relations*, 4(3): 487–509.

Robinson, N. (2012) 'Videogames, Persuasion and the War on Terror: Escaping or Embedding the Military-Entertainment Complex?', *Political Studies*, 60(3): 504–22.

Roe, P. (2004) 'Securitization and Minority Rights: Conditions of Desecuritization', *Security Dialogue*, 35(3): 279–94.

Roe, P. (2012) 'Is Securitization a "Negative" Concept? Revisiting the normative debate over normal versus extraordinary politics', *Security Dialogue*, 43(3): 249–66.

Rogers, P. (2013) 'Peace Studies', in Collins, A. (ed.), *Contemporary Security Studies*, Oxford: Oxford University Press.

Rogers, R. (2008) 'Terrorism', in Williams, P. (ed.), *Security Studies: An Introduction*, London: Routledge.

Rogers-Hayden, T., Hatton, F. and Lorenzi, I. (2011) '"Energy Security" and "Climate Change": Constructing UK Energy Discursive Realities', *Global Environmental Change*, 21(1): 134–42.

Rose, G. (1998) 'Review Article: Neoclassical Realism and Theories of Foreign Policy', *World Politics*, 51(1): 144–72.

Ross, A. (2006) 'Coming in from the Cold: Constructivism and Emotions', *European Journal of International Relations*, 12(2): 197–222.

Rothschild, E. (1995) 'What is Security', *Daedalus*, 124(3): 53–98.

Rourke, A. (2012) 'Julia Gillard's Attack on Sexism Hailed as Turning Point for Australian Women', *The Guardian*, 12 October. Available at: http://www.guardian.co.uk/world/2012/oct/12/julia-gillard-sexism-australian-women?newsfeed=true.

Rowley, C. and Weldes, J. (2012) 'The Evolution of International Security Studies and the Everyday: Suggestions from the Buffyverse', *Security Dialogues*, 43(6): 513–30.

Ruane, J. and Todd, J. (2005) in Booth, K. *Critical Security Studies and World Politics*, (London: Lynne Rienner).

Said, E. (2003) *Orientalism*, London: Penguin.

Salter, M. and Mutlu, C. (eds) (2013) *Research Methods in Critical Security Studies*, Abingdon: Routledge.

Salter, M. (2013) 'Introduction', in Salter, M. and Mutlu, C. (eds), *Research Methods in Critical Security Studies: An Introduction*, Abingdon: Routledge, pp. 1–14.

Saurette, P. (2006) 'You Dissin Me? Humiliation and Post 9–11 Global Politics', *Review of International Studies*, 32(2): 495–522.

Sayer, A. (2000) *Realism and Social Science*, London: Sage.

Schmidt, B. (2004) 'Realism as Tragedy', *Review of International Studies*, 30(3): 427–41.

Schmidt, B. (2007) 'Realist Conceptions of Power', in Berenskoetter, F. and Williams, M.J. (eds), *Power in World Politics*, London: Routledge, pp. 43–63.

Schweller, R. (1997) 'New Realist Research on Alliances: Refining, Not Refuting, Waltz's Balancing Proposition', *American Political Science Review*, 91(4): 927–30.

Scott-Clark, C. and Levy, A. (2003) 'Spectre Orange', *Guardian Online*, 29 March 2003. Available via: http://www.theguardian.com/world/2003/mar/29/usa.adrianlevy, accessed 22 November 2013.

Scully, G. (1997) 'Murder by the State', *National Center for Policy Analysis*, No. 211. Available via: http://www.ncpa.org/pub/st211, accessed: 9 October 2013.

Shaheen, J. (2003) 'Reel Bad Arabs: How Hollywood Vilifies a People', *The ANNALS of the American Academy of Political and Social Science*, 588(1): 171–93.

Sheehan, M. (2005) *International Security: An Analytical Survey*, London: Lynne Rienner.

Shepherd, L. (2008) 'Power and Authority in the Production of United Nations Security Council Resolution 1325', *International Studies Quarterly*, 52(2): 383–404.

Shepherd, L. (2010) 'Women, Armed Conflict and Language: Gender, Violence and Discourse', *International Review of the Red Cross*, 92(877).

Shepherd, L. (ed.) (2013) *Critical Approaches to Security: An Introduction to Theories and Methods*, Abingdon: Routledge.

Simon, S. and Benjamin, D. (2000) 'America and the New Terrorism', *Survival*, 42(1): 59–75.

SIPRI (2014) 'Recent Trends in Military Expenditure'. Available online via: http://www.sipri.org/research/armaments/milex/recent-trends, accessed 1 July 2014.

Sisler, V. (2008) 'Digital Arabs: Representation in Video Games', *European Journal of Cultural Studies*, 11(2): 12–31.

Sjoberg, L. (2009) 'Introduction to Security Studies: Feminist Contributions', *Security Studies*, 18(2): 183–213.

Sjoberg, L. and Horowitz, J. (2013) 'Quantitative Methods', in Shepherd, L. (ed.), *Critical Approaches to Security: An Introduction to Theories and Methods*, Abingdon: Routledge, pp. 113–17.

Smith , S. (1996) 'Positivism and Beyond', in Smith, S., Booth, K. and Zalewski, M. (eds), *International Theory: Positivism and Beyond*, Cambridge: Cambridge University Press, pp. 11–44.

Snyder, G.H. (1991) 'Alliances, Balance and Stability', *International Organization*, 45(1): 121–42.

Snyder, J. (1984/5) 'Richness, Rigor, and Relevance in the Study of Soviet Foreign Policy', *International Security*, 9(3).

Spalek, B. and Imtoual, A. (2007) '"Hard" Approaches to Community Engagement in the UK and Australia: Muslim communities and counter-terror responses', *Journal of Muslim Minority Affairs*, 27(2): 185–202.

Spalek, B. and Lambert, R. (2008) 'Muslim Communities, Counter-terrorism and Counter-radicalisation: a critically reflective approach to engagement', *International Journal of Law, Crime and Justice*, 36(4): 257–70.

Spencer, A. (2006) 'Questioning the Concept of "New Terrorism"', *Peace, Conflict & Development*, 8: 1–33.

Spencer, A. (2008) 'Linking Immigrants and Terrorists: The Use of Immigration as an Anti-Terror Policy', *The Online Journal of Peace and Conflict Resolution*, 8(1): 1–24.

Steans, J., Pettiford, L., Diez, T. and El-Anis, I. (2010) *An Introduction to International Relations Theory: Perspectives and Themes*, 3rd edn, Abingdon: Routledge.

Stokes, D. (2009) 'Ideas and Avocadoes: Ontologising Critical Terrorism Studies', *International Relations*, 23(1): 85–92.

Suhrke, A. (1993) 'Pressure Points: Environmental Degradation, Migration and Conflict', prepared for the workshop on 'Environmental Change, Population Displacement, and Acute Conflict', held at the Institute for Research on Public Policy in Ottawa in June 1991. Available at: http://www.cmi.no/publications/1993%5Cpressure_points.pdf. And see later, 'Environmental Degradation and Population Flows', *Journal of International Affairs*, 47(2).

Suhrke, A. (1997) 'Environmental Degradation, Migration, and the Potential for Violent Conflict', in Gleditsch, N.P. (ed.), *Conflict and the Environment*, The Hague: Kluwer.

Suhrke, A. (1999) 'Human Security and the Interests of States', *Security Dialogue*, 3(3): 265–76.

Suhrke, A. (2004) 'A Stalled Initiative', *Security Dialogue*, 35(1): 365.

Sylvester, C. (2002) *Feminist International Relations: An Unfinished Journey*, Cambridge: Cambridge University Press.

Sylvester, C. (2013) 'Experiencing the End and Afterlives of International Relations/Theory', *European Journal of International Relations*, 19(3): 609–26.

Taliaferro, J. (2000) 'Security Seeking Under Anarchy: Defensive Realism Revisited', *International Security*, 25(3): 128–61.

Teo, P. (2000) 'Racism in the News: A Critical Discourse Analysis of News Reporting in Two Australian Newspapers', *Discourse & Society*, 11(1): 7–49.

Thomas, C. (2001) 'Global Governance, Development and Human Security: Exploring the Links', *Third World Quarterly*, 22(2): 159–75.

Thomas, C. (2008) 'Poverty', in Williams, P. (ed.), *Security Studies: An Introduction*, London: Routledge.

Thompson, M. (2011) 'The 5 Trillion War on Terror', *Time*, 19 June 2011. Available at: http://nation.time.com/2011/06/29/the-5-trillion-war-on-terror/

Thrift, N. (2008) *Non-Representational Theory: Space, Politics, Affect*, London: Routledge.

Tickner, J. (1997) 'You Just Don't Understand: Troubled Engagements Between Feminists and IR Theorists', *International Studies Quarterly*, 41(4): 611–32.

Tickner, J. (1999) 'Why Women Can't Run the World: International Politics According to Francis Fukuyama', *International Studies Review*, 1(3): 3–11.

Tickner, J. (2004) 'Feminist Responses to International Security Studies', *Peace Review: A Journal of Social Justice*, 16(1): 43–8.

Toal, G. (1996) *Critical Geopolitics: The Politics of Writing Global Space*, London: Routledge.

Toft, M. (2007) 'Getting Religion? The Puzzling Case of Islam and Civil War', *International Security*, 31(4): 97–131.

Tucker, D. (2001) 'What's New About The New Terrorism And How Dangerous Is It?', *Terrorism and Political Violence*, 13(3): 1–14.

UCDP (200142014) Uppsala Conflict Data Programme. Available online at: http://www.pcr.uu.se/research/UCDP/, accessed 1 July7 2014.

UK Cabinet Office (2012) 'United Kingdom National Risk Register of civil emergencies'. Available online at: http://www.cabinetoffice.gov.uk/sites/default/files/resources/CO_NationalRiskRegister_2012_acc.pdf, last accessed 16 April 2014.

UNDP (1994) 'Human Development Report: New Dimensions of Human Security', available at http://hdr.undp.org/en/reports/global/hdr1994/chapters/, last accessed 16 April 2014.

United Nations (2000) *Millennium Development Goals*, available at www.un.org/millenniumgoals/.2014accessed 1 JulyUnited Nations (2011) *Annual Review of Millennium Development Goals Report*.

United Nations (2014a) 'The Responsibility to Protect', Office of the Special Adviser on the Prevention of Genocide, available at: http://www.un.org/en/preventgenocide/adviser/responsibility.shtml, accessed 1 July 2014.

United Nations (2014b) *The Universal Declaration of Human Rights.* Available online via: http://www.un.org/en/documents/udhr/, accessed 1 July 2014.

United Nations Department of Economic and Social Affairs (2010) *The World's Women: Trends and Statistics*, New York, NY: United Nations.

United Nations Development Programme (2010) *What Will it Take to Achieve the Millennium Development Goals?* Available online at http://content.undp.org/go/cms-service/stream/asset/?asset_id=2620072, accessed 13 June 2012.

United Nations Environment Programme (2009) *Protecting the Environment During Armed Conflict: An Inventory and Analysis of International Law.* Available via: http://postconflict.unep.ch/publications/int_law.pdf, accessed 22 November 2013.

United Nations Food and Agriculture Agency (2012) 'Globally almost 870 million chronically undernourished – new hunger report'. Available online at: http://www.fao.org/news/story/en/item/161819/icode/. Accessed 1 July 2014.

United Nations Millennium Campaign (2014) 'End Poverty 2015'. Available online at: http://www.endpoverty2015.org/, accessed 1 July 2014.

United Nations Office of the Special Advisor on the Prevention of Genocide (2014) 'The Responsibility to Protect'. Available online at: http://www.un.org/en/preventgenocide/adviser/responsibility.shtml. Accessed 1 July 2014.

United States Department of Homeland Security (20142014) 'What is Security and Resilience', available at: http://www.dhs.gov/what-security-and-resilience. Accessed 1 July 2014.

van Dijk, T. (2001) 'Multidisciplinary CDA: a plea for diversity', in Wodak, R. and Meyer, M. (eds), *Methods of Critical Discourse Analysis*, London: Sage, pp. 95–120.

Van Veeren, E. (2012) 'Guantanamo Ten Years On', University of Sussex, http://www.sussex.ac.uk/ir/newsandevents/?id=11379

Vaughan-Williams, N. and Stevens, D. (2012) 'Public Perceptions of Security: Reconsidering Sociotropic and Personal Threats', Paper prepared for the annual Elections, Public Opinion and Parties meeting, 7–9 September, Oxford.

Vertovec, S. and Cohen, R. (2002) 'Introduction: Conceiving Cosmopolitanism', in Vertovec, S. and Cohen, R. (eds), *Conceiving Cosmopolitanism: Theory, Context, and Practice*, Oxford: Oxford University Press, pp. 1–22.

Vuori, J. (2010) 'A Timely Prophet? The Doomsday Clock as a Visualisation of Securitizing Moves with a Global Referent Object', *Security Dialogue*, 41(3): 255–77.

Waever, O. (1993) 'Societal Security: the concept', in Waever, O. Buzan, B.

Kelstrup, M. Lemaitre, P. (eds), *Identity, Migration and the New Security Agenda in Europe*, Continuum International Publishing.

Wæver, O. (1996) 'The Rise and Fall of the Inter-Paradigm Debate', in Smith, S., Booth, K. and Zalewski, M. (eds), *International Theory: Positivism and Beyond*, Cambridge: Cambridge University Press, pp. 149–85.

Walker, R.B.J. (1987) 'Realism, Change and International Political Theory', *International Studies Quarterly*, 31(1): 65–86.

Walker, R.B.J. (1993) *Inside/Outside: International Relations as Political Theory*, Cambridge: Cambridge University Press.

Walker, R.B.J. (2010) *After the Globe, Before the World*, Abingdon: Routledge.

Walt, S. (1991) 'The Renaissance of Security Studies', *International Studies Quarterly*, 35(2): 211–39.

Walt, S. (1997) 'The Progressive Power of Realism', *American Political Science Review*, 91(4): 931–5.

Walt, S. (1998). 'International Relations: One World, Many Theories'. *Foreign Policy*, 110: 29–46.

Walt, S. (1999) 'Rigor or Rigor Mortis? Rational Choice and Security Studies', *International Security*, 23(4): 5–48.

Waltz, K. (1979) *Theory of International Politics*, New York, NY: McGraw-Hill.

Waltz, K. (1981) 'The Spread of Nuclear Weapons: More May Better', *Adelphi Papers*, Number 171, London: International Institute for Strategic Studies.

Waltz, K. (1986) 'Laws and Theories', in Keohane, R. (ed.), *Neorealism and Its Critics*, New York, NY: Columbia University Press, pp. 27–46.

Waltz, K. (1990) 'Nuclear Myths and Political Realities', *American Political Science Review*, 84(3): 731–45.

Waltz, K. (2001) *Man, the State and War: A Theoretical Analysis* (revised edition), New York, NY: Columbia University Press.

Ward, H. (1996) 'Game Theory and the Politics of Global Warming: The State of Play and Beyond', *Political Studies*, 44(5): 850–71.

Weber, C. (2005) *International Relations Theory: A Critical Introduction*, 2nd edn, Abingdon: Routledge.

Weber, C. (2014) 'Why is There No Queer IR Theory?', *European Journal of International Relations*, published online ahead of print.

Weitz, R. (2010) 'Illusive Visions and Practical Realities: Russia, NATO and Missile Defence', *Survival*, 52(4): 99–120.

Weldes, J. (1996) 'Making State Action Possible: The United States and the Discursive Construction of "the Cuban Problem", 1960–1994', *Millennium: Journal of International Studies*, 25(3): 361–98.

Weldes, J. (1999a) 'Going Cultural: Star Trek, State Action, and Popular Culture', *Millennium: Journal of International Studies*, 28(1): 117–34.

Weldes, J. (1999b) 'The Cultural Production of Crises: U.S. Identity and Missiles in Cuba', in J. Weldes, M. Laffey, H. Gusterson and R. Duvall (eds), *Cultures of Insecurity: States, Communities and the Production of Danger*, Minneapolis: University of Minnesota Press, pp. 35–62.

Wellcome Collection (2014) 'AIDS Posters'. Available online via: http://www.wellcomecollection.org/explore/sickness—health/topics/aids-posters/images.aspx?view=aids-the-death-warrant, accessed 1 July 2014.

Wendt, A. (1992) 'Anarchy Is What States Make of It: The Social Construction of Power Politics', *International Organisation*, 46(2): 391–425.

Wendt, A. (1995) 'Constructing International Politics', *International Security*, 20(1): 71–81.

Wendt, A. (1998). 'On Constitution and Causation in International Relations', *Review of International Studies*, 24(5): 101–18.

Wendt, A. (1999) *Social Theory of International Politics*, Cambridge: Cambridge University Press.

Wheeler, N. (2002) *Saving Strangers: Humanitarian Intervention in International Society*, Oxford: Oxford University Press.

White, H. (1980) *The Content of the Form: Narrative Discourse and Historical Representation*, Baltimore: Johns Hopkins University Press.

Whitworth, S. (2005) 'Militarized Masculinities and the Politics of Peacekeeping', in Booth, K. (ed.), *Critical Security Studies and World Politics*, London: Lynne Rienner.

Wibben, A. (2010) *Feminist Security Studies: A Narrative Approach*, Abingdon: Routledge.

Widmaier, W. (2007) 'Constructing Foreign Policy Crises: Interpretive Leadership in the Cold War and War on Terror', *International Studies Quarterly*, 51(4): 779–94.

Widmaier, W. W., Blyth, M. and Seabrooke, L. (2007) 'Exogenous Shocks or Endogenous Constructions? The Meanings of Wars and Crises', *International Studies Quarterly*, 51:4: 747–59.

Wiebe, S. (2013) 'Affective Terrain: approaching the field in Aamjiwnaang', in Salter, M. and Mutlu, C. (eds), *Research Methods in Critical Security Studies: An Introduction*, Abingdon: Routledge, pp. 158–61.

Williams, M. (2003) 'Words, Images, Enemies: Securitization and International Politics', *International Studies Quarterly*, 47(4): 511–31.

Williams, M. (2007) *Culture and Security: Symbolic Power and the Politics of International Security*, Oxford: Routledge.

Williams, P. (2008) 'War', in Williams, P. (ed.), *Security Studies: An Introduction*, Abingdon: Routledge.

Williams, P. (ed.) (2013) *Security Studies: An Introduction*, 2nd edn, Abingdon: Routledge.

Winch, P. (1990) *The Idea of a Social Science and its Relation to Philosophy*, Abingdon: Routledge.

Wirtz, J. (2007) 'Weapons of Mass Destruction', in Collins, A. (ed.), *Contemporary Security Studies*, Oxford: OUP.

Wodak, R. (2001) 'What CDA is About – a summary of its history, important concepts and its developments', in Wodak, R. and Meyer, M. (eds), *Methods of Critical Discourse Analysis*, London: Sage, pp. 1–13.

Wolfers, A. (2011) 'National Security as an Ambiguous Symbol', in Hughes, C. and Meng, L. (eds), *Security Studies: A Reader*. Abingdon: Routledge, pp. 5–10.

World Health Organization (2014) Malaria Fact Sheet, available at http://www.who.int/mediacentre/factsheets/fs094/en/index.html. Accessed 1 July 2014.

World Trade Organization (2008) *Ten Benefits of the WTO Trading System.* Available online at: http://www.wto.org/english/thewto_e/whatis_e/10ben_ e/10b00_e.htm, accessed 20 May 2012. (Accessed 6 June 2012.)

Wright, K. and Holland, J. (2014) 'Julia Gillard, Leadership and the Media: Gendered Framings of the Sexism and Misogyny Speech', *Australian Journal of Political Science*, forthcoming.

Wyn Jones, R. (1999) *Security, Strategy and Critical Theory*, London: Lynne Rienner.

Wyn Jones, R. (2005) 'On Emancipation: Necessity, Capacity, and Concrete Utopias', in Booth, K. (ed.), *Critical Security Studies and World Politics*, London: Lynne Rienner, pp. 215–35.

Zehfuss, M. (2002) *Constructivism in International Relations: The Politics of Reality.* Cambridge: Cambridge University Press.

Zehfuss, M. (2009) 'Hierarchies of Grief' and the Possiblity of War: Remembering UK Fatalities in Iraq', *Millennium: Journal of International Studies,* 38(2): 419–40.

Žižek, S. (2013) 'If Nelson Mandela really had won, he wouldn't be seen as a universal hero', *The Guardian*, 9 December 2013.

Zulaika, J (2009) *Terrorism: The Self-Fulfilling Prophecy,* University of Chicago Press.

Index

Printed in Great Britain
by Amazon